TARQUIN'S SHIP

The Etruscan Wreck
in Campese Bay

By the same author

The Coal-Scuttle Brigade
Black Saturday
Strike from the Sky
The Golden Wreck
HMS Bounty
The Friendless Sky
From Merciless Invaders
Caen: Anvil of Victory
Gordon of Khartoum
Vimy Ridge
Farming the Sea
History under the Sea
The Race for the Rhine Bridges
King Henry VIII's *Mary Rose*
Death Raft
The Queen's Corsair
Ice Crash
Into the Blue
Dresden 1945: The Devil's Tinderbox
How We Found the Mary Rose

TARQUIN'S SHIP

*The Etruscan Wreck
in Campese Bay*

Alexander McKee

SOUVENIR PRESS

ISBN 0 285 62652 3

Filmset and printed in Great Britain by
BAS Printers Limited, Over Wallop, Hampshire

CONTENTS

DEDICATED IN GRATITUDE TO

all those members of Southsea Branch of the British Sub-Aqua Club who took time and trouble to record the wrecks of Giglio and Giannutri before their destruction more than twenty years ago and who, soon after, were by many long years the first of what was to become a multitude of supporters for my project to locate, excavate and lift King Henry VIII's *Mary Rose*.

ACKNOWLEDGEMENTS

I am indebted to William Heinemann for permission to quote from translations of various Greek and Roman authors, published in the Loeb Classical Library; to Penguin Books Ltd for permission to quote from their translation of *The Voyage of Argo* by Apollonius of Rhodes (1979); to Dr John Reich for permission to quote from translations of Herodotus and Virgil published in his book *Italy Before Rome* (Elsevier-Phaidon, Oxford, 1979); to Ellen Macnamara for permission to quote from her translations of various classical authors published in her book *Everyday Life of the Etruscans* (Batsford, London, 1973); to Brian Phillips for permission to quote from his translations of various classical authors published in the English edition of *The Etruscans* by Mauro Cristofani (Orbis Publishing, London, 1979); to *The Sunday Times* for permission to quote from an article by Dilys Powell which appeared on 15 August, 1954; to *Diver* magazine (Eaton Publications) for permission to quote from the translation of an article which first appeared in *Mundo Subacuatico*; to Routledge & Kegan Paul plc for permission to quote from *The Collected Poems of Sidney Keyes* (London, 1945).

My thanks to Aldo Scoppa for giving me the benefit of his great knowledge of Etruria and the Etruscans; to the many other modern historians whose works I have consulted; to Roger Hale and John Towse for their help with the events of the 1960s; to Brenda Bumstead, Jane Pannell and David Swan for their recollections of the Oxford expeditions of the 1980s; and to my editor, Tessa Harrow, for a skilful and almost painless cutting of an over-long manuscript.

For permission to reproduce photographs I am indebted to the Istituto Geografico Agostini, Novara; Scala/Firenze, Florence; Emilio Valerioti, Tarquinia; *The News*, Portsmouth; Phillip Burner; Roger Hale; John Towse; Victor de Sanctis. For the artwork I must thank Edgar Taylor and Maurice Young.

In a few cases, although every effort has been made, it has not been possible to contact the owners of copyright.

PREFACE

I have seen old ships sail like swans asleep
Beyond the village which men still call Tyre,
With leaden age o'ercargoed, dipping deep
For Famagusta and the hidden sun
That rings black Cyprus with a lake of fire . . .
James Elroy Flecker, *The Old Ships*

Adventure is when things go wrong. A normal dive is like a short visit to Mars: a swift succession of scenes and impressions of a world totally different from that in which we live for most of the time. Hard even to recall them all, almost impossible to describe to anyone who has never seen them. Besides, the scenery of the submerged continents varies at least as much as that of the land surfaces of the globe.

Some of the most fascinating, colourful and spectacular in the world are to be found in British waters, where luxuriant jungles of weed change continually with the seasons, even from week to week. The barren seascapes of winter give place without warning to the riotous exuberance of spring, suddenly alive with fish.

Some of the darkest, fastest and most dangerous waters are to be found there, too; and, in contrast, many of the most barren and boring, and not a few of the foulest.

Occasionally, some of these factors may combine to preserve almost perfectly much of the hull and contents of a particularly important ship, such as King Henry VIII's *Mary Rose*, sunk off Portsmouth in 1545, close to where I now live. As long ago as 1962 I had come to suspect that she might be much better preserved than was popularly thought and had begun a long process of enquiry and deduction as to the precise location of the wreck site, which was to culminate in the raising of her great hull in 1982. Twenty years passed between that dream and its fulfilment.

In the interval a great many things happened, including yet another dream which also took twenty years to come true—although with much less effort on my part than with the *Mary Rose* search and excavation saga.

In 1962, more than twenty years younger, and much less experienced, we were literally exploring an unknown world, suddenly opened up to us by the aqualung, a simple if primitive means of staying down under-water without too much fuss, expense or bother. In all of human experience—in perhaps two, three or more million years—this had never happened before.

9

Like mechanical flight, it all came to pass within a single century. The pioneers were very fortunate, and even those who came after them early on were uniquely privileged, amateurs though we were. For instance, I started learning to fly in 1933 and soloed at the age of 15 in 1934. Yet the number on my Royal Aero Club certificate is 13516. I began snorkel diving without tuition in 1958 and joined the British Sub-Aqua Club the following year as diver number 6437. (But I had already done a brief course in helmet diving with the Royal Engineers in Hamburg in 1951–1952). When I learned to fly I was a schoolboy, but I was a middle-aged historian when I first began to dive around Britain.

Flying and diving have a lot in common. Because one is not pinned to the earth by gravity, there is a delightful sense of freedom. However, few of our underwater experiences could be described, strictly speaking, as adventure. To the eternal bafflement of film-makers and cameramen, most underwater hazards are not visual. The really deadly processes are internal; they take place within the diver's own body, as a result of breathing various gases under high pressure. An inadequately trained novice is like a blind and deaf man trying to cross a motorway. He's dead before he knows what hit him.

Even in the days of helmet diving, with all its restrictions, it was fashionable to say that no one would pay you to dive; it was what you did when you got down there that mattered. The diving apparatus was merely a means of transport to one's place of work, like a motor car or bicycle. This was, and is, largely true. A professional diver has to be master of many trades which he happens to follow underwater.

There were, and are, very few professional divers; and I am not one of them. The aqualung brought in the true amateur who, because he was not paid—indeed, actually paid for everything himself—had leisure to swim, stop and stare if he wished. As an historian, I could hardly help choosing to study history underwater, because that was what interested me. I had no employer to tell me to stop wasting his money and my time, and get on with welding this or that.

In two respects, however, a task performed underwater may differ markedly from the same job at the surface. Firstly, if there is a considerable degree of hazard involved—great depth, fast currents, black water—part of the diver's attention must be given to considerations of his own survival, which may detract from the performance of the job in hand. Secondly, if the depth is very great the diver may be affected by nitrogen narcosis, which often has much the same effect on his performance as alcohol. There is a third, more shadowy reason. If conditions are good and the scene interesting, there is an insidious desire just to relax and enjoy being underwater, browsing and looking in a perfectly delightful, weightless way.

Twenty years ago land archaeologists used to deny that there could be such a thing as underwater archaeology at all. No one talked about jungle archaeology (if the ruins happened to be in a jungle) or mountain archaeology (if the site happened to be at high altitude), so what was so special about underwater?

But it *is* different. Physically, because one is adapting to life in another environment—one lives in a liquid and not in a gas mixture. Academically, because much of the subject matter for study is specialist—ships, cargoes, sea routes, coastlines, ports. Above all, the sea. The sea as an environment, with all its different laws (at that time, mostly unguessed at by archaeologists). An archaeologist is only a kind of historian, dealing with things rather than people and documents, and claiming special knowledge of how to dig them up without destroying all the evidence. Twenty years ago, archaeologists had no such knowledge where underwater sites were concerned. Even today, most ship specialists would deny the right of any ordinary archaeologist to excavate a ship hull without assistance from nautical experts.

That is the background to this particular story, which spans more than twenty years, beginning when underwater archaeology was a very questionable proceeding and ending when a degree of knowledge and respectability has been gained. For me, it began on 25 August, 1962, about 150 feet down the slope of an underwater island in the Tuscan archipelago. A trail of broken amphorae led down the slope to even greater depths. I fanned away the sand, uncovering the graceful handle broken off an amphora an immensely long time ago. Because I nearly died from the effects of nitrogen narcosis farther down the slope, I still retain an impression of its steepness, of a gulley dropping away between flanking rocks. In spite of the narcosis I did not let go of the tube-worm encrusted handle. That was fortunate, although at the time I did not realise just how significant that handle was to prove to be.

I had always been moved by Flecker's poem, which goes on:

> It was so old a ship—who knows, who knows?
> —And yet so beautiful, I watched in vain
> To see the mast burst open with a rose,
> And the whole deck put on its leaves again.

As a child I had seen the bay where St Paul was wrecked off Malta in AD 60, and felt close to ancient history. But this broken ship down in the dim twilight of deep water was to be something else again; far older, more enigmatic—a key into the dark world of the Etruscans.

I began to question those who had found it and carried on questioning those of my friends who continued to dive the site over the years, trying to find out what had been taken from the ship, so that even if it was to be entirely plundered, still some record would have been made. Eventually, I was able to publish. It had become quite clear that, although there were other wrecks around that island, both Roman and Greek, this ship— even if not a great deal now remained—was the most important of all. Possibly it was unique. Perhaps there was nothing else like it in the world.

Chapter 1

THE MYSTERIOUS
ETRUSCANS

When I began to talk about an Etruscan wreck, people would look puzzled and ask, 'A *what* wreck?' And when I had hesitantly half-explained, they would instantly demand, 'But *where* is it?' Hard to say, because there are no famous cities anywhere near Giglio, Rome being far to the south, Pisa and Florence well to the north; best to reply that, on a good day, one could see the islands of Elba and Montecristo, with Corsica just down over the horizon. As for Etruria itself, modern Tuscany is smaller than the territory occupied by the ancient Etruscans who drove south of Rome and north of the Apennines. The next question, '*When* did it happen?' is easier to answer. The heyday of Etruscan expansion came in the sixth century BC, a hundred years before the classical age of Greece; our ship therefore dated from a time before the 'Elgin marbles', was older than the buildings on the Acropolis of Athens.

A harder question to answer would be, '*Who* were the Etruscans and what language did they speak?' That they were different from all other peoples is sure; the nature of the differences was debated in their own time and is still contested. It would be rash to declare that we were dealing with an unknown ship belonging to an unknown people speaking an unknown language, but that would not be so very far from the truth. The Etruscans are indeed an enigma, because the evidence is so sparse and ill-balanced. A ship from that time would be more than ordinarily important.

The earliest surviving history was written in the fifth century (probably about 430 BC) by Herodotus, a careful Greek historian who merely set down the story told by the Lydians regarding events many centuries in the past. Their country lay in what is now Turkey, inland of later Greek settlements on the Aegean coast of Asia, just to the north of Halicarnassus where Herodotus was born.

In the reign of Atys, son of Manes, a terrible famine occurred throughout Lydia . . . but when things got no better they began to look for something to help and came up with a number of devices. It was during this time that they invented dice, knucklebones, ball

13

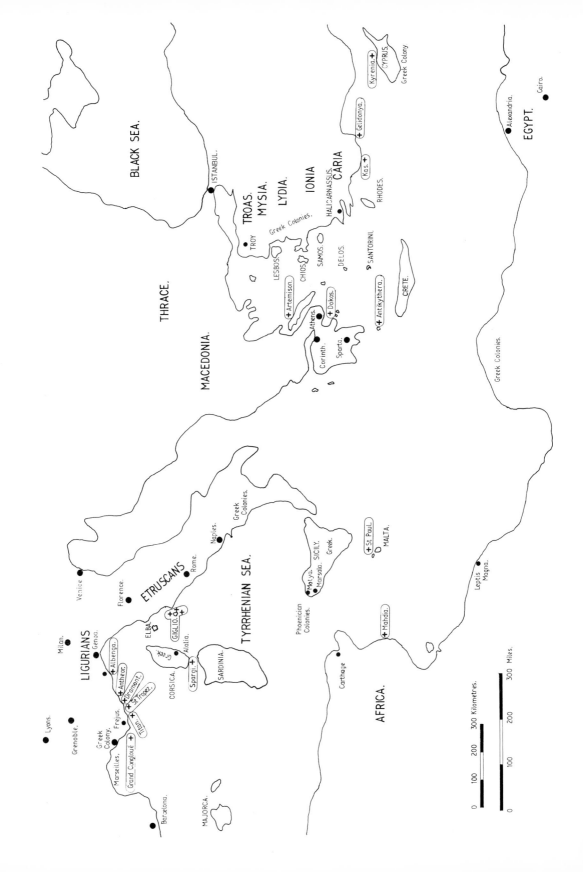

games and other games (but not checkers). They used these to distract them from their hunger by, on alternate days, playing continuously one whole day so they would not think about food, and
eating on the following day without playing. In this way they got
through 18 years. Things got worse, however, rather than better, and
the king therefore divided all the Lydians into two groups and drew
lots to decide which should stay and which should emigrate, putting
himself at the head of those who were to remain and appointing his
son, who was called Tyrrhenus, as the leader for those who had to
leave. Those Lydians whose lot it was to leave went down to Smyrna
and built boats on to which they loaded all their possessions and sailed
away to seek a life elsewhere. After sailing past many lands they came
to Umbria in Italy where they built cities and still live to this day,
changing their name from Lydians to Tyrrhenians after the king's
son Tyrrhenus who had led them.

Hellanicus of Lesbos, another Greek historian writing in the fifth century
BC, mentioned a group of Pelasgians who arrived in Italy and there
changed their name to Tyrrhenians.

Roman authors confirmed an eastern origin for the Etruscans. Virgil
(70–19 BC) referred to the town of '. . . Cerveteri, built on an ancient rock
where once the Lydians, a race distinguished in war, settled the hills of
Tuscany.' And Seneca (who died in AD 65) stated that '. . . Asia claims
the Etruscans as her own.' Tacitus (first to second centuries AD) accepted
the story as told by Herodotus. Other tales also locate the Etruscans in
Asia Minor, linking them with the Pelasgians; and refer to Tyrsenians
or Tyrrhenians on the islands of Lemnos, Imbros and Lesbos, just off the
Asian coast in the northern Aegean, and on Delos, the holy island in the
centre of the Cyclades.

The Etruscans referred to themselves as Rasenna, but to the Romans
and Greeks they were Etrusci, Tusci, Tyrrheni, or Tyrseni. To the modern
Italians they are still Etrusci and the name of the Etruscan Sea is still
the Tyrrhenian, after perhaps 3,000 years.

But in the first century BC, a dissenting voice spoke up. Dionysius,
another Greek historian from Halicarnassus, writing four centuries later
than Herodotus, declared a different finding:

I do not believe that the Tyrrhenians were a colony of the Lydians,
for they do not use the same language as the latter, nor can it be
alleged that, though they no longer speak a similar tongue, they still
retain some other indications of their mother country. For they

◀   The Mediterranean in the time of the Etruscans. *Drawn by Maurice Young*

neither worship the same gods as the Lydians nor make use of similar laws or institutions . . . Indeed, those probably come nearest the truth who declare that the nation migrated from nowhere else, but was native to the country, since it is found to be a very ancient nation and to agree with no other in its language or in its manner of living.

Arguing about the distant past can be inconclusive, but Dionysius was living at the same time as the Etruscans. Although they had by now been subjugated by the Romans, they still remained distinctive. According to his testimony, in two respects the Etruscans resembled no other nation—in their language and in their manner of living. But what exactly were those differences?

Specialists claim that there is no mystery about the Etruscan language. Some 10,000 inscriptions have been found, and clearly the letters have been adapted from a Greek alphabet, based in turn on a Phoenician or Semitic source. Although the letters can now be understood, the words are a different matter. Etruscan resembles no known language, although there are connections with inscriptions found on the island of Lemnos, off the coast of modern Turkey opposite the Dardanelles, and with some place and proper names on the nearby coast of Asia Minor. It does not belong to the Indo-European family of languages. Bilingual inscriptions have been found, notably a recent discovery at Pyrgi, just up the coast from Rome, which held both Punic and Etruscan texts. But, alas, the hopes were not realised—the texts were not exactly comparable, for one was full and the other merely a precis. So what of the 10,000 inscriptions?

Very many of them read like this:

Laris Pulenas, Larces clan, Larthal papacs, Velthurus nefts, prumts Pules Parisal Creices.

And because there are so many such as this it is now possible to translate the inscription as:

Lars Pulenas, son of Larce, nephew of Larth, grandson of Velthur, great-grandson of Laris Pule, the Greek.

Similarly, from funerary inscriptions for females, we now know that *puia, ati* and *sec* or *sex* mean respectively 'wife', 'mother', and 'daughter'.

The 10,000 texts span the seventh to the first centuries BC. By far the longest is a religious liturgy: it numbers 1,190 words (or about three or four pages of a modern book). The next longest numbers 300 words (less

◄ Cerveteri: Steps into the underworld of an Etruscan tomb, seen from inside the tomb itself. *Photo: Alexander McKee*

than a modern page) and is a prescription for funeral ceremonies. Two or three more exceed 100 words, about a dozen are slightly in excess of 30 words. Most, so far as they can be translated, appear to be religious formulae, epitaphs for the dead, enumerations of proper names and titles, plus some oddities. There is a boundary stone, some coins, a lead disc with an inscription written in a spiral, a bronze model of a sheep's liver apparently inscribed with the signs of the zodiac as used for divination, pottery inscriptions, dice and so on. The materials on which these were written were imperishable. But everyday writing, on waxed wooden tablets, has hardly ever survived. It is from this evidence that attempts have been made completely to understand the Etruscan language.

It is as if the English language (and, one hopes, the history of England) were to be understood when the evidence consisted of one extract from the Bible (possibly part of the Sermon on the Mount), the order for burial at sea, a section of *Burke's Peerage*, a number of souvenir Coronation mugs and several thousand headstones from various cemeteries scattered throughout the country.

Livy, the Roman historian who lived between 59 BC and AD 17, wrote of the Etruscan city of Caere in the fourth century BC:

> I have authority for believing that in that age Roman boys were regularly schooled in Etruscan literature, as nowadays they are trained in Greek.

There was, then, an Etruscan literature ranking with Greek and Latin; but none of it has yet come to light. So, although we know more now than we did, the Etruscan language may still be rated as mysterious.

More is known about the Etruscan manner of living, which was a scandal to their neighbours, the Greeks and Romans. For a start, they ate too well, too often, and ostentatiously. Their slaves were far too smartly dressed and even the women were 'intrepid drinkers'. Dionysius of Halicarnassus complained:

> The Tyrrhenians were a people of dainty and expensive tastes, both at home and in the field, carrying about with them, besides the necessities, costly and artistic articles of all kinds designed for pleasure and luxury.

Another first century Greek, Diodorus Siculus, was equally scathing:

> Twice a day, they spread costly tables and upon them everything that is appropriate for excessive luxury, providing gaily coloured couches and silver drinking cups of every description and servants-in-waiting in no small number.

Vulci: The lintel of an Etruscan temple. *Photo: Alexander McKee*

As if consuming two square meals a day was insufficient to condemn the Etruscans as irresponsible gourmets, Diodorus accused them of degeneracy:

> In general they have abandoned the valiant steadfastness that they so prized in former days, and by their indulgence in banquets and effeminate delights they have lost the reputation which their ancestors won in war.

Their new reputation was for unspeakable orgies (but not quite as unspeakable as all that, for a number of historians found themselves fully capable of description). Athenaeus, a Greek grammarian of the third century AD, came too late to give a personal eye-witness account, and had to rely instead on fellow Greeks, Timaeus and Theopompus, both of whom had lived in the fourth century BC.

Among the Etruscans, who had become extravagantly luxurious,

19

Timaeus records in his first book that the slave girls wait on the men naked. And Theopompus in the forty-third book of his *Histories* says that it is customary with the Etruscans to share their women in common; the women bestow great care on their bodies and often exercise even with men, sometimes also with one another; for it is no disgrace for women to show themselves naked. Further, they dine, not with their own husbands, but with any men who happen to be present, and they pledge with wine any whom they wish. They are also terribly bibulous, and are very good-looking. The Etruscans rear all the babies that are born, not knowing who is the father in any single case. These in turn pursue the same mode of life as those who have given them nurture, having drinking parties often and consorting with all the women. It is no disgrace for Etruscans to be seen doing anything in the open, or even having anything done to them; for this also is a custom of their country. And so far are they from regarding it as a disgrace that they actually say, when the master of the house is indulging in a love affair, and someone enquires for him, that he is undergoing so-and-so, openly calling the act by its indecent name. When they get together for companionship or in family parties they do as follows: first of all, after they have stopped drinking and are ready to go to bed, the servants bring in to them, the lamps being still lighted, sometimes female prostitutes, sometimes very beautiful boys, sometimes also their wives; and when they have enjoyed these, the servants then introduce lusty young men, who in their turn consort with them. They indulge in love affairs and carry on these unions sometimes in full view of one another, but in most cases with screens set up round the beds; the screens are made of latticed wands, over which cloths are thrown. Now they consort very eagerly, to be sure, with women; much more, however, do they enjoy consorting with boys and striplings. For in their country these latter are very good-looking, because they live in luxury and keep their bodies smooth. In fact all the barbarians who live in the west remove the hair of their bodies by means of pitch-plasters and by shaving with razors.

These stories were believed. Among those who accepted them were the Greek philosopher Aristotle (fourth century BC), the Roman poet Plautus (third century BC), and another Roman poet, Horace (first century BC). But what should we believe?

To me, Diodorus Siculus, condemning the loss of warlike prowess through luxury, echoes that diabolical armchair British patriot who lamented the introduction of the gunshield before the First World War as 'not in the true tradition of the artillery'. His opinion was based on

historical ignorance, technical ignorance of recent changes, and a willing-
ness, from a position of perfect safety, to expose others to needless wounds
or death.

A serious point could have been made by the ancient critics, that anyone
serving up the sharp end, who necessarily must live in the open in all
weathers and often on short rations, needs to be hard; and if he is not,
then he needs to be acclimatised. We are anyway talking about the young
men who fight wars, not the older civilians they later become, who may
wallow in luxury without detriment to the national interest. But Dionysius
and Diodorus are not making serious points; they are merely criticising
excess kit and over-eating on campaign. And not even their own campaign.

Athenaeus, through the otherwise lost histories of Timaeus and
Theopompus, introduces a different issue. Regarding the forward attitude
of women in Etruscan social life, it must be admitted that he is blinkered
by the Greek custom of keeping the women at home, while the men go
out feasting with the lewd girls (and boys); this makes him highly cen-
sorious towards a social system, such as the Etruscan, where the women
in many spheres (but not quite all) were treated equally with men, and
husbands actually sat down to meals together with their wives. Failure
to sympathise with alien customs is a trait to which many of us could plead
guilty; but Athenaeus is guilty of hypocrisy as well. For, having smitten
the Etruscan foe naked hip and naked thigh, he goes on to praise the habits
of fellow Greeks, as recorded by earlier Greek historians:

> The Spartan custom of displaying the young girls naked before
> strangers is highly praised; and in the island of Chios it is delightful
> just to walk to the gymnasia and running tracks to see the young
> men wrestling naked with the young girls, who are also naked.

In the final analysis, one wants to ask how balanced is the account of
Etruscan orgies, how representative; and one is inclined to answer that
Athenaeus would have been in his element as a reporter for one of the
more sensational Sunday newspapers of modern Britain.

Popular papers of this kind are, of course, primarily picture papers,
which prompts us to check on the classical equivalents, for pictures—and
statues also—we do have from Greece, from Rome, from Etruria. The
Greeks can be gracefully erotic, the Romans often crudely pornographic.
The Etruscans are different, possibly because most of their surviving pictures are paintings on the walls of their tombs. They often show happy
scenes. Frequently, men and women are depicted in the dance, leaping
as if to a steady, driving beat, although that seems unlikely, as the musicians are playing the lyre and the flute. Flutes occur most often, usually
the double-flute, occasionally the single. There are a few sombre pictures,

A buxom dancing girl, based on a damaged painting in the Tomb of Hunting and Fishing at Tarquinia. *Drawn by Edgar G. Taylor*

almost invariably historical, showing single combat or the execution of prisoners.

The tomb pictures are wordless in the narrative sense—there are no captions to tell you what is happening. Virtually the only words we have are Roman: those of Livy who reflects the surprise of Roman audiences when for once their virile live-combat shows were replaced by the softer Etruscan music-and-movement spectacles.

> To appease the gods, the idea of staged games was conceived, something quite new for a race of warriors accustomed only to amphitheatre games. Without any singing, without imitating the action of singers, players who had been brought in from Etruria danced to the strains of the flautist and performed not ungraceful evolutions in the Tuscan style. This kind of spectacle spread and the actors were called *histriones*, from the Etruscan term *hister*.

There seems nothing orgiastic about that, although the tomb paintings suggest a gaiety bordering on eroticism; Etruria, it must be remembered, is hot. Of all the tomb paintings, the great exception is a kind of crude panorama painted on the wall above an interior lintel. On the left is a bull gazing peacefully at the backsides of a couple engaged in heterosexual intercourse; in the centre is a bull charging with stiffened penis at a standing couple on the right engaging in homosexual intercourse. Modern historians seem unable to interpret this. Some doubtfully suggest that the picture may be a moral tract, implying that the wages of sin are to be gored by a bull *in flagrante delicto*. To me, it might be likened to a wartime cartoon on the lines of 'Famous Last Words'. This is truly an enigma of the Etruscans.

One of the tombs contains a delightful mural of men hunting and fishing, another shows a diver curving gracefully down to the water, and a further hunting scene shows the hunter wearing a bright red, shady hat, tied on firmly by cords under the chin. Although the Etruscans were credited by their neighbours with the invention of the war trumpet (not primarily a musical instrument but a means of transmitting brief orders through the chaotic roar of the fighting), a detailed description of an Etruscan hunt by the Roman scholar Varro (116–28 BC) is curious. Normally, strong and dangerous animals are driven by the sound of dogs, beaters and the blare of the hunting horn towards either traps or a spread-out line of marksmen armed with bows or (in my own personal experience) with rifles. Even with a ·303 bullet travelling at 2,440 feet per second, a large boar is not all that easy to knock over instantly. Anyone who was prepared to take on beasts like that with handspears alone, has my sincere admiration. But what Varro describes is something different, almost incredible.

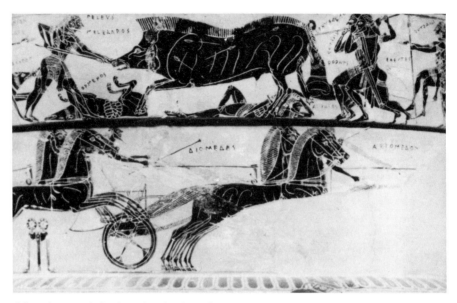

A boar hunt and chariots, showing how dangerous an animal this was to men armed only with spears. From a drinking vessel dated 570–60 BC, now in the Archaeological Museum in Florence. *Photo: Scala, Firenze*

It is said in Etruria, where wild pigs and stags are caught with nets and dogs in the usual manner of hunters, that success is greater when music is used as an aid . . . Nets are stretched out and all kinds of traps set in position. Along comes an experienced piper. He avoids so far as possible regular melodies and loud sounds and plays the sweetest tunes the double pipe can produce. In the silent solitude, his airs float up to the tops of the mountains, into the gorges and thickets, into all the retreats and breeding grounds of the game. At first, when the sounds reach their ears, the animals are terrified and filled with fear. But later they are irresistibly overcome by enjoyment of the music. Enraptured, they abandon their young, their lairs, their familiar trails from which they would normally be unwilling to stray. Thus the wild beasts of the Tyrrhenian forests are gradually attracted by the powerful music and they draw near, bewitched by the sounds, till they fall, overpowered by music, into the snares.

Not quite the Pied Piper of Hamelin, but almost as unbelievable. One would dismiss the story totally, but for the fact that the legendary tales from the classical world of boys riding on dolphins have been amply corroborated in modern times. There might be a basis of truth, if only that music played a great part in the life of the Etruscans.

Less easy for us to grasp is the Etruscan attitude to religion, which seems to have been allied to haruspicy or soothsaying. The Etruscans were regarded as masters in foretelling the future and even averting catastrophe, and high-ranking Romans often had Etruscan soothsayers on their personal staffs. Julius Caesar, for instance, employed a member of the Etruscan Spurinna family in this capacity and in 44 BC was warned to beware of the Ides (the 15th) of March. Caesar's personal protection proved inadequate, however, and the Etruscan prophecy came true.

The Roman historian Cicero (106–43 BC), writing of the founding of Rome (traditionally in 753 BC), recorded that:

In the first place, the founder of our city, Romulus, is said not only to have founded it in obedience to the auspices, but also to have been himself an augur of outstanding skill. After him the other kings also had recourse to soothsayers; and when the (Etruscan) kings had been driven out (of Rome), no state business was ever transacted, whether in time of war or peace, without reference to the auspices. And as the science of haruspicy seemed to be very successful both in seeking to obtain omens by consulting nature and in understanding and averting evil portents, they introduced the whole of this science from Etruria so that no kind of divination should be neglected.

A statue of a member of this college of *haruspices* exists. The costume is weird, with a fringed mantle, high conical hat like a Welsh wizard and a curved stick like a bent Field Marshal's baton. One can appreciate the remark by the Roman historian Cato (second century BC) that he could not understand how one 'soothsayer doesn't laugh when he sees another soothsayer'.

The Etruscans' view of god, unlike that of the Greeks and Romans, was not personalised in human form. They had an intense belief in nature, difficult to appreciate in the twentieth century AD when we are guided more by street lights than by the stars. One has to go to a place like the Sinai desert fully to appreciate what an uncontaminated sky and a clear atmosphere are like. With small populations and no means of harnessing electricity, nature tended to dominate man rather than the other way round, although already the Romans were tending to think rationally, if not accurately. Seneca, the Roman philosopher and dramatist, wrote:

There is this difference between us Romans and Etruscans. We believe that lightning is caused by clouds colliding, whereas they believe that clouds collide in order to create lightning. Since they attribute everything to the gods, they are led to believe not that events have a meaning because they have happened, but that they happen in order to express a meaning.

This was the basis for the Etruscans' efforts to foretell the future or identify trends from observing nature. Nevertheless, they were not impractical. For instance, a tomb find shows that they knew how to manufacture false teeth, using gold as the material for the bridge work.

The archaeological evidence of the tombs, with all their costly contents, and the use of gold in dentistry, together with all the comments by Greeks and Romans on their over-eating and obnoxiously luxurious life-style, shows that, at the height of their power, the Etruscans were rich. But how did they become rich? Where did all this wealth come from, to elicit the envy of their foes and rivals?

Basically, from agriculture and industry. However, to understand the ancient authors, we must first learn the military geography. Italy is approximately 1,000 miles long and 100 miles wide, with a mountainous spine going up to 6,000 feet in places and virtually impassable in winter. From the central spine mountainous ribs branch out to the seas, those on the western side often dog-legging down to the coast. On the west there is a practical front (for living and the advance of armies) of between 20 and 25 miles; on the east coast it is only 5 to 15 miles wide. The Etruscans occupied much of the west coast, and its division by dog-leg ribs and river valleys tended towards the formation of semi-independent city states, each with a strongly individual character. Sometimes they fought each other, as European nations do. They rarely combined against an outside foe, and this was to be their downfall.

There were about a dozen such states, of which the most important were Caere (modern Cerveteri), Tarquinii (modern Tarquinia), Vulci, Rusellae (modern Roselle), Vetulonia, Volsinii (modern Bolsena), Clusium (modern Chiusi), Perusia (modern Perugia), Cortona, Arretium (modern Arezzo), Volaterrae (modern Volterra), and Veii. When Veii fell to the Romans after a long and epic siege, it was replaced by Populonia. Not all the Etruscan names for these cities are known with certainty, but Populonia in Etruscan was probably Pupluna or Fufluna. Latin Caere, modern Cerveteri, in Etruscan was Chaisre, as near as we may make it, for the Etruscan script makes exact equivalents difficult.

Diodorus Siculus, in the first century BC, borrowed a description of the Etruscan countryside from an earlier Greek writer of the late second century BC.

The earth bears much fruit and, by the effort they put into cultivating it, the inhabitants can make it yield an abundance of produce,

The sarcophagus of the bride and bridegroom from Cerveteri, now in the Villa Giulia Museum in Rome, and dated to the second half of the sixth century BC. Typically Etruscan are the woman's headdress and shoes, and also the fact that she lies beside her husband as an equal. *Photo : Istituto Geografico De Agostini-Novara*

beyond what they require for their own sustenance . . . The fields consist of vast plains, interspersed with many hills, and they are well cultivated. The land is fertile because it is very humid, in summer as well as in winter.

Not all Etruria is like that, but the Maremma, the coastal plain from Orbetello and the Argentario peninsula northwards to Follonica and also south towards the Tiber, is still fertile and, in summer, shimmers with heat at the foot of the mountains.

Property divisions were at least as important then as now, together with the rule of law. There is a text in the Latin collection of *Gramatici veteres* in which a divinity, the nymph Vergoia, speaks to Arruns Veltumnus:

Know that the sea was once separate from the sky. When Jupiter thereafter claimed the land of Etruria for himself, he laid down and commanded that its fields should be measured and the boundaries of cultivated areas marked out. Knowing the greed of men and their desire for land, he insisted that all should be divided up and boundaries marked out.

The time shall come, however . . . when someone shall be overcome with greed and shall interfere with the divisions and with what has been granted, and men shall illegally interfere with the divisions and with what has been granted, and men shall illegally interfere with, touch and move the stones which mark the boundaries. But whosoever shall touch them or move them in order to increase his own property and diminish that of others shall be punished.

If it is done by slaves, their condition shall be made worse; if they do it with the complicity of their master, his house shall soon suffer ruin and all his race shall perish.

The guilty shall be afflicted with terrible ills and diseases, which will reduce them to a state of utter physical debility. The earth shall be rent with storms and floods which shall throw it into complete confusion. Crops shall be damaged by rain and hail, dried up by the heat of the sun and destroyed by mildew. There will be great civil strife. Know that this will happen when crimes of this kind are committed. Therefore you must not be false or speak with two tongues. Retain these teachings in your memory.

The laws referred to public land as well as private property; the amazing fertility of the Etruscan plains and valleys owed much to vast hydraulic works. However, the richest source of Etruscan wealth by far was the mines. Etruria had the greatest concentration of metals in the ground—of iron, tin and copper—in the entire central Mediterranean. It lay in the hills running down to the Maremma, along the river valleys like Cecina, in the Tolfa mountains north of Rome, and on the island of Elba off Populonia. From about 750–700 BC, for over 400 years, from Elba alone, it is thought, as much as 10,000 tons of iron ore a year were extracted and shipped to the mainland and to foreign customers. This is why the Etruscans were rich and could afford to eat well twice a day off pretty, flower-patterned tablecloths, and drink expensive wines out of silver cups. But, as with most industrial complexes, there was a penalty to pay in the spoliation of the environment. Diodorus Siculus described the Elba mines in the first century BC.

Near the city of Populonia there is an island called *Aithaleia*. It is about 100 stades from the coast, and was given its name because of the smoke (*aithalos* in Greek) which completely envelops it. For the island is rich in siderite, which is broken up for smelting, to secure the iron contained in it in large quantities. Those who carry out this work crush the stone and bake it in specially constructed furnaces. The heat causes the metal to liquefy in the furnaces and it is then shaped into ingots of medium size which look like sponges in form. Large quantities of these ingots can be bought from those who deal in them, and they transport them as far as Dichaearcheia or other trading stations.

Greek Dichaearcheia is Roman Puteoli (modern Pozzuoli on the Bay of Naples), one of many such Greek trading posts and colonies established on the Italian peninsula during the period of Etruscan expansion.

Sometimes Greeks and Etruscans worked together, at other times they were rivals or foes; but it must always have been easier to ship the heavy ingots as ballast by sea than to move them great distances on land. Such valuable cargoes must also have tempted pirates and perhaps received protection. Certainly a general command of the sea would have been required.

There is an earlier but still contemporary picture of the contrast between an agricultural economy and an industrial one in the ancient world. Apollonius of Rhodes, writing in the third century BC of the semi-mythical Voyage of Jason and the Argonauts long before, nevertheless described a scene which must have been familiar to him:

At nightfall on the following day they reached the land of the Chalybes. These people do not use the ploughing ox. They not only grow no corn, but plant no vines or trees for their delicious fruit and graze no flocks in dewy pastures. Their task is to dig for iron in the stubborn ground and they live by selling the metal they produce. To them no morning ever brings a holiday. In a black atmosphere of soot and smoke they live a life of unremitting toil.

Just so must life have appeared to many in Etruscan times. The other main type of manual labour—on the land—meant working under a searing sun for long hours; no wonder the Etruscan paintings show a wide-brimmed hat as a popular item of wear! For the top people, of course, there was fashionable clothing; shoes of elaborately Etruscan type with oddly curled-up toes are often depicted. Nothing so unsuitable for the summer climate as trousers were worn; instead, different kinds of cloak-like garments hanging from the shoulder, and often and understandably, many men worked naked to the waist.

Etruscan civilisation flourished from about 1000 BC until about 300 BC when they were overpowered by the Romans, lost their independence and merged with Rome. This was the swing of a pendulum which, at the start

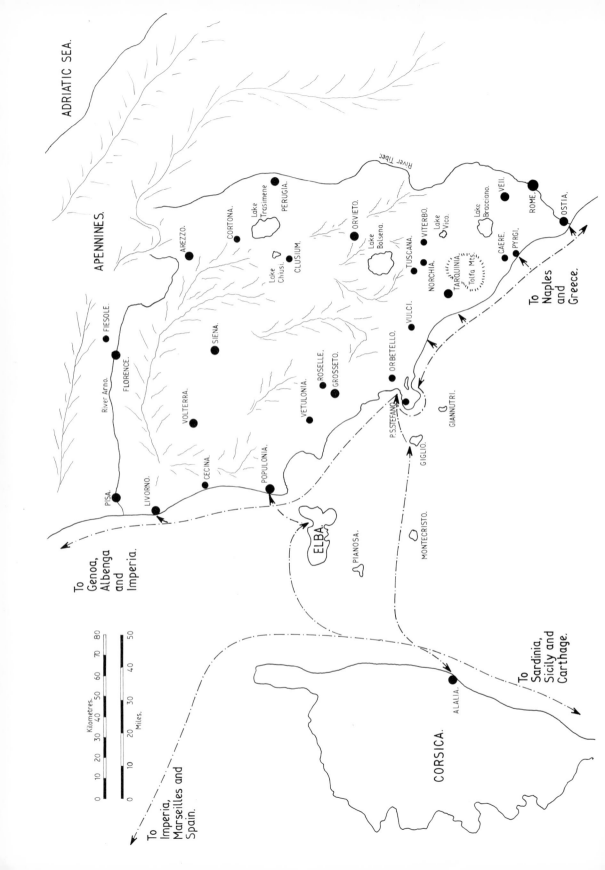

of the story, had gone the other way, southwards to Rome. The Etruscans supplied three known kings to the city of Romulus, from Lucius Tarquinius Priscus in about 616 BC, through Servius Tullius (about 579–533 BC), to Tarquinius Superbus (Tarquin the Proud) from 533 to about 509 BC. The latter was expelled and took refuge in Etruscan Clusium, the city of Lars Porsenna. Here, the names ring bells from one's childhood schooling, with vague recollections of Macaulay's *Lays of Ancient Rome*.

That story began in the middle of the seventh century BC, according to the Roman historian Livy, writing some 600 years later. (The first history of Rome was not written until 200 BC, by Q. Fabius Pictor, but this failed to survive except for a few quotations to be found in other authors.) What Livy says is that a Greek nobleman, Demaratus of Corinth, left Greece in the mid-seventh century BC during a political crisis and, bringing Greek artists with him, settled in the Etruscan city of Tarquinia, just north of Rome. (Dionysius of Halicarnassus implies that he was in the shipping business, 'taking Greek goods to the Etruscans and Etruscan goods to Greece', and this may well have been so.) In any event, he married an Etruscan lady and they had two sons.

One of these sons was named Lucomo (a word really meaning 'chief' or 'king'), and he married a forceful Etruscan lady called Tanaquil. But because he was only half Etruscan himself, he found his career blocked in Tarquinia and, urged on by Tanaquil, decided to move to Rome where the society was freer and his opportunities would be better. They climbed into their vehicle and then, wrote Livy:

> They had come as far as Janiculum, when as they were sitting in their carpentum (covered wagon), an eagle poised on its wings gently descended upon them and plucked off Lucomo's cap, after which, rising noisily above the car and again stooping, as if sent from heaven for that service, it deftly replaced the cap upon his head and departed on high. This augury was joyfully accepted, it is said, by Tanaquil, a woman skilled in celestial prodigies, as was the case with most Etruscans.

The reigning king of Rome was a Sabine, Ancus Martius. The Roman kingship was not hereditary, but by election or selection among a small aristocracy, as in many political parties today. The position until then had been alternated between the two main peoples involved, the Romans and the Sabines. After the probably mythical Romulus (in 748, 735, 751, 728 or 753, according to which ancient author you pick) came the Sabine, Numa Pompilius, who was followed by a Latin, Tullus Hostilius, who was

◀ Etruscan sites and trade routes. *Drawn by Maurice Young*

succeeded by Ancus Martius. From this Sabine king, the position went quite peacefully to the half-Greek, half-Etruscan Lucomo and his wholly Etruscan wife, Tanaquil. He now became Lucius Tarquinius Priscus (Tarquin the First). He was credited by ancient authors with improving the city centre of Rome, a story confirmed by recent archaeological excavations, and was then assassinated.

The Roman Emperor Claudius (10 BC–AD 54) is our next witness from the past. The first of Claudius' four wives was Platia Urgulanilla, an Etruscan girl who spoke her native language. Claudius, who was a respectable scholar if a trifle informal in public affairs, wrote (in Greek) a history of the Etruscans in 20 volumes and another of the Carthaginians in eight volumes, which he caused to be read aloud once a year in the library of Alexandria. When one is a Roman Emperor, there are few problems in publishing or in getting one's work known. But making sure that it survives the next cosmic disaster or little local revolution, or even an outbreak of puritanism, is a different matter. Claudius was unlucky in that respect, and so are we. If both these works had survived, it would have transformed our knowledge of antiquity in general and of the Etruscans in particular. But they did not, and all we have left of them is a fragment from a speech made by Claudius at Lyon, in which he drew on his studies of previous writers:

> Between Tarquinius Priscus and his son or grandson (Tarquin the Proud)—the sources do not agree on this point—must be placed Servius Tullius. According to Latin writers, his mother was the slave Ocresia; according to Etruscan writers, he was a close friend of Caelius Vibenna and was involved in all the latter's adventures. After a series of events, he went to Etruria with the remainder of Caelius's troops, and occupied Mons Caelius, which he named after his general; and having changed his name to Servius Tullius (he was called Mastarna in Etruscan), he held sway there to the immense benefit of the state.

According to Verrius Flaccus, the brothers Caelius and Aulus Vibenna, together with Mastarna (or Macstrna), had come to Rome originally in the train of Tarquin and Tanaquil. Rarely does a tomb speak, but there is an Etruscan tomb at Vulci which is an exception; rather like a strip-cartoon but with captions restricted to name and nation only, a linked series of paintings shows two of these people in action, with Macstrna (or Mastarna) freeing Caelius Vibenna, and then a number of single-combats, in one of which a warrior from Vulci, Marce Camitlnas, is driving a sword into a man identified as Cneve Tarchunies Rumach (that is, a Roman Tarquin). The scenes were probably painted in the fourth or third centuries BC, much nearer to the events than Roman authors, who do not mention them. This hints at appalling gaps in our knowledge of early Roman history.

Macstrna (or Mastarna), in his Roman name of Servius Tullius, is credited with reorganising the Roman Army and creating the basic unit, the Century of one hundred men. Many of the symbols and organisation we think of as typically Roman seemed to have been introduced by the Etruscan kings. These include the twelve lictors who attended on the king; the fasces, the symbol of power which they carried; the curule stool and toga of the magistrates.

Like Tarquin the First, Servius Tullius was removed by assassination and succeeded by Tarquinius Superbus (the Proud), who was driven from his throne allegedly because of the rape of Lucretia by one of his sons, but possibly because he had become a tyrant. To recover his fortunes, the last Tarquin fled to Clusium, the capital of Lars Porsenna, then king, not merely of an Etruscan city state, but of all Etruria—the only king of whom that is said. Varro, the Roman antiquarian, writing in the first century BC, described Porsenna's great tomb at Clusium, 300 feet square. Under his warrior leadership the Etruscans, united for once, drove north through the Apennines to the fertile plain of the Po valley, south to Rome and beyond into Campania.

The Romans attempted to assassinate Porsenna. According to Livy, the Roman agent, Mucius Scaevola, got into the Etruscan camp during pay parade:

> The scribe was sitting next to the king, wearing very similar clothes to his, and was very busy as all the soldiers sought his attention. Scaevola dared not ask which of the two was Porsenna for fear that his ignorance would give him away, and he killed the scribe, mistaking him for the king.

Tacitus (first to second centuries BC) implies that Porsenna went on to take Rome. Pliny the Elder (AD 23–79) adds that he granted Rome a treaty, and Dionysius of Halicarnassus says that the Roman Senate offered Porsenna the emblems of kingship. But there is an alternative tale, passed on by Livy, of the defence of the Pons Sublicius, a wooden bridge across the Tiber built in the reign of King Ancus Martius the Sabine, by Horatius Cocles (the 'one-eyed') and two companions, who held off the Etruscans until the bridge could be cut down behind him. This is the story Macaulay used in his *Lays of Ancient Rome*, taught to many generations of schoolchildren:

Lars Porsena of Clusium
  By the Nine Gods he swore
That the great house of Tarquin
  Should suffer wrong no more.
By the Nine Gods he swore it,
  And named a trysting day,
And bade his messengers ride forth,
East and west and south and north,
  To summon his array.

The number of modern historians who believe Livy's story is as near nil as makes no matter, let alone Macaulay's telling of it. They suspect it to be Roman propaganda. This does not mean that no bravery or skill was shown by the defeated. It is quite likely that there may have been a bitter rearguard action at the Pons Sublicius and that, inevitably, some Romans were left on the wrong side when the bridge went down. And they may well have swum for it. But that might not have been the end of the affair. The next stage would be an assault river crossing and the erection of a temporary military bridge, and, most probably, that is what happened at Rome in 509 BC or soon after. But no Tarquin ever ruled there again, although perhaps Lars Porsenna did.

What is important to remember is that, in spite of everything, the Etruscans remain a strange and mysterious people whose history has never been written in modern times, because it cannot be: the evidence is not there. Not one of the ancient historians whom I have been able to quote was an Etruscan. They were all Greeks or Romans, rivals and often foes of the Etruscans. And not one of them has produced a history of the Etruscans which has survived. In almost every case, except that of Claudius, they are merely commenting on some aspect of Etruscan life, often just because the history of their own country was affected by the Etruscans in one sphere or another for a short time. This is the worst type of historical evidence.

The archaeological evidence is similarly flawed: it is unbalanced and partial. Nevertheless, it is important.

Chapter 2

ACROPOLIS AND NECROPOLIS

Cities of the Living, Cities of the Dead

Rome remember, remember the seafowls' sermon
That followed the beaked ships westward to their triumph.
O Rome, you city of soldiers, remember the singers
That cry with dead voices along the African shore.

Rome remember, the courts of learning are tiled
With figures from the east like running nooses.
The desolate bodies of boys in the blue glare
Of falling torches cannot stir your passion.
Remember the Greeks who measured out your doom.
Remember the soft funereal Etruscans.

Sidney Keyes, killed in Tunisia, 1943, aged 20

I suppose my early knowledge of the Etruscans was much the same as most people's—Macaulay's verses and a few vague snippets. One of the snippets was the poem written by Sidney Keyes and published in 1945, when I was in Germany. An infantryman, Keyes had ended up on a hillside near Medjez-el-Bab, 'missing'. He had been a history scholar at The Queen's College, Oxford, and had been fascinated by the classical world— as I was myself; possibly that was why I never forgot some of his poems, but this one above all. When, because of the Etruscan ship, I came to study the Etruscans for my own satisfaction, I now thought Keyes had been quite wrong. The Etruscans had been neither soft nor funereal. However, after reading what their contemporaries had said, and having studied what many of the modern historians had written, I decided to go and have a look at the Etruscan sites on land—or as many as I conveniently could. And afterwards I came to the conclusion that the Etruscans had indeed come to that melancholy state when their civilisation ended in conquest by Rome. The sites I saw covered, almost every one, the history of the Etruscans for nearly a thousand years: from primitive beginnings, through the years of full flowering during the sixth and fifth centuries BC, to the sad decline and often disappearance in the last few centuries before Christ.

Because of their relevance to the wreck lying off the island of Giglio,

I was particularly interested in the cities near the coast—those with ports—but I also wanted to see some of the inland places. I started in the south and worked north up the coast before branching inland, and everywhere I went I listened to what local experts had to say about their mysterious forebears; it was interesting to compare their views with those of the scholars—Italian, German, Scandinavian, British—whose books I had lately been reading. Facts were not really in dispute, but the emphasis could be different, the interpretative and value judgements striking. The time of the year was important. It was spring, the second half of May.

England had been chilly, above all monotonous, with dull winter lasting many months too long, one felt. In the first hour in Etruria, the warmth was absorbed to the bones. It was not just the sun, for there had been sunny days in England, too, but with a cold, chilling wind which also went to the core. With the new warmth, one felt relaxed, pleasantly non-aggressive, easy-going. The drive north from Rome to the shores of Lake Vico took a little over an hour, passing almost the full length of Veii, the first Etruscan state to fall to the Romans. I had decided to base myself at Ronsiglione, looking out over the lake whose deep, cold waters are the result of the flooding long ago of a huge volcanic crater. On the far shore of Lake Vico rose the wooded hills of the Cimmerian Forest.

In ancient times this forest had a fearsome reputation as the abode of dangerous monsters, and this is true enough even today, for there are wild boar in there still and there is hazardously close undergrowth which can mask the presence of large animals. I took part in wild boar hunts in Germany just after the war and killed one of some 300 pounds on my very first hunt; I found that a bullet which would knock a man over like a rabbit did not have such a decisive effect on a large wild animal, even at the close range of 20 feet. I stopped it with my first shot, but it took four more bullets before it fell over and died. A man armed only with a spear might well come off second best. It is no use running away, for the beast can travel much faster than you can. So what hits you are two tusks with up to 500 pounds' weight behind them, moving at 30 miles an hour. How to charm that with the music of the double flute, as the Etruscan are said to have done, would appear to present a problem. But I can believe that the deadly reputation of the Cimmerian Forest was well earned in the days when the standard weapon was a bronze or iron blade on the end of a pole.

Although here in Etruria one can see breeds of animals different from those in the rest of Italy—different horses, dogs, cattle—one should not take too literally some of the foreign plants, such as the lotus, or strange animals, such as the lion, which are depicted in Etruscan art. These will have been the work of foreign painters who settled in rich Etruria, as many scholars have noted. There were, however, many surprises as I drove across Southern Etruria: for instance, in many country areas I saw no smoke at all from factories, not even on the horizon. They are still completely agricultural, with sometimes only a dozen people to the square kilometre; although, close to the coast near Vulci, I did pass a sign reading 'CENTRALE NUCLARE'. The locals there had fought a long battle against the building of a nuclear power station—and lost.

Just as the Etruscans did against the Romans. Their city states did not band together, perhaps from local indifference or emnity but perhaps also from the difficulty of communications by land. They allowed Rome's first victim, Veii, to fall after an epic siege of ten years, in 396 BC. When the last of Etruscan independence was gone, everything went—the language, the literature, the luxury. Almost all of it was steam-rollered out of history by the conquerors and their successors and, since the Etruscans used many impermanent materials in their buildings, the physical evidence of their civilisation eroded away to ruin where it was not built upon in later times. So they became a mysterious, vanished race, to be recalled only by digging underground—and lately by explorations under the sea.

One cannot help feeling out of sympathy with the ancient Romans in relation to the Etruscans. They were after pomp and power, whereas the Etruscans opted for a happy life in a pleasant climate, with time for luxury and art. They believed in having a good life on this earth and that a good (but even better) life awaited them after death. They were not funereal or sad. On the other hand, Roman ideals have an appeal for many people, because it can be said that theirs was a society of free men, whereas the Etruscan states were ruled by over-powerful autocracies. Perhaps that is why the Romans won. After their conquest, by law they made everyone speak Latin—so the Etruscan language died out and the Etruscans became poor and disillusioned. Later the Church, for religious reasons, ignored them and this also helped to erase them from history.

Some scholars have said that the Romans may have been so jealous of the Etruscans—because they owed so much of their civilisation and customs to them—that they found it convenient to ignore the debt and to pretend that they had done it all themselves. There are many modern parallels.

As the southern border of inland Veii runs along the river Tiber on which Rome stands, so does that of its next-door coastal neighbour, Caere. Its modern name, Cerveteri (literally 'old Caere') is closely derived from the Etruscan Chaisre or Kysry (although the Greeks called it Arylla). In 1883, when the historical traveller George Dennis came here, all he found was a poor village of 300–400 people and some fourteenth-century fortifications—nothing else.

What we see now, almost exactly a century later, is a complete city of the dead which has appeared from under the ground as a result of excavation. It goes on for miles, the tombs on either side of the streets (some of which are paved—and rutted by carts) having been constructed internally to represent contemporary houses. The volcanic rock has been cut so that the ceilings of the rooms seem to be supported by beams; similarly, beds and furniture inside them have also been shaped from rock, and there are carved representations of objects supposedly hanging from hooks on the walls and pillars—knives, axes, jugs and so on; even a carved dog or two. Many represent the one-family three-room houses of around the sixth to fifth centuries BC, which the Romans later made fashionable. There are also remains (sometimes in the form of funerary urns) which depict the huts of an earlier time, called by the archaeologists Villanovan, after a distinctive culture found at a site near Bologna. In about 900 BC these people were making fine bronze armour and weapons, but by about 800 BC they were using mostly iron and trading in ores with the Greeks,

Cerveteri: (*Below*) A street of tombs in a great city of the dead. (*Opposite*) Ruts made in the roadway by carts more than two thousand years ago. *Photos: Alexander McKee*

so there may exist somewhere the wrecks of Villanovan ships.

Their village communities later coalesced to form the nucleus of the Etruscan cities; these were sited on high ground (easy to defend), near a river (for transport and trade), close to fertile land (for agriculture), not too far from mineral resources, and preferably with an opposing height across a valley. On that far height they would build a replica city to house their dead (who were not really dead but had merely gone on to a far better life in another world which was still close at hand). Whatever they wanted to take with them over that mysterious border was placed with the bodies in the tomb. And it was these objects which told historians so much about the lives of these dead Etruscans and which put them into a race with the tomb robbers who, starting with the Romans and continuing with professional plunderers (sometimes working for well-known modern museums), make a good living out of the grave goods of the dead. The areas to be explored are so vast that what one actually sees is often only a fraction of what is there, and more often it is the necropolis (the tomb city on a hill) which has been revealed rather than the acropolis (the city proper on the opposing height).

In the case of Caere the acropolis is ringed by burial heights—Banditaccia, Sorbo, Monte Tosto, Monte Abatone, Monte Abatoncino. The city gates look directly towards the shining sea five kilometres away. Two roads once led to the coast, one going to the port of Alsium, the other serving first Pyrgi, the harbour used by the Greeks, and carrying on to Punicum, the port probably used by Phoenician ships. But it was at Pyrgi that the discovery of the three gold strips was made recently (they are now in the Villa Giulia in Rome, the finest Etruscan museum in the world). Two of the strips contain Etruscan writing, the third is written in Phoenician. It is a dedication by the King of Caere, Tefarie Velianas, to the Etruscan goddess Uni (who was also the Phoenician goddess Astarte). But, alas, the latter is not a word-for-word translation of the Etruscan, but a precis. The find, although useful, is not an equivalent to the Rosetta Stone which proved to be the key to understanding ancient Egyptian. We still know only 52 words of Etruscan.

What we do know about the Caeritans, however, is that they were a considerable seapower. Herodotus, writing about 430 BC, states that, in approximately 535 BC, 60 ships from Caere joined a similar fleet of 60 Phoenician vessels and engaged 60 Phocaean (Greek) ships in a famous sea fight off the coasts of Corsica or Sardinia, now known as the Battle of Alalia. The figures of ships seem a little too regular to be true. Herodotus, who was a Greek, accuses the 'Tyrrhenians' (Etruscans) of killing their prisoners by stoning and adds that they had to expiate this atrocity by carrying out penances laid down by the Oracle at Delphi. But he had no time for the Phocaeans, whom he condemned as pirates. Afterwards, he says that Caere extracted tribute from Corsica in the form of resin, wax and honey; items we might not think of as normal ship cargoes.

Caere traded with the Phoenician-held areas of what are now France and Spain (including Massilia—modern Marseilles), but according to Diodorus Siculus, relying on Timaeus (fourth century BC), also had ambitions to expand out into the Atlantic, possibly to what is now Madeira. So they must have had ocean-going merchant ships. An Etruscan vase found at Caere shows two war galleys of quite different type apparently in head-on conflict on a sea filled with fish, squid and turtles. Apart from Alalia, at the height of Etruscan power, there was a devastating sea raid on the port of Pyrgi by Dionysius of Syracuse in 384 BC, when it was beginning to decline. There certainly were savage sea battles as an adjunct to the activities of the trading ships.

Some of the tombs at Caere are dug very deep in the ground and have narrow catacomb-like passageways. Others, of a different period, have floors more nearly flush with the ground outside. It seems clear from the homelike appearance of many of them that the Etruscans communed with the dead. To them, they weren't really dead. In the same way, Italian women today will go and sit by the graves of their husbands and ask:

'Where are you . . .?'

And in their minds receive the reply:

'I am here.'

And then tell them about the day's events, the small worries and triumphs.

*   *   *

To the north of Caere, the next city state with a coastal strip and ports is Tarquinia (in Etruscan, Tarchuna). Not surprisingly, the ports were situated near the mouths of rivers, partly because the rivers provided waterlanes inland, but also to provide shelter for the ships, for the coast is very exposed with little natural protection. There are three known harbours: Gravisca (with a Roman port on top of the Etruscan one), Martanum, near the mouth of the Marta, and Rapinium, near the mouth of the Mignone along the border with Caere. Excavations both on land and in the shallow sea have revealed extensive breakwaters, moles and quays. Indeed, one can see the areas of broken water offshore which point to the remains of moles. The prevailing winds here are the same as in England—in an arc centred at south-west—which means that they blow onshore for much of the time. Difficult often, dangerous sometimes.

There was an established Greek colony at Gravisca in the sixth and

42

fifth centuries BC. The finds made there can be traced to the Greek colonies in what is now Turkey and their offshore islands from Mytilene, south of Troy, through Chios and Samos off the coast of Lydia, through Cos off the coast of Ionia opposite Halicarnassus, to Rhodes off Caria.

The Etruscan Tarquinia, built on hills five miles inland from the port of Gravisca, is linked to the basic story (or legend) of the Etruscans as a whole. It is supposed to have been founded by Tarcon, brother of the leader who originally brought the Etruscans from Lydia to Italy. And it was from Tarquinia, in the seventh century BC, that the Etruscans began to move south to the conquest of Latium and Rome, with Tarquins on the throne as a ruling dynasty until the advent of the Roman Republic.

More than six thousand tombs have been discovered so far. The method used is to plot where the tombs are likely to be on the pleasant hilltops, given the known position of the inhabited city. Various instruments are then employed to search out anomalies in the ground. Once found, a tomb is inspected visually by putting down a periscope and can be measured by means of sound-waves. But nowadays, an excavation is decided upon only if it appears that important new facts may result from it. Several of the unexcavated tombs can be seen. When a tomb is opened here, and found to contain wall paintings—which at Tarquinia is very likely—the excavator has acquired a responsibility to preserve them. The Greeks, we know, produced great paintings, but virtually nothing of this aspect of their art has survived; so the Etruscan works are nearly unique. Unfortunately, when exposed to air—and the changes in humidity and temperature which result when streams of tourists daily occupy the confined spaces of the tombs to view the paintings—then those paintings deteriorate. So visits to the tombs have to be rationed; some tombs are open only on some days.

When I visited Tarquinia, I missed two of the paintings I most wanted to see—the delightful Hunting and Fishing picture, innocuously happy (of 520 BC, or alternatively 540–530 BC, depending on your authority), and the (some say) mid-fifth century BC ship, the only representation of an Etruscan freighter that I know of, and so damaged that it leaves lots of unanswered questions.

There are two bold, bouncy dancing pictures—one of a girl alone in the Hunting and Fishing tomb, apparently leaping to a pounding beat; and a high-stepping couple facing each other in the Tomb of the Lioness (last quarter of the sixth century BC), both of which I saw. Faded, but still exciting with spontaneous movement. In the Tomb of the Jugglers, games and dancers are shown, including a clearly Eastern, perhaps Egyp-

◄ Cerveteri: The entrance to an Etruscan tomb. *Photo: Alexander McKee*

tian woman executing some formal and decorative movements, with pointed fingers and pointed toes. This is from around 550–500 BC. In the Tomb of the Warrior, a soldier with helmet, shield and spear is shown. And there is the Hunting Pavilion, where the tomb is painted to represent the inside of a campaigning tent, so that anyone who enters feels that he is looking out from it at the surrounding countryside. There are many, many more, nearly all happy pictures. You can almost hear the music of the flutes and lyres, the dancing feet, the prancing horses, the wing-flapping birds, the leaping dolphins smacking down into the waves at the end of their jump. These paintings are from the 'happy time' of the Etruscans, around the sixth and fifth centuries BC. But after another two hundred years have passed, and we are looking at the third century BC—the time of the Romans—a sad and morbid tone prevails; later, even an actual funeral procession is shown. Now there is no gaiety beyond the grave.

In the museum of modern Tarquinia, several miles away from the Etruscan site, there is a staggering sculpture of two winged horses (displayed most effectively on a wall against a black background). This still produces a shock, for here is Pegasus. And the Vanths, the well-covered winged females of which statuettes survive here and there, are they not angels?

*　　　*　　　*

The approach to Vulci is utterly misleading. Very little of the city can be seen today, although excavations date from 1783, the most famous worker in that field being Lucian Bonaparte who began to dig there in 1828. Illegal excavations probably date from 280 BC, when Vulci was defeated by the Romans, and continue to this day. The site is a large and lonely place, six miles from the sea and hard to police, particularly when tomb robbers operate by night. Like its neighbours, Vulci (in Etruscan, Velcha or Velx) possessed a long coastline with three ports, Cosa, Orbetello and Talamone, and may also have ruled the three Tuscan islands off the Argentario peninsula south of Elba: Giglio, Giannutri and Montecristo.

But as you drive up to the acropolis, dominating the skyline are the high walls and towers of Badia Castle and the hump-backed bridge outside it which spans the river Fiora far below. The water table is lower now than in Etruscan times, which gives another misleading impression. The foundations of that bridge are Etruscan; on top of that there is Roman work, and on top of that once more, mediaeval—matching the castle which is now the museum of Vulci. Inside the castle, on the day I explored it, I found the courtyard covered with chairs, laid tables, and decorations.

Tarquinia: The famous winged horses, excavated nearby, but now displayed in a
Renaissance building turned into a museum of Etruscan artefacts. *Photo: Alexander McKee*

The Tourist Board, I discovered, were having a banquet—the sort of thing
the Etruscans were famous for, and here, 2,500 years later, they were still
at it. They immediately invited me to join in, handing round glasses of
the marvellous local red wine, and plates of delicacies. Consigning various
old Greek and Roman authors to the dustbin marked 'prigs', I accepted
the offerings; and came back for more.

Nevertheless, I was able to walk the recent excavations on the acropolis
nearby. A large plinth (120 feet by 80 feet), the base of an Etruscan temple,
had only just emerged from the raw, red-brown earth; but most of the
exposed ruins appeared to be Roman (with presumably the Etruscan
underneath). The remains of brick buildings, about as high as the average
English village church, were the most striking feature of the landscape;
they are Roman but their function is unknown.

Most of the large areas of the city exposed by excavation over the last
two centuries or so have been almost completely erased by a combination
of hostile factors: land reclamation, agriculture and the natural forces of
erosion by wind and weather. Wild boar and herds of Maremma cattle
wander at will over this landscape, the farmers being more akin to the

45

Vulci: Recent excavation has revealed the base of an Etruscan temple. *Photo: Alexander McKee*

'cowboys' of the American plains than to Italy; while the tomb robbers and the police wage their feuds over the still unknown and unseen graves.

The tombs face the sunset, and that is the best time to see them.

Those which have been opened demonstrate that Vulci dates from the beginning of the ninth century BC. Probably, like Veii, the majestic city was ruined and abandoned by the first century AD.

The most famous tomb was discovered in 1857 by two Frenchmen, Noël des Vergers and the engineer François. Dating from the fourth century BC, its central room contains two brilliantly painted and sharply preserved frescoes. The first action-painting shows the sacrifice of the Trojan prisoners by Achilles—a story from the distant past, whether it be truth or myth. The second deliberately echoes the first—but the story is more recent and is certainly history, because it illustrates what is known elsewhere from fragments of text, including part of a speech by Claudius in which he refers to the 'adventures' of Servius Tullius and Caelius Vibenna. It is a picture of slaughter with edged weapons and appears

46

to depict the raid in which Mastarna (later Servius Tullius) freed the captive Caelius Vibenna, held prisoner in the enemy camp. The enemy is Rome or, rather, the current rulers of Rome; a Tarquin was killed during this struggle, Mastarna eventually emerging as Servius Tullius, king of Rome. So here at last we have Etruscan history in pictures. The paintings show heroically muscular strongmen, some naked, some yellow-haired, stabbing each other with sword or dagger point, or cutting a throat with the edge of a blade. In effect, 'action men' of more than two thousand years ago, but real enough to make you feel the pain. And none of them at all like the obese luxury-lovers sneered at by the Greeks and Romans.

This is probably the most important find from the tombs of Vulci which, by robbery or licence, has supplied the world's museums with tens of thousands of Etruscan artefacts over a period of several hundred years.

*   *   *

The most northerly of the coastal cities I visited was Roselle (Rusellae), still being excavated. This was a long journey, past Norchia, across the hillside of Tarquinia, to the Via Aurelia, before entering the much-truncated Tuscany of modern Italy, with a motorway system imposed on the older routes. Past Vulci with its nuclear installation, along the coastal road within sight of Etruscan villages like Capalbio and probable Etruscan ports like Orbetello and Porto Ercole. But so much of this area has been built on, dammed or otherwise altered, that the Etruscan past is impossible to discern clearly. I drove to the quayside of Porto San Stefano, but Giglio over the water was hidden by rainclouds and the harbour, clear as glass right down to the seabed when I first saw it in the 1960s, was opaque with fuel and other contaminants.

I continued through the 'safari' countryside of the Maremma, between the sea and the hills, and climbed up to the village of Istia on the Ombrone river. The village restaurant, apparently a notable Tuscan gourmet spot for miles around, as far away as Grosseto, laid on an unexpected banquet—was it 13 courses? One was certainly wild boar salami. And there was only red wine to wash it all down with—no preparation for examining an Etruscan acropolis.

In Etruria, as in Greece, every way is up. Roselle is no exception. But here there are no tombs. This is the city site, mostly overlaid by Roman construction, including an arena which only lacks its spectacle of lions.

Excavation of what is obviously an extensive site was a long way from completion when I was there, but Etruscan manufacturing areas, as well as living sites, were beginning to appear. The most striking aspect of Roselle is the view—looking out over a flat valley hundreds of feet below,

Roselle: A typical Etruscan hilltop site, which is still being excavated and contains workshops as well as houses, often overlaid by Roman constructions. The view over the valley was breathtaking. *Photo: Alexander McKee*

with other hills as a backdrop. Without motor cars and lorries, it must have been a tiresome climb for the farmers with their produce, and for men bringing the raw materials to the factories, presumably in carts or on animal back. Only stark necessity could have dictated the choice of such a site. The enemies were not only Romans; other Etruscans, too, were a danger.

*   *   *

When the city was deep inland and had no harbours, and for this or other reasons was not particularly important to the Romans, the Etruscan influence tended to live on into modern times and in the most curious ways. At Tuscania, for instance, where a fortified mediaeval city stands on top of an Etruscan necropolis—both much disturbed by an earthquake in

1971—there is an extraordinary church, St Peter's. There are Etruscan ornaments on the west front, Etruscan sarcophagi inside, as well as Roman columns. A mix of artefacts, including carved devils found in the ground nearby, have been added to a Christian church.

No one, without spending a lifetime on it, could look at all the discovered tombs of Etruria; one should aim to see contrasting styles, which reflect both regional differences and a history not all that short of one thousand years, if one includes the first few centuries of Roman occupation, before Etruria lost its identity and language. At Orvieto, for instance—a fortified mediaeval and Renaissance city crowning a vast rock rearing from the plain, like the hull of a battleship spouting gun turrets and control towers— at this spectacular site, the tombs are outside the city, planted in a kind of niche against the backdrop of the hill. They date from the sixth century BC, when the Etruscans ruled Rome, and are boldly constructed out in the open, exactly like a new housing estate: rows and rows of 'terraced' tombs facing each other, the designs identical, and a little carving outside the front door to show whether the body inside is that of a man or a woman—domes for women, columns for men.

A completely different and varied range of tombs is to be found in the territory of Tarquinia at Norchia (ancient Orcla) and Barbarano. Whereas the Orvieto necropolis is easy to get to, these are difficult of access, being situated in deep ravines eroded out of the sheer volcanic rock, the tufa, which is soft and easy to cut. The number of tombs is endless, and most have been sculpted to show in the cliff face the front elevations of the Etruscan houses of the time. The appearance of an Etruscan town is therefore preserved, something we would otherwise never have known, because the buildings were erected out of fragile material which generally has failed to survive. Representing the height of Etruscan power, the tombs are boldly cut, openly facing out over the river valley far below, lovely with flowers and glittering water. I even disturbed a viper which was lying happily in the sun until he heard me coming.

But at another site not far away, the way is harder and much, much gloomier. The tombs are virtually hidden away, concealed by foliage and deeply waterlogged in a very low valley, with streams which have to be jumped or waded. The whole scene is damp, dim and unpleasant, as though the people had wanted to conceal their dead from strangers. New tombs are still being found and explored here. One of them, excavated in November, 1983, is full of iron and bronze objects and also a cart to carry the occupant, a woman, to the next world.

My longest trip was to Florence, still recovering from the disaster of 1966. The Etruscan section of the museum had been on the ground floor— and had gone underwater in the floods. Many pieces were missing, taken

away for restoration, although the famous bronze Chimera was there, and a large Greek amphora showing Jason and the Argonauts (but lacking the stern half of their light galley). This picture, like that of the Etruscan freighter, had long been familiar to me, together with many of the other representations of ancient ships. It was an experience to see the original.

From Florence I went further on to Fiesole, another Etruscan town, but most of the Etruscan buildings were buried under the Roman and later constructions.

Florence is the most Etruscan city that one can see today. Politically, it has always followed the tradition of the Lucomo—the autocratic chief, often a merchant. The Medici were exactly like the leaders of the Etruscan city states must have been. Then, the people themselves had taste. And still have it. They make beautiful shoes, handbags and so on. Why did the Renaissance start in Florence? Why did it not start in Sicily, for instance? One only has to remember the parallels between the Etruscan paintings in tombs and the paintings in the Christian churches of the area. More than one Italian I met insisted that Western civilisation began in Etruria and emanated from the Etruscans.

*　　　*　　　*

While some of the Etruscan engineering and hydraulic works remain, their great public buildings were not built of imperishable stone, like those of the Greeks and Romans, so they do not make a powerful visual impact today. Visually, for me, there were three great moments during my exploration of ancient Etruria. Coming down the hill and then, as the view opened out through the trees, the sight of Orvieto, like a battleship, towering up from the valley floor. An Etruscan site, of course, but it was the mediaeval works which made the impact. The second time was actually in Orvieto; walking up an ascending street into the cathedral square, you suddenly come on part of the cathedral, and instead of bare stone you are confronted by a glittering silver and gold wall, totally unexpected. And the final scene was to come out on to the high platform on which stands the giant statue known as the Apollo Belvedere, overlooking that stupendous view out over Florence in a stunningly bright golden light. After that, it was hard to go back to Portsmouth, which glories in not less than two of the very worst buildings to be designed in the last 7,000 years, anywhere in the world.

In touring Etruria I deliberately went along a variety of routes to see as much of the country as possible. There is no doubt that the landscape

◀　Barbarano: Doorway of a tomb in the cliff necropolis. *Photo : Alexander McKee* is a military nightmare today; for the attacker, that is. The defender would be laughing. In around 600 BC it might not have been quite so bad, because the available firepower was so short-ranged and much less important. It would still have been very, very difficult country, full of little hills, twisting valleys and blindspots.

Communications through much of the area are not all that good today; in ancient times they must have been very poor. Control and movement would have been difficult. One can see why the city states did not unite and rarely all acted in concert. Physically moving an army along existing routes would have been a major feat.

Clearly, the basic judgement of the scholars is correct. The Etruscan cities used mainly water transport along the rivers to the coast; and the entire economy would have depended upon control of the Tyrrhenian Sea.

From that it follows that much of their missing history may lie beneath the sea. Until lately, no Etruscan ship had been found, let alone excavated. But they have been waiting in the silent depths. We are the fortunate generation, the first to see them for 25 centuries.

Orvieto: An Etruscan city may lie beneath later buildings. The Etruscans liked to build on hilltops, which are easily defensible. *Photo: Alexander McKee*

Chapter 3

ISLAND IN THE SUN

Summer 1961 was one of the most successful seasons of the Club Aquatique, our Aqualung Diving School. The many discoveries made by Club members were mentioned in the Italian press and television and a museum was opened on the island to house the antiquities found. This year new members will have a chance to take part in these exciting archaeological searches, while at the same time enjoying the thrill of mastering a new element and the exhilaration of weightlessness in a shimmering world of fish and corals.

Holiday brochure, 1962

In 1961 Roger Hale had returned from diving off the Tuscan island of Giglio, full of enthusiasm for the clear water, the spectacular fishlife, and the thrilling archaeological discoveries that were being made. He had even been taken on himself as a part-time instructor by the British aqualung diving school which had just opened there.

This word-of-mouth recommendation in our diving boat decided others of us—like Roger, members of Southsea Branch of the British Sub-Aqua Club—to visit Giglio in 1962. Eight people went out in all, including experienced divers like John Towse, Alan Lee, Jack and Pat Millgate, and Roger Hale himself, plus two girls, one of whom was a diver from London Branch of the BS-AC. The experienced people went by road in a van which carried their diving gear and a small hard-boat. I elected to go out by air with the travel company, which would also loan me diving gear on the spot and provide a hard-boat, the *Sea Laird*, from which to dive. Inflatable boats were then almost unknown.

In 1962 the diving scene was different. The image of the '80s is of a mass of macho teenagers immersed not only in a sub-tropical sea but in an immensely tough, demanding sport. In the '50s and '60s there was no trace of that. I should imagine that the average age of the amateur divers in Southsea Branch then was about 35. A good few of us had been around 20 when World War II began, others were perhaps 20 when it ended. And there were girls and married women among us, although in regrettably small numbers.

The real pull was two-fold. Firstly, the actual sensation of being under the sea and free to manoeuvre as an aeroplane in the sky, but solidly supported by the water, gravity absent, was sensuous and delightful.

However, the greater attraction was that the underwater environment was the last unknown continent to be explored. In those days we were going—not necessarily with boldness but rather with sensible caution—where no one in the long history of man had gone before. Workmen had dived, yes, restricted by their task, and by clumsy gear. But we were the first explorers, unpaid, unorganised, eager and excited.

The British Sub-Aqua Club itself had not been formed until 1953, and the aqualung was an invention of the French some ten years earlier. Virtually all underwater territory was virgin, unexplored, open to the first venturer.

*   *   *

When I stepped out of the aeroplane in that August night of 1962, the heat was like the blast from a sharply-opened oven. Pisa airport, named after a great explorer of the heavens, Galileo Galilei, was the first stop on the route to Giglio. Next morning, before catching my train to Orbetello, I had time to go out and buy a copy of *Mondo Sommerso*, a superb magazine of the Italian underwater world. It beat all rivals—American, British, French or German—into cheap, tiny pieces. The costly colour photographs were startling, both in conception and technique, particularly those credited to Maurizio Sarra, who seemed to be Italy's top underwater photographer. One could not expect to achieve anything like that in our home waters around Portsmouth which, with objective truth, we even then dubbed the 'Solent Sewer'. Now I was to go into Italian seas. I could hardly wait.

The train ran down the coastal plain of Tuscany, with the mountains of Etruria on the left and the Tyrrhenian Sea on the right. Where the mountains stopped only at the coast, the rocks plunged breathlessly down to a sea the colour of ultramarine. Sometimes the road south to the sun was close on our left; somewhere to the west, out across the tempting blue water, lay Elba.

Ninety-five miles south of Pisa, the railway line began to curve round to the right, and from the low, parched, rust-brown hills of summer the hunched height of Monte Argentario appeared like a sprawled lion looking out to the islands of the Tuscan sea. I alighted at Orbetello, a small country town, once one of the three ports of the Etruscan state of Vulci, while the train thundered off south on the seventy miles to Rome. The next stage was a short bus journey across the causeway bordering a series of reeded lagoons which separated the Argentario peninsula from mainland Italy. From this exceedingly restful scene, the bus lurched on to the hot quayside of Porto San Stefano. I unloaded my luggage and, while waiting for the little island steamer to arrive, gazed fascinated at the fish swimming deep in crystal-clear water; it was as if nothing but a sheet of glass lay between me and the harbour bottom. At Portsmouth, in similar depths, one would have seen nothing at all—except perhaps the odd Coca-Cola tin floating on the scummy surface, foul with fuel oil.

The sea journey to Giglio took about an hour over water the colour of dark grapes. Very deep water, obviously. Coming from a naval area like Portsmouth, one tended to use the Navy's word for the ocean. They call it the 'oggin, a word perfectly descriptive of the liquid surrounding most of the British Isles, but sacrilegious to apply to the Tyrrhenian Sea in full summer. It is an immensely deep, rich blue. The phrase used by ancient writers, and translated as 'wine-dark sea', can only be descriptive in terms of blue-black grapes today, but perhaps the old wines, from the resin used to coat the amphorae, really did resemble that tremendous blue.

I was permeated with happiness. A sea that colour would be warm, like bath water. One could live in it a long time. Quite unlike the British brand which, to a foot thrust incautiously into it out of season, hits back exactly like an amputation. Even in summer, aided by wind-chill, it can be lethal. But here, the wind was warm—like a summer kitchen. Not a thing to worry about, I thought.

Giglio was in view ahead all the way. A high mountainous island, the offshore counterpart to Monte Argentario, the rocks sweeping steeply from 2,000 feet down into the sea, there was clearly going to be very deep water close to shore. The first thing a diver should do in his reconnaissance is to study the land around his diving site, not the sea. He should read a little geology, for the shape of the land will tell him what to expect under the waves and may help him understand what he sees down there. The Portsmouth area, for instance, is mostly flat; and the seabed likewise; and is shallow except for the river valleys which were drowned again by the last great rise of sea level in geological (not historical) time. This explains why Portsmouth and Southampton are great ports (standing on the banks of long-drowned major rivers, which still flow), while nearby Brighton will never be anything but a seaside resort. A supertanker or aircraft carrier approaching Brighton would run aground while still many miles from shore.

Only a few years before, when making my first snorkel dive from a club boat two miles out to sea off Hayling Island and, in my then untutored state, expecting to find 60 feet of water at least, I had been amazed to reach the bottom on one breath in three seconds or so. There was only 14 feet of sea under our boats. Giglio was bound to be totally different. Or so the leaflet from the travel company said. Among the photographs inside was one of Roger Hale with amphorae and other items from one of the wrecks I was soon to see for myself—the incredibly old ship at the foot of the *secca* in Campese Bay. For the cost of £62.5s.od I was to have 12 days of this, and much more.

> The Island of Giglio itself is charming and unspoilt ... Undeveloped as a tourist centre, its rocky coastline provides incredibly clear water for diving and tiny isolated coves for sunbathing. Expeditions are made in the Club diving boat, the *Sea Laird*, to neighbouring islands such as Giannutri, which is populated only by butterflies and pheasants and has the ruins of a Roman villa to explore. Evenings on Giglio are spent open-air dancing or visiting Giglio Castello, the old walled town that dominates the island from 2,000 feet.
>
> Beginners first learn to use fins, mask and breathing tube before graduating to the aqualung ... Grouped according to ability, they are guided underwater by experienced instructors in exploratory dives increasing in scope and depth. Newcomers require only average swimming ability but should be thoroughly at home in the water. Instruction in Snorkel swimming and Spearfishing is given by a member of the British Team.
>
> The school will again be directed by Reg Vallintine of the British Sub-Aqua Club.

Everything the man wrote proved to be right. But this was the Swinging Sixties. As the ship nosed into the quay at the small fishing harbour of Giglio Porto that evening, the discs being played at the open air café were the Twist and the Madison, sung by continental groups like Harry Madison et son Squartett and Peppino di Capri e i suoi Rockers; I expect there were British and American noises as well, but I cannot recall them. It was the time of Brigitte Bardot and St Tropez; of cheerful fun and freedom; an end to five years of war and rationing followed by what felt like fifteen years of peace and rationing—twenty years in all of being told to do what was good for us.

The sub-aqua scene proved to be just as free-and-easy; dominated by the continentals and continental equipment (because it was often the best), but with some American gear. Most divers were using the Cousteau-type twin-hose demand valves, although a few American single-hose regulators were on the market. The cylinders we would use were big, high-pressure continental types, far better than the ex-Air Ministry oxygen bottles which some of us owned. Not only were lifejackets not compulsory, they were almost unheard of in those days, either at home or abroad; instead, if

Giglio, showing the principal wreck sites explored in 1962. *Drawn by Maurice Young* ▶

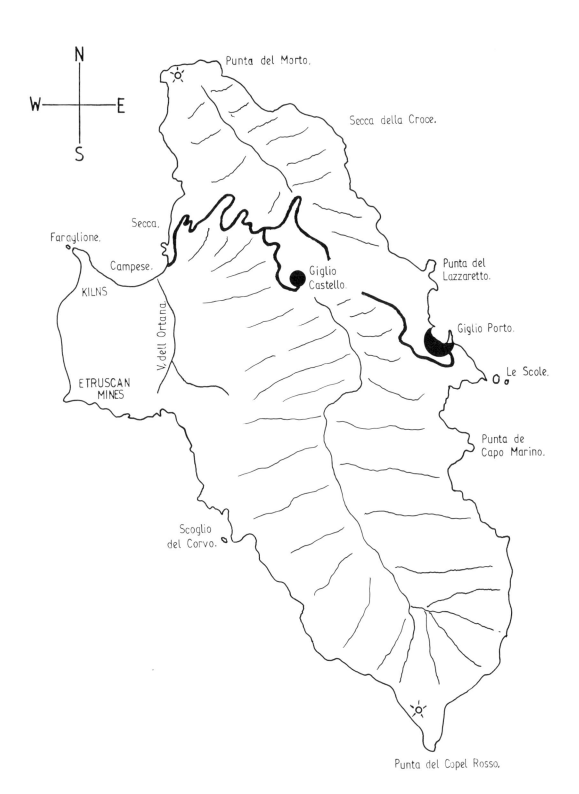

N
W   E
S

Punta del Morto.

Secca della Croce.

Secca.

Faraylione.

Campese.

KILNS

V. dell Ortana.

ETRUSCAN
MINES

Giglio
Castello.

Punta del
Lazzaretto.

Giglio Porto.

Le Scole.

Punta de
Capo Marino.

Scoglio
del Corvo.

Punta del Copel Rosso.

in trouble, we were trained to ditch our weightbelts. There was a variety of cases for underwater cameras, bulky and drag-causing in varying degrees, like my own. Reg Vallintine, the head of the diving school, was wearing a new invention, the DCP or decompression meter which, with a little luck, might solve the problem of how to avoid 'bends'. Wet-suits were now generally available, although my first dive with an aqualung, two years before, had been made in British waters wearing nothing but swimming trunks and three thick jerseys. Indeed, most of our weightbelts and harnesses were still home-made. But accidents were rare and due to unusual causes (such as the snorkel diver shot through the head by a rifle-man who had mistaken him for a seal). Not so at Giglio, although Reg's school had an accident-free record.

Giglio Porto then consisted of the small waterfront where everyone con-gregated, with a few residential streets behind; all at the foot of rocky mountains which rose steeply to the central ridge of the island. The Club Aquatique was based in the Pensione Bahamas, a few minutes' walk up the hill from the quayside where the diving boat was moored. As I dumped my kit in the hall, the first thing I noticed was a so-called 'shipping amphora' (with a pointed base to go into a cargo rack); the encrustations on it showed that this large storage jar had come from under the sea. We were to dive next day on the site from which it had been taken, a late Roman wreck of the fourth century AD.

Already staying at the hotel were the Southsea group who had driven out in a van carrying their boat on the roof. John Towse and Roger Hale, both in their late twenties, were experienced; John I know had done 100 dives. Alan Lee was younger, I think; the Millgates were certainly older. But at 41, Jack was three years younger than I was.

Just 44, I still thought of myself, physically, as being 15—the peak per-formance age for surface swimmers. I had done a fair amount of snorkelling (that is, breath-hold diving without apparatus), but otherwise was inex-perienced. In 1951 and 1952 I had done a short course in helmet (or 'hard-hat') diving in Hamburg, as research for a Forces Radio feature pro-gramme. I had taught myself snorkel diving in 1958 and in 1959 had joined the Southsea Club—the first club trip I went on was a visit to HMS *Vernon*, the Navy diving school, where I was promptly put down in Portsmouth harbour using an oxygen set (as opposed to the compressed air used by sport divers). Breaking a leg during book research in 1959 had set back my aqualung training, and at this time I had logged only 22 dives with an aqualung, and the deepest of these was only to 75 feet. The only

The author (with camera in watertight case) and Reg Vallintine about to dive at Giglio ▶
in 1962. *Photo: Victor de Sanctis (from colour slide)*

hazardous one had been a 65-foot dive on Bullock Patch, looking for a lost anchor, in three-feet visibility, a racing tide, and with fast-moving, rough, heaped-up water above. One went down the anchor rope streamed out like a flag in a gale. And if one surfaced astern of the boat, one could not fight the tide and was certainly invisible to those on board. Compared to that, Giglio would be a doddle.

With few words, Reg Vallintine disabused me of this notion. Minimum visibility would be 80 feet, down a steep slope which reached 400 feet very close to shore. Swimming parallel to the slope, there was not the impression of increasing depth one gets when descending an anchor line. It was only too easy to go fatally deep without realising it.

Next morning, at a civilised hour around ten o'clock, we gathered at the jukebox café on the quayside, had a coffee and then got into *Sea Laird*, a comfortably sizeable hard-boat. No cylinders or weightbelts to carry— they were all stacked on board. Just our own kit, and not too much of that. I personally was only going to wear a wet-suit jacket and a hood. Out of the harbour we turned right towards Le Scole, and I suited up; it was terribly hot inside the neoprene. Reg led a typical Mediterranean Cousteau-type group dive (impractical in low visibilities), with two young-sters, Julian Nott and Kenneth Merron, and myself tagging along in a gaggle loose enough to stop and look at things. My depth gauge showed around 70 feet most of the time, possibly we touched 100 feet. I wrote in my log:

> Don't really remember much about this dive; all too strange, not exactly what I had expected. My last memories of the Med were when aged $8\frac{1}{2}$ and as a surface swimmer. Slightly overwhelmed.

This turned out to be a fairly general initial reaction, particularly where British divers were concerned. On Bullock Patch, for instance, at depths between 65 and 75 feet, I had been unable to see my own flippers; to this add cold and gloom. Now there was glistening light and vast rocky land-scapes in full view falling away to blue depths, and clouds of hovering fish. But one soon got used to it. After slipping the aqualung off my shoulders and dropping the weightbelt, I got back into the water for a snorkel dive.

> Shot a half-cassette on Julian and Kenneth who were lunging in the shallows around 30 or 40 feet. I seemed to go down surprisingly easily, and to have no breath-holding worries, the water was so warm. I was struck by the 'rain curtains'—the stream of bubbles ascending from three or four divers swimming below me in a line.

These breath-holding dives were so easy because there was no nervous

A typical group dive at Giglio in 1962. *Photo : Alexander McKee*

tension. In poor visibility, where you can't even see your own length, let alone the bottom below you, there is the subconscious fear of being trapped in some unknown entanglement—nets, lines, wreckage—and if you are not carrying an air supply down with you, then you have very little time in which to free yourself. Here, however, everything was in plain view below. And there was the bonus of warm water; holding the breath in cold water, when you're beginning to shiver, is much harder. Back in England, my best performance on one breath had been 35 feet; at Giglio that was easy and once I managed 50 feet. Reg, however, a former member of the British spearfishing team (no aqualungs allowed) could do 100 feet in British waters, as could several members of my own club. During our time at Giglio we were all spending at least as much time snorkel diving as aqualunging—one simply did not want to waste those wonderful conditions.

That afternoon we did a second lung dive. Reg had waited long enough for the nitrogen, which had been forced into our bloodstreams by the pressure, to come out slowly. We went down to 75 feet for 25 minutes, to the right of the port, off the rock called Le Scole. The Roman wreck lay there, deeper still, around 160–165 feet. We were wearing big yellow cylinders, either singly or two yoked together as a pair to give double the submerged time of a single bottle. The safety measure was continental, not British. In place of a pressure gauge to show how much air you had left, there was a thin wire handle at the back of the cylinder which, when pulled downwards, released a reserve air supply good enough for perhaps 5 minutes (exact time would depend on the depth and how heavily you were breathing). We learned the two vital signals. Showing a clenched fist to your partner was a warning, telling him (or her) that you had pulled the reserve lever and would be leaving shortly, if not before. If you not merely clenched your fist but shook it violently, that meant that you had been unable to pull the reserve lever, probably because the wire tended to be elusive among the straps of the aqualung, the weightbelt, or whatever, and would he/she please pull the lever pretty damn quick or you would drown. My log entry shows that the previous dive in the morning had been sufficient to acclimatise.

I abandoned the suit jacket. No rain here for four months, blue 'oggin and hot as an oven. Took my camera this time, as I was assured we would not be going too deep. I was overweight to start with, so surfaced and ditched 4 lbs back into the boat, then went down again and caught up with the others, easily tracked by their rain curtains. This isn't diving, it's undersea mountaineering. The twin peaks of Le Scole which appear above the surface are the summits. I glided over valleys filled with fish and saw an Italian pupil find an amphora above the site. I suppose the wreck hit these rocks, then sank sternfirst down the slope.

What I did not realise at that moment was that the wreck was being looted and that the broken amphorae higher up might just as well have been debris from the plundering as cargo lost overboard on the day the hull went swaying down to the base of the cliffs, perhaps even striking an outcrop during its plunge.

An Italian boat came alongside *Sea Laird*, an Italian girl in it asked Reg for a lesson, paid her lire, kitted up and went down. She was pretty and well built, so I put on mask and flippers, plus camera, and tried to use her as an underwater model. It was very difficult to frame her properly. The camera lens, buried deep inside the heavy metal box built to withstand great pressures, was well below the framing wires at the top of the case,

Undersea mountaineering off Giglio. A typical scene anywhere off rocky coasts in the Mediterranean. *Photo : Alexander McKee*

so the parallax error was quite remarkable; I tended to cut off either heads or tails, like the owner of an early box Brownie. Then, to alter the setting of aperture or focus, I had to turn the box round, look into the darkness inside, twiddle some knobs on top and try to make out what the results, if any, had been on the 'f' numbers or shutter speeds. Sometimes, if the rubber gearing slipped, nothing happened at all, except to my temper.

*   *   *

My second day's diving at Giglio introduced further problems: depth and light. Instead of wandering around acclimatising at around 70 feet or so, we were to go straight down to a wreck lying at twice that depth— 140 feet—and stay there as long as our air lasted. I would be wearing one of the twin-sets and therefore would be able to stay down for almost half-an-hour. The first photographic problem associated with depth is that the best conditions in the Mediterranean are found in the top 50 feet. At 70 feet the light is beginning to fade and many of the colours have gone. Sea water acts exactly like a colour filter to a camera lens—in British 'oggin it's a green filter, in the Med it's a blue filter. If you cut yourself, the blood is not red but green; and deeper still, it becomes black. There is very little contrast and there are no shadows (except just under the surface). Of course, artificial light brings up the true colours again—or reveals unexpected ones on dull surfaces—but to fit a flashgun to my already clumsy, blunt camera case would cause still further drag, which could prove fatal if an emergency developed. We all disliked the 'Father Christmas' effect of carrying too much gear, and preferred to be stripped down as much as possible. I decided to put into the camera a fast black and white film, and overdevelop it to produce the contrast which would not in fact be there.

All that now remained was to hope that the heavy metal box, with its thick glass porthole for the camera lens, would not 'weep' or even implode under the pressure. At 33 feet down, pressure has doubled. And it goes on building as you go down. The aqualung supplies you with even more compressed air as you descend, so that it exactly balances the pressure of the water around you; but my camera case would still contain air at comparatively thin surface pressure.

The wreck site lay off the southern headland of Giglio, overlooked by a lighthouse, and was called Punta del Capel Rosso. I suppose 'Red Cape' might be a useful translation. There was a strong local legend that a Spanish galleon had been sunk there at some time. Vallintine thought that it might be, not one wreck site, but several; perhaps as many as three ships intermingled. This was certainly the sort of feature which would be bound to collect ships at night, in fog or in bad weather. Giglio lies 12 miles offshore, on the main coastal trade route from southern Italy to France and Spain, even England. The southern headland would collect north-bound ships while the northern headland, ominously called Punta del Morto, would trap some of the south-bound traders.

We went down a steeply sloping rock face in fantastic visibility of 100 feet or more and, from high above, saw a mast sticking out of the sand slope at the foot of the rocks. We passed from the warm bath water of the upper layer to the slight chill beyond an invisible temperature barrier.

▲ The Etruscan town of tombs at
Orvieto. The shape of the stones
outside the doorways indicates
the sex of the person buried
there. *Photo: Alexander McKee*

Painting of a boat with 'eyes' ▶
from the Tomb of Hunting and
Fishing at Tarquinia, dated to
550–525 BC—the time of the
Campese Bay ship.
*Photo: Istituto Geografico De
Agostini-Novara*

▲ Lake Vico, a flooded volcanic
crater in the heart of Tuscany,
with the hills of the Cimmerian
forest in the background.
Photo : Alexander McKee

◀ Painting of musicians, showing
the double flute, from the Tomb
of the Leopard at Tarquinia.
*Photo : Istituto Geografico De
Agostini-Novara*

Light and life were suddenly left behind as we entered the grey world below 100 feet, where all colour had been filtered out by the blue water; and then we were down on the unstirred sand, where waves never reach, and the fish seemed like grey ghosts.

My first reaction was to re-set my camera aperture, to allow for the dim light. I discovered an extraordinary thing: I was thinking in slow motion. It required an actual effort of will, first to decide that the setting should be f5·6, and then physically to alter the setting. I felt that I did not really want to bother, but was content instead to browse around till the end of time in this graveyard of dead sailors.

After taking one indifferent photograph, I began stirring the sand gently, and this revealed deck-planking a few inches below its surface. I then made a potentially deadly error: I turned round and began to go down the steep sand slope, following the trail of surface debris along the buried hull.

There were plates—dishes—sticking out of the sand. I grasped one, but it would not come free. Then Vallintine tapped me on the shoulder, and pointed up the slope.

I had a big twin-set on my back, and plenty of air, and I was full of joy at being able, for once, to see a wreck site as a whole in splendid visibility. I was, therefore, somewhat annoyed; but as my depth gauge had flooded under the terrific pressure and was no longer working, I followed him grudgingly, keeping my eyes on the sand. There was a cache of musket balls or grapeshot; and lying among surface debris near the mast a number of heavily encrusted iron tubes of one-and-a-half inch diameter—possibly swivel guns or, equally, hexagonal iron bars sunk so long that all the iron had vanished into the surrounding crust. The wreck mound of the 'galleon' was well-defined by debris on the sand slope parallel to the foot of the submarine cliffs; but fairly high up that slope was a typical litter of broken amphorae from a wreck much older. And to one side, in a crevice at the base of the rocks, was an anchor. As I pounced on this, a slight misting of my new wide-vision mask became really irritating.

Without thinking twice, because I had been trained to do it, I pushed the mask up, instantly flooding it and blotting out all vision 125 feet down; then I refitted it, full of water which cleared the misting; and finally blew out the water with an exhalation or two through the nose. When I looked round again, all the others had gone, so I rose up off the sand and went leisurely up the rock cliff.

Suddenly, I was in sunlit water, and the dulled, slow-motion feeling had vanished. I was thinking normally again. On my way back up the cliffs I came across the Southsea party swarming around the pinnacles as part of their decompression routine. No one had then shown conclusively which particular gas, under high pressure, affects the brain in this way; but the concensus favoured nitrogen.

The symptoms seem to occur shortly after one passes through the 125 foot level, and are aggravated by exertion. But in Hamburg, back in 1952, I had also experienced a similar slight drunkenness in only about 10 feet of water, while wearing the old-style helmet gear. That was definitely CO_2 poisoning, caused by too-rapid breathing of compressed air inside a helmet, so that the pump could not remove the stale air fast enough. I was then making a recording for the British Forces Network, so everyone could hear how my speech deteriorated to a drunken babble, in which I described myself as 'schwimming like a fisch and crawwling like a crawb'—and the instructor's voice cutting in sharply: 'Stop moving, diver!' After I had ceased shuffling my feet for a few seconds, my voice and commentary came back to normal. That was CO_2 poisoning, not a doubt of it, the breathing of bad air under pressure.

Stale air is immediately poisonous, of course, but compressed nitrogen seems to require much greater depths in excess of 125 feet in order to be really noticeable; while the oxygen content of the compressed air does not become toxic (so I'm told) until the diver reaches 270–280 feet, by

The underwater paradise in the 1960s: one of Reg's pupils surrounded by fork-tailed fish. *Photo: Alexander McKee*

which time he is being poisoned by both nitrogen and oxygen, and perhaps some of the other gases as well. And all of them, in addition, affecting the mental faculties at depths where false decisions may be fatal.

We just could not get enough diving in such wonderful waters; we always wanted more. Those of us who had gone deep with twin-sets in the morning could not go deep again for many hours without risking a 'bend', which might mean paralysis or death. So we went snorkelling instead, watching the people who had used only single bottles in the morning lunging in the shallows off the headland. Tom, a British pupil, reported that he had wounded a big fish while snorkelling with a speargun, but was unable to find it again. I had nothing against spearfishing, so long as it was for food, but preferred a camera. In my log I wrote:

> I found I could go down a long way, but not so deep as Tom or the Italian pupil, who seemed to be reaching 50–60 feet with ease. We snorkel dived two different sites, but I cannot remember the details; just a haze of heat, hard rocks rising out of the water, hundreds of fish, many brilliantly coloured, black sea urchins on stone, water like warm milk, an incredibly clear blue sea.

*   *   *

Next morning, 25 August, we were to dive what was described as a 'Roman' wreck. I duly logged it as such, but I think the word was being used loosely to mean a wreck of antiquity, which none of us was qualified to identify. As far as I knew then, only the Le Scole site had been shown without doubt to be Roman. All the amphorae recovered from it appeared to be of identical type—slim, with pointed bases. The site we were to see now was very different. I had heard a whisper from a departing London diver that someone had got a bronze helmet from it; and not a standard Roman battle-bowler either, but more enclosed, like the Greek model.

My knowledge of the place and the period was patchy. I did know quite a bit about ships, aircraft and weapons, but somehow I had neglected to study the pottery of antiquity. On the other hand, I had absorbed a certain amount of Mediterranean background from a two-and-a-half year stay in Malta when I was a boy. The first archaeological sites I saw started with the hypogeum, dated to around 4000 BC, followed by the traces of a succession of conquerors or traders—the Phoenicians in 1450 BC, the Greeks in 700 BC, the Carthaginians in 480 BC, the Romans in 215 BC, and the catacombs of the early Christians around the third century AD.

It was at about this time, too, that I first saw Giglio—from the rail of the Italian liner *Roma* on her maiden voyage from Genoa in 1926. Mussolini had devalued the lira, so my family took advantage of the favourable exchange rate to have a two-month holiday. We visited Tripoli and Tunis in North Africa, Cagliari in Sardinia, then Genoa to see Rapallo. We returned to Genoa to catch the *Roma* (missing seeing Mussolini by ten minutes). We sailed through part of the Ligurian Sea and through all the Tyrrhenian, past Corsica on one side and Elba, Giglio and Giannutri on the other, trailed by dolphins down to Naples. And from there we caught another ship going to Syracuse in Sicily and finally Malta again. At some moment on that voyage, I think off either the Ligurian or the Tuscan coast, I saw a sailing ship distant under the land, coasting quietly through the haze, as if it were some Roman trader out of the past. I have never forgotten it, so strong was the feeling of contact with antiquity. In my mind's eye, I can see it still.

But of course it was no ghost, merely one of the last of the real sailing ships—a genuine merchant vessel engaged in the coasting trade, essentially unchanged since, when? Certainly since the time of the Phoenicians, three or four thousand years ago. And now, about to become extinct. In how many years? Ten? Twenty? No more. In so short a time the old technology was to pass away. In my own life time.

But now—now I was going to see one of those old ships in fact. Indeed, more than one, for a great many wrecks of antiquity had come to grief on the volcanic rocks of Giglio and Giannutri—and the more obvious ones had been discovered, it seemed, within the last twelve months or so. There would never again be anything like this—the sea was giving up her dead, all over the Mediterranean. Wrecked ships no man or woman had seen for 1,600, 2,300, 2,600 years could be picked over by a favoured few. But for so short a time. For in the picking over the old cargoes were being dispersed and the remains of the vessels themselves carelessly destroyed with no records taken; I suspect without the divers realising what they were doing, not thinking of hulls and decks and sails and ropes as history, or the traces which must still be there of the men who had sailed them, and perhaps died in them.

Reg Vallintine told us what the Italian law was—that all items recovered from shipwrecks were the property of the government—but that it was not his job to enforce the law. As far as I could understand, the law was similar to the British one and was based on the premise that all accessible wrecks were modern, with known owners—which until lately had indeed been the case. Understandably, the lawmakers had not taken historical wrecks into calculation, where the valuations could have a different basis. A common coarseware pot, such as an amphora, might now be worth several hundred pounds as an antique; while fineware might be very valuable indeed. On land, there had been a flourishing trade in such things for at least several hundred years. On the other hand, the ship and its gear, valueless in one sense now, as historical information might be priceless, particularly if both ship and cargo were meticulously excavated and recorded. But no one would do that until it had first been established what the ship was and its value as an historical document assessed—and that meant taking significant samples.

Both in England and in Italy, central governments act slowly. So Vallintine had taken the initiative and, with the idea of eventually seeing a museum of marine antiquities established on the island, had come to an unofficial agreement with local authorities which might save many finds from being dispersed. The size of the problem was quite obvious, every time the ships came in from Porto San Stefano carrying visitors from the mainland. Many of those who surged off the gangways were clearly divers, carrying big twin-sets on their backs. Perhaps most of them were Italian, but there were Germans and British, too. The numbers were extraordinary, for back home the British Sub-Aqua Club had about 4,000 members; and the sight of a diver or two on the beach would bring all the kids running with wild yells of 'Frogmen!'

In Italy, however, there were so many divers, even in 1962, that they attracted no notice from the ordinary public. No one showed the slightest interest when we gathered each morning at the quayside and got on board *Sea Laird*, led by Reg Vallintine who—short, stocky, bearded and wearing a sensible straw hat—rather resembled, I thought, Sir Francis Drake in a heatwave about to snap up a Spanish galleon or two.

On this particular morning we were accompanied by an important Italian diver, Victor de Sanctis. Among his kit was a compressed-air speargun so large that its prey might well have included American aircraft carriers, and also the very first example I had seen of the Calypso Phot, a camera designed specifically to operate underwater. There was no clumsy case, just a miniature camera slightly smaller than a Leica; the body of this camera *was* the case, as de Sanctis explained. The controls were all easy to hand, aperture, focus, shutter speed altered instantly without fumbling, even if one was wearing gloves, but because of the camera's small size and weight it would be no hindrance in the water; could be used, indeed, as a reporter's tool, recording at will what one found. The camera had been developed in France for the Cousteau group and was marketed by Henri Broussard of Cannes, a famous pioneer aqualung diver. I was instantly converted and arranged to buy it off de Sanctis once he had finished testing the camera for a report in *Mondo Sommerso*.

* * *

Sea Laird went out of Giglio Porto into a choppy sea, towing Victor de Sanctis's boat, turned left out of the harbour, rounded the northern head-land of Punta del Morto and anchored in Campese Bay on top of a *secca*, an underwater mountain reaching to within 10–20 feet of the surface. The southern headland was marked by a *faraglione*, a column of rock rearing dramatically out of the sea, as at Capri and Heligoland; the most promi-nent building at Campese was the Medici Tower, a small fortress guarding the tiny boat harbour. Behind Campese, 2,000 feet up, one could just make out the battlements of Castello, the fortified town which crowns the island. Only after the deep dive did Reg point out the white cross on the rocks opposite, marking the death site below us from which two Italian snorkel divers never surfaced, presumably lost by anoxia while after a great fish which had its home in a cavern some 70 feet down. With it was a plaque:

GORGONA CLUB PISA
Marco Tito Fortunati
Gianfranco Nannichini
29 MAGGIO 1959

Sea Laird in Campese Bay with the Medici Tower in the background. Although this was at the height of the holiday season, there were few boats in the little harbour. *Photo: Alexander McKee*

Depth to the wreck was 140 feet and, as it was my turn to have a single bottle only, my time below would not be long. Things went wrong from the first, even while we were stacking up under the boat, like airliners waiting their turn to land. Eventually, the party was complete, and Reg Vallintine tipped over and led the way down. They all followed him, except for me. My mask had two straps and, while I was still stacking at 10 feet, one of them broke. The tension slackened and the mask began to flood, the water level in it rising up my face to the eyes. With the others already beginning to stream away down, I had to tighten the one remaining strap, then blow the water out of the mask with blasts of compressed air through my nostrils and, that done, put on a burst of speed to catch up the others. All this spelt effort, instead of the slow, leisurely, relaxed form of swimming which is normal and more than ever necessary when going to great depths.

Finning like the clappers, I caught them up before they reached the highest part of the wreck, which was lying on a slope, marked only by a downward trail of broken amphorae. I picked up and examined the base of a wide-bellied pot; and found de Sanctis looking at me, making gestures for me to pose for his Calypso with the broken amphora. So I

Reg Vallintine diving with a pupil. *Photo: Alexander McKee* balanced it on the palm of one hand, feeling unaccountably giggly and irresponsible and (it makes me grit my teeth to think of it) even larking around a bit, so that my fins kicked up a cloud of mud and sand. De Sanctis gestured irritably.

I was now well within the cold layer, wearing only swimming trunks, but, eager to examine more of this wreck which had produced a bronze helmet, I went on down the slope from 140 feet. I chose a likely spot and began to dig by fanning away the sand with water waves powered by the palm of one hand. Almost instantly, fresh wreckage was exposed. Among the pieces was the curved tubeworm-encrusted handle of an amphora still attached to part of the pot itself: a worthwhile, ultimately-identifiable piece which would also make a graceful souvenir and, because it had been broken long ago, represented, from the archaeological aspect, only a relatively tiny sin.

Probably I was now at around 150–160 feet, but, still holding my amphora handle, I went on again farther down that steep slope, past rocks, to where I thought I saw, only another 10 or 20 feet down, another, similar handle lying in the sand. Suddenly the air I was breathing had a metallic taste. Now that other amphora handle seemed not a handle after all, but more like a curled sea cucumber, and although I was diving down on it, hand outstretched to grab it, it seemed to come no nearer. I was perfectly, delightfully happy, but a cold, frightened individual, existing quite separately inside my brain, whispered, 'If you go down farther, you will die.' Into my head slipped a sentence from Jacques Cousteau's book, *The Silent World*: 'Nitrogen has a dirty taste.'

Dimly I realised that I was experiencing what the poetic French call 'raptures of the great depths', known to the down-to-earth British as 'the narks'. I vaguely remembered the cure. Go up slowly, not necessarily as far as the surface, and the drunk-and-incapable feeling will vanish. So, at certainly not less than 160 feet, but perhaps much, much more, I turned to escape up the slope, away from the split-mind hallucinations of the depths. And my air ran out.

Instead of satisfying lungfuls, I found myself sucking a sparse breath or two with great effort. The surface was a long, long way above me, and I was still half hallucinated. I groped behind me for the loop of the reserve lever which, if I could find it among the straps, would give me enough air to get back to the sunlight. I located it at last, pulled the loop sharply downwards, and the sweet air gushed into my mouth again. The despairing feeling that I had let myself in for deep trouble and was doomed, faded away. Still holding the first amphora handle, but knowing that the reserve air would not last long at depth, I did not try to swim back up the slope between the rocky cliffs but broke away for the surface, finning vertically upwards. Without warning, as I reached the sunlit area of the sea, giddiness swept over me and I felt as if I was beginning to black out.

Simultaneously, I was surrounded by other people's bubbles, presumably from the two-bottle men still swimming up the slope far below; glistening, metallic, swelling, expanding as they plumed up in great curtains towards the surface. I suffered a moment of blind panic. I still had the amphora handle in one hand, but was ready to drop it; with my other hand I felt for the quick-release of my weightbelt (which I had tested in the boat), ready to 'bale out' before I became totally helpless. I was really frightened, not having heard of such symptoms before and vaguely thinking they must be connected with the narcosis. In fact, they were nothing of the sort, as Towse told me later, but were caused by the transition from the cold water of the depths through the thermocline into the warm water layer above, which affects the organs of balance in the ears.

Nevertheless, it was a very shaken McKee who surfaced, handle in hand and weightbelt still on, to find that there was no sign of *Sea Laird* or any other boat. I was apparently alone upon a wide, wide sea, abandoned by my friends. (In fact, they had not left me; I, by coming up vertically from the wreck instead of along the upward slope of the *secca*, had left them.) This, however, did not bother me. In Southsea Branch we did a good deal of snorkelling over long distances. Knowing my air must be almost out, I changed the aqualung mouthpiece for the snorkel mouthpiece, and set out to swim to shore. It might be a long haul, but after the Solent Sewer such a surface swim must be a snip—no vicious currents or cruelly cold water. Then I saw the boat a few hundred yards away and headed slowly for it.

*   *   *

The whole experience had been traumatic, not to say chastening. In a far more significant way, however, it had also been very important. I made a careful note, separate from my log, of what I had seen at the foot of the *secca* in Campese Bay:

> This is not a very well defined wreck. A jumble of fat-bellied amphorae, broken bases and handles, starting at 140 feet and trailing down a very steep slope among rocky spurs. Noticeably, the amphorae were of different sizes, as well as different shapes.

Although my main job was as a writer of factual war books, I edited on a part-time basis the house magazine of a group of coal and oil companies which handled coastal shipping in British waters; and had added some merchant navy background to that obtained from being the son of

73

a Naval Officer. From all accounts, as well as my own brief observation, this cargo seemed extraordinary.

On another level altogether was the psychological impact of contact with the relatively undisturbed relics of some much older civilisation than our own twentieth century mixture of industrial grime and technological gloss which many find profoundly unsatisfactory. Once on board, in brilliant sunshine, the curved pottery handle was indeed beautiful, glowing in shades of milk-white and pink, not visible before. This was caused by sea creatures which had left their shells on it long ago, plus the light of our world. In the depths, they had had no colour. Not, at least, to human eyes.

I had taken the piece as a harmless souvenir which might tell us a bit more about the wreck, which I had been told was Roman. I had no idea how important that handle was to be in the future. I had yet to learn that the wreck had been anything but Roman. Greek, Punic, Etruscan, perhaps—but certainly not Roman.

That handle was a relic from a century so far away, from a ship so old, that the Romans had yet to conquer even Italy. Rome was then just a trading town with the civilised Etruscans at the gates and Etruscan ships supreme upon the sea.

Campese Bay with the faraglione pillar in the background. I had just dived the Etruscan wreck for the first time—note the amphora base and also the amphora handle which I had brought up. *Photo: Alexander McKee*

Chapter 4

HEADLAND OF DEATH

The wrecks had been a surprise, a bonus. No one had imagined such a thing, for no word had reached England of what was going on in the Mediterranean, apart from certain parts of Provence associated with the Cousteau team. This was because French divers such as Cousteau and Diolé had written books which had been published in English editions. There were indeed English versions of works written by Italian divers such as Folco Quilici, Gianni Roghi and Francesco Baschieri, but their subject was primarily the hunting of big game below the waves; and to do this and to secure really ideal conditions for it, they had deserted the, to us, marvellous Mediterranean waters around Italy for the Red Sea. There were ancient wrecks there also, but in the 1950s and 1960s these had still to be found.

Spearfishing was a minor interest for British divers, however. Primarily we had come to Italy because of the warm water, the wonderful underwater scenery, the visibility to appreciate that world fully, to swim with and perhaps photograph exotic sea creatures. By definition, where you yourself live is non-exotic, sordid, boring, and inhabited by creatures similarly unexciting. What we wanted was to see something rich and strange. And we were not disappointed.

On the morning of 26 August we headed north out of Giglio Porto for a scenic spot called the Secca della Croce, and anchored alongside the boat being used by Victor de Sanctis and Maurizio Sarra, the photographer of *Mondo Sommerso*. The cover photograph of the current issue was one of Sarra's, as were the unbelievable photographs of a shoal of big fish, dentex, on the inside pages. I had yet to see dentex, but when I did, I found Sarra's pictures even more incredible.

With the advanced group, I went down the anchor rope to 120 feet, then turned upwards for a roam around; the greater the depth, the shorter is the time for which your air lasts. I had a big twin-set on and was able to make a minute search for wildlife. I looked under all rocks and into every crack and crevice. A seabed may look barren, but there are perhaps ten thousand eyes watching you. I swooped into a horizontal crack in the rock and met a small fish head on. We halted nose-to-nose and considered.

Who has right of way on an Italian underwaterway? Clearly, the boys from the big battalions. He moved over and let me pass. I spotted a large pinna shell and collected it; and then a king-size growth of gorgonia coral (a glorious pink colour) which I also collected. Their delicate tracery resembles a fan.

The next specimen I discovered was Reg. He was pointing a speargun at a spotted creature lying under a rock. Rocks tend to be undercut and provide many lurking places for wildlife, both in British and Mediterranean waters. Vallintine continued to point the gun, but did not fire. As I was wandering around with a knife in my hand, I assumed that he as host was giving me as tourist the honour of stabbing the thing. Dutifully but nervously, I advanced, mindful of electric rays which I had read up in a wildlife recognition book before my flight out. This was a big, nasty-looking flattie and I did not care for it at all. Therefore I was relieved when Reg made a violent gesture of a nature not in the Diving Manual, but which plainly spelt: NO! This was a ray (he told me later), and as most rays caught around Giglio were electric, this most probably was a shocker.

I went round the corner of the next rock and came on de Sanctis. I still had the knife in my hand and was looking suitably ferocious, so when once again he gestured to me to pose for an underwater photograph, I immediately assumed a suitably aggressive attitude. I knew at once it was de Sanctis because of the Calypso camera he was wearing round his neck, which I could hardly wait to get hold of. He was legendary for spending four hours a day underwater, using a big twin-set and an oxygen set. He always obtained amusement from our questions as to how he could go to 70 feet on pure oxygen without convulsing, when, according to our manuals, that type of set should not be used below 30 feet. We knew, of course, that the Italians had pioneered the offensive use of divers equipped with oxygen re-breathers, which send no telltale bubbles to the surface, and had been brilliantly successful in sinking British battleships in their own harbours. The French had meanwhile been pioneering the aqualungs we were now using, because they are safer, will allow you to go deeper and require little maintenance. For an expert professional like de Sanctis, however, the vastly superior endurance obtained from a re-breather was obviously an acceptable risk. With aqualungs we were always fretting at the comparatively short time one could stay down, a basic situation which still exists.

Like Campese, this site, too, was another underwater mountain, or completely submerged island, offering splendid scenery in the shallows. Circ-

Reg Vallintine leading a dive. *Photo: Alexander McKee* ▶

ling its uttermost crag, I saw a spotty, dun-coloured flattish object. What would a flatfish be doing on top of a Mediterranean rock? I carried on as if I had not noticed the creature, then turned and came in on it from behind and above. Eventually I could look down at part of it (a part which did not include its eyes) and could see that it was half in and half out of what could be either a rock crevice or an undercut shelf. From under the body I glimpsed a tentacle.

Not wanting to hurt the octopus, but curious about its living habits and homelife, I prodded the poor beast with the flat of my knife, at which it hurried inside and shut the door. He (or she) had clearly built a little fort to live in, for an old beer bottle and some shells were piled up in front of the entrance as a barricade. The true-blue British lobster does this, too, for his claws are in fact specialised hands—one for crushing, the other for cutting.

Reg Vallintine than arrived and we made signals at each other. Reg was trying to tell me: *Go up.* And I was trying to tell him: *There's an octopus down there, let's get it.* After some moments of mutual incomprehension, I returned to the boat and reported: 'I've just seen an octopus sucking on a beer bottle.' Reg had in fact been rounding up his strays from the advanced group before leading a new dive with the beginners. I still had air in my twin-set, and joined them immediately.

First of all, I had to find the octopus again. It had a great area of rock at its disposal in which to remain unnoticed, one volcanic rock looking much like another; so I circled round and round that rock pinnacle, keeping high up, partly to save air, partly to stay with the beginners, partly to keep warm. At last, I recognised the general area where the octopus had its lair. I lay motionless in the water, moving only my head as I scanned the terrain. Reg came up beside me; and he was the first to spot it, a little to my left.

There followed an epic battle before an audience of thousands (of tiny fish), stepped up in layers almost to the ceiling, like a crowd in the dress circle. Gouts of excited air burst from Reg's regulator, as he began to breathe harder and harder; writhing tentacles whipped the water as the frightened octopus went into its defensive routine.

The diver was grabbing at the octopus and trying to get a good grip on it; the octopus was hanging on to the walls of its home with some of its tentacles, and with the others was shoving out broken bottles and sharp shells at Vallintine, on which he cut his hands. The outcome of the battle was still uncertain when my air became 'stiff' and I had to pull the reserve

Reg surfacing with the octopus. It had taken him many minutes to extract the creature from ▶ its cave. *Photo: Alexander McKee*

lever. I hung fascinated above the struggle, while keeping a sharp eye on the whereabouts of the *Sea Laird*'s ladder which projected down from the hull hanging in the sky above. When at last my air was all gone, I surfaced and made for the ladder.

A few minutes later Reg came up with the octopus, which changed colour rapidly on the boat's engine cover—from white to brown to red. When we put it back it clung round Reg's neck. Then it changed colour again and vanished downwards at top speed, jetting ink. I had seen no inkscreen during the battle. I did not measure it, but it seemed to be about four feet across.

* * *

We returned from the Secca della Croce in company with a boatful of Italian divers, including the legendary photographer, Maurizio Sarra, who was larking about in an exaggerated manner. It was the 'done thing' then to indulge in a kind of Battle of Britain-type boasting, on the lines of 'There was I, old boy, upside down at 40,000 feet . . .' But Sarra seemed to be overdoing it, as if he were under some strain. He certainly was not ill, as we realised that evening at a dive called the White Dolphin.

Reg Vallintine had rigged up a room with the usual nets and baskets to indicate seafood, but with an extra dimension: a pool in the floor containing amphora sherds, pinna shells and so on; it was quite colourful and atmospheric. Many of the Italian divers and their girl friends were there, too, and a Twist session developed. Maurizio, whose physical image did not suggest the brilliance and beauty he could capture underwater, but rather that of an Apache, was, it seemed the winner of a Twist competition in Paris, so he led for the Italian side. On our side we could field Angela Keef, who was a professional dancer as well as an excellent amateur diver. That was quite an exhibition! But not a single Italian song was played or sung. It was all either Twist or Madison, to which I was a stranger. However, I knew my duty as a father and wrote home immediately to tell my wife to tell my daughters the vital social news, that 'all the Italians are Twisting'.

* * *

The following day we spent visiting the neighbouring island of Giannutri which was waterless and uninhabited, although this had not always been so. All my fellow Southsea members were on *Sea Laird* this time, sunbathing on the foredeck as we rolled south over the Tyrrhenian Sea, sighting dolphins as we approached. The coastline, much lower than Giglio but rising

The Southsea party, including Roger Hale and John Towse, aboard *Sea Laird* off the cliffs of Giannutri. *Photo: Alexander McKee*

vertically out of the sea in some places, would be a nightmare for shipwreck survivors if any sea at all were running. We came in close to investigate a great cavern with an arch of rock, then stopped engine farther along off an equally sinister stretch of bone-breaking coast. John Towse took the water temperature: 77 degrees Fahrenheit!

To make sure we all found the wreck we had come to see, Reg swam the anchor down himself, but I did not see him go because I was dressing; for once, I put on a wet suit jacket instead of wearing just a neoprene hood and an anti-sunburn singlet. Last in, I swam down the line to the anchor. There was no one there. The anchor had hooked on to a rock surrounded by scattered amphorae sherds and an imitation forest of large pinna shells, growing upright in the sand patches; fish began to gather round me. I took a couple of photographs in the grey light, before Reg emerged out of a smokescreen hanging about farther down the slope, obviously made by the main party, and beckoned me down. I didn't envy him his job of swimming sheepdog on a lot of curious tourists likely to stray aside to examine this and that at depths where time—and life—was strictly limited.

I followed him and found myself hovering above hordes of tumbled amphorae, many broken. It looked as if the wreck had burst her sides on impact when she hit the floor; but that was merely the impression. It was much more likely that the sides had fallen only when the wood became water-weakened and the frames and planks began to droop like a dead flower's petals, eventually being consumed by shipworm. I tried to take pictures but clouds of white dust kicked up by the other tourists, rolling among the wreckage, made the water indistinct, with the shapes of black-suited divers moving about like ghosts. Incongruously, old (but not *that* old) buckets and bottles lay among the shipping-jars of antiquity.

I let out my breath and sank right down among the chaotic mass of amphorae. Turning to look up for the invisible surface ceiling 110 feet above me, I now sensed a real feeling of an ancient shipwreck; of being surrounded by the rubble of her cargo; and for the first time at Giglio, I had some sense of human drama instead of a coldfish appraisal of the scene combined with my own survival considerations. How had they died? Probably, the ship was driven by high winds on to that horrible rocky shore far above and splintered, leaving the sailors to be beaten to death by the waves. Then, filling, the ship might sway or somersault down, shedding cargo on the way, strike higher up the slope, with more cargo falling out, then lurch silently down to her last resting place amid an enormous white cloud of disturbed sand. And wait there through unnumbered centuries until this time of discovery.

The reason why this cargo stood up so high from the muddy plain below the rock slope could be that there was rock just underneath the mud and sand. Or possibly that the ship had been high-piled with empty amphorae. I never found out.

I had been given only a single cylinder aqualung, so my air was soon exhausted. I pulled the reserve lever and was sufficiently confident now not to go directly for the surface, but to climb steadily up the slope, at a constant altitude of 10 feet or so above ground, looking for objects of interest.

The first items I saw were enormous pinna shells lying flat on the floor, obviously dead, instead of in up-standing forest formation. Clearly, these could be simply picked up, instead of struggled out after much wrestling and see-sawing, for which I lacked sufficient air. Breathing slowly and cautiously once every fifteen seconds or so, I plumed down and chose the largest pair of shells, nearly two-and-a-half feet long, which would make a nice 'souvenir from the seaside'.

Holding them carefully, I climbed up again to cruising altitude, still rising with the slope, and as I mounted towards the *Sea Laird*'s anchor, I glimpsed through the corner of my mask a Cressi diver's knife in a blue plastic sheath. Thinking it had been lost by one of the Italians who were diving with us, I turned back down the slope, swooped, and picked it up with my free hand.

My air supply was now almost exhausted and it was hard to breathe. I was sucking on the bottle without getting very much, so I turned upwards and began to fin fast vertically towards the surface, thereby shortening the ascent distance and, once I reached the lower pressures, getting a breath or two. I slowed down for the last 30 feet, which is the critical area, and arrived virtually out of air. In order to get a breath, I now had to take out the aqualung mouthpiece and exchange it for the mouthpiece of the snorkel tube. Doing this with both hands full of souvenirs proved awkward, but I managed it without dropping anything.

Once back on board, I looked around for the owner of the knife I had saved, but they all disclaimed it. Easing the catch, I took the knife out of its sheath—the blade was rusty and the hollow plastic handle was full of water. So it had been down there some time.

Some of the others had got better souvenirs. Complete amphorae tops were coming up all round, glowing with vivid colours, mainly red and purple, from the seagrowth on them. Roger Hale of Southsea had chosen a technically interesting item—a large piece of lead, not unlike the chest-weights used with standard helmet diving gear. The question was, however, did this piece actually belong to the wreck or was it a later intrusion, like the buckets, bottles and my Cressi 'floating-type' diver's knife?

My own most important discovery of the day was the formulation of a heresy. I noted:

> The old archaeologists' data-fed, computerised dictum, that a ship-wreck is always a 'closed find', with everything related to everything else, and of approximately the same date—was exploded.

My heresy was to remain a heresy for some twenty years, with phrases like 'time capsule' and 'closed find' being batted to and fro by innocent enthusiasts; but lately, other people have made the same discovery for themselves.

Undated and unidentified, this wreck seemed to be another recent discovery. Reg had been shown it for the first time a matter of seven weeks earlier, on 9 July, by the two Italian divers Claudio Ripa and Maurizio Sarra.

Pat Millgate in the Roman villa on Giannutri, a palace said to have been built for a relative of Nero. *Photo: Alexander McKee*

Reg now made a second, shallower dive with the party of beginners, and I got into the water again, but without a bottle, to photograph their ascent. The light was very bright and the water so warm that I could go deep and stay down easily; so much so, that I was still snorkel diving when the anchor was hauled up to hang just under the boat.

We then went round to Attracco cove, formerly the harbour for the island's Roman villa. According to the local story, this had been built by a relative of Nero, or by a family which had flourished on both islands during his reign. It was certainly a wonderful place and superbly sited on a small hill above the sea. After lunch, we walked over to what remained of the buildings. The cliff edge, with the blue Tyrrhenian far below, was shrouded by bushes and trees; inland, tall white columns crowned by capitals stood 15 feet high. The lower parts of the walls still remained and some of the flooring, including a broken mosaic of dolphins; in some rooms, however, the underfloor central heating system was exposed. But this was August; there was a breeze, sweet-scented with flowers, and shade, yet the air was burning warm even out of the sun; the only sound was the ceaseless rustling of the cicadas. There was a sense of ease, of peaceful luxury, of life unhurried, even idyllic. A few miles away over the water lay the Italian coastline, running southward to Rome which had been mighty, and violent, and brutal; a knife-edged city, literally, for men and women engaged in politics. No doubt they needed this retreat. And through this channel, between Giannutri and the coast of Tuscany, had passed the sea traffic to and from Ostia, the port of Rome; and further south, to and from the Greek colonies around Naples and Salerno, where the three temples of Paestum had stood before there ever was a Roman Empire; when it was the Etruscans and not the Romans who had ruled this strait and all the nearby seas.

Not far from the villa, in 140 feet of water, lay the remains of what Roger Hale told me appeared to be a small cargo ship, known as the 'Plate' wreck,

Campanian ware from the 'Plate Wreck' off Punta Scaletta, Giannutri. The entire cargo consisted of plates dating from around 300 BC, which had obviously been tightly packed into crates. The wreck lay at 140 feet off the headland topped by the Roman villa, not far from a small harbour which may have served the villa. *Photo: Roger Hale*

because it was full of black dinner plates, stacked each inside the other, upright. Reg believed that the first time this wreck was seen was on 15 June, 1961, when he came across it while diving with Siegfried Koster of the Munich Underwater Club. Plates and bowls from the site were to be identified by the British Museum as Campanian ware of about 300 BC, and later, in 1963, the Italian frigate *Daino* was to be base ship for a three-month excavation of the site by Professor Nino Lamboglia. It puzzled me to learn that, while delicate ship sites were being plundered, the *Daino* had been employed mainly on mapping ancient submerged harbour works, such as the Roman remains at Baia, in the Gulf of Naples, and, more interestingly, the Etruscan port of Pyrgi. It seemed to me that submerged docks and quays, particularly massive Roman ones, might quite safely be left for a few years, whereas the ancient ships were visibly disappearing, piece by piece, daily. One could hardly blame the souvenir hunters because, if diver A did not remove a piece, diver B certainly would. If, however, it was known that certain sites were to be properly excavated in the immediate future, most (though not all) amateur divers would tend to respect them.

I never saw the 'Plate' wreck because Reg was teaching a French tourist to dive in the shallow waters of the cove (and had probably accumulated too much nitrogen in his system to allow a deep dive to 140 feet on top of the other two dives he had done in the morning). For the rest of us, he had left two weightbelts on the bottom of the cove in 20 feet or so, for those who were interested to pick up and bring back to the surface, snorkel diving only, without bottles. This was good basic practice; snorkel diving is more difficult and more physically demanding than aqualung diving, but often more rewarding.

What struck me about the cove were features resembling submerged quays, but with no facing stones visible; instead, a rather ragged, undercut wall. I had noticed much the same thing in Giglio Porto in shallower water; but this was more elaborate as well as deeper, it really did suggest quays. Above water, I had noticed no such geological formation. The coast seemed to consist of folded volcanic rock with curious 'string courses' here and there.

*　　*　　*

The next morning found us off the north cape of Giglio, diving at a spot near the modern lighthouse marked on the charts as Punta del Morto. In plain English—Headland of Death. It was an obvious accident black spot for any ship heading south in fog or bad weather, just as the headland at the opposite end of the island, called Punta del Capel Rosso, or Red

86

Cape, would be an obvious obstruction to any ship heading north and slightly off course in similar conditions of poor visibility. Similarly, the rock of Le Scole, which had collected the late Roman wreck, formed another awkward projection, the most easterly point of the island, bearing in mind that these were sailing ships, which would not always take the path that their captains wanted, operating in an area where sudden and drastic changes of wind direction occur. The Campese Bay wreck was different, Reg said; he believed he had found traces of burnt timber and assumed a battle with pirates. On the other hand, the *secca*, the underwater island, was another obvious ship trap if sea level had been only a little lower in those days.

This morning's wreck, I was told, was an underwater junk shop with everything broken; so if one wanted a souvenir, this was the place. Although complete amphorae were valuable prizes, parts of broken ones were worthless, commercially at least. Some of the other divers that day were after graceful souvenirs for the shelf—necks with twin handles. I wanted evidence for dating—a top would serve that purpose, true, but so would a base. Besides, one could use a base as an old Roman ashtray (for we still thought of all these wrecks as Roman). I rather fancied telling my friends: 'Mind how you knock out your pipe—that thing's 2,000 years old!'

I was still the complete novice, and careless tourist, for on this morning I was too keen to get into the water to think first. Yesterday I had worn a suit jacket (which is buoyant and requires extra weight), but today I was going to wear only swimming trunks and would require some 6 lbs less lead. But I just picked up the same weightbelt I had used at Giannutri and put it on, without removing any of the weights.

So when I got into the water I sank fast and easily, taking photos on the way of Reg doing guide dog for us. We arrived at a steep gulley in the rocks at about 100 feet; its winding floor was littered with broken amphorae down to about 125 feet. It looked as if the ship had struck the rocks at the head of the ravine; and when it broke, the cargo went pouring down the slope in a typical 'cascade' of amphorae, shattering completely. There was no sign of a hull and I never expected to see one on terrain like this. Not that there were all that many amphorae, certainly not a full cargo for a big ship. So perhaps just a small vessel, or a larger one riding 'light'; or more probably, a great many pieces had been pillaged already. Reg had first seen this wreck site on 29 July, 1961; and he was not the discoverer. A great many people who would have respected an archaeologically reconstructable site, might have had no hesitation in taking a souvenir or two here. And one could share their feelings. The old wine jars, although made for mundane cargo-handling purposes, for some

Punta del Morto: A fish nosing among broken Greek amphorae (fourth to third century BC) at 140 feet. *Photo: Alexander McKee*

reason struck us all as extremely graceful, perfectly satisfying to the eye. To us, they were Art. Part of an ancient world more perfect than ours.

I went nose first down the gulley, choosing three interesting pieces, to where the 'cascade' petered put at around 125 feet. I noticed a curiously-shaped growth on a rock, like a dolphin's head, and hacked it off with my knife for easier examination in air. I had far too much weight on my belt; three heavy and clumsy pieces of amphorae (including one top and one base) in my hands; a heavy and clumsy camera-case round my neck; and, of course, only a single-cylinder aqualung, which at that moment ceased to supply me with air. This time, it was not merely difficult to find the reserve lever—it was impossible. I groped around at the back among the straps, without success. Looking round, I spotted Reg watching over his charges, swam over to him and made the correct signal. He activated the reserve, and I had a full supply of air again. But not for long, not at that depth.

What followed was a performance to make a shark laugh. I was at the bottom of a steeply sloping rock gulley, both hands full, and heavily over-weighted. I literally climbed back up that gulley on my hands and knees like any normal mountaineer, scraping a leg on the rocks as I did so. At the very top, well, there was perhaps 80 feet of pure water directly above me; between me and the surface. That distance, I would have to swim.

Reg, who was following me closely, signalled: 'Are you OK?' I made a despairing sign with my amphorae-laden hands, intended to convey the message, not in any manual, that I was too heavy and was looking upwards for either the boat or a snorkel diver, and couldn't see either.

I took off from the topmost rock for the surface and part-way up sighted a snorkeller, like a great waterbeetle clawing his way across the mirror-like surface. I changed my course slightly to intercept him, and surfaced nearby. Momentarily, from pure exhaustion, I stopped finning—and promptly sank ten feet. I flipped up again, attracted the attention of the snorkeller, who was not one of us but an Italian, and gave him my load of old amphorae to hold. Then I changed over mouthpieces, to snorkel from aqualung, but was still too heavy. And the boat was too far away.

I decided to do a leisurely bale-out like a gentleman. I was over deep water, where any ditched weightbelt would be lost, so I ploughed over to a high white rock which was only about eight feet below the surface, and most conspicuous; pulled the quick-release, making sure the weights did not slip off the belt, and then laid it down carefully on bare rock where I could find it again. I gratefully collected my amphorae samples from the helpful Italian and swam them back to the boat. I would have gone back for the belt, but Reg, following in my wake, had already picked it up. I had just removed my aqualung, now empty, when I heard a loud cry in Italian:

'*Morane! Morane!*'

I quickly put my fins, mask and camera back on and went over the side. A moray eel was a creature I was keen to see and photograph. They were popularly supposed to be purple and ferocious, descendants of eels fed on slaves by Tiberius (or was it Nero?). Anyway, it was a jolly good story of which I didn't believe a word. Now was the chance to test it.

About 25 yards away an Italian girl, knife in hand, was warily snorkel-diving around a small hole in a sloping rock face. I dived, too, putting my mask at the entrance to the hole but seeing nothing inside. John Towse, a ten-times better diver than I was, arrived and started snooping around lower down for connecting holes which might link with the upper one where the girl had first seen the moray, for the rocks were honeycombed with passages. With all this commotion going on, one could hardly blame the purple eel for going away and locking himself up in the lavatory.

For lunch, we went round the north tip of the island, beyond Punta del Morto, and put into Campese Bay where there was a sand beach with a restaurant at the back of it. A development was under way, but the place was still distinctly untouristy, with only a dozen or so people sunbathing. *Sea Laird* nosed into the sand and we went ashore. This beach, one of very few on Giglio, was about a mile from the *secca* where I had been 'narked' on that ancient wreck with the strange cargo, and from the cross marking on shore the death site above it of the two Italian divers, lost there in 1959.

I was very hot and dying to get into the water. Perhaps I could blame it on the wine; certainly, I had got used to great depths close inshore. At all events, once on board, I went to the stern, put on mask, flippers and snorkel and, holding the mask tightly to my face (to prevent it being pushed off by the impact of the water), I jumped over the side. And landed in a sea so deep that the waves just about came to my knees. There were nearly fatal casualties among my Southsea friends who were laughing so much they could hardly float.

I suppose, really, it was the song of the sirens. The water so warm, so clear, so still, so beautiful. How could it kill you? In England one was totally convinced that the sea could be lethal in any one of many different ways. A cold diver cloaked in darkness is a coward, whereas a warm diver swimming down in limitless visibility is brave and bold, until it is too late.

We went out of Campese's tiny harbour and turned left round the headland marked by a single rock stack, a *faraglione*, rearing lonely from the sea. We came to a dark and forbidding coast of harsh cliffs rising almost sheer, and anchored close to a small rocky island, the peak of a submerged mountain known as the Scoglio del Corvo, or Rock of the Crow.

This time I was nervous. The place not only looked and felt ill-omened. It really was so. 'Skeleton Cove' was its nickname now. A year ago Reg had found the headless skeletons of two German divers, Ponnerier and Eisenschmidt, at a depth of 220 feet. They also, like the two Italians at Campese, had disappeared without trace in 1959. Assisted by Roger Hale of Southsea, Reg had recovered the bodies for burial.

Hale was also diving here today and it was my turn to have one of the twin-cylinder aqualungs, so I would be able to stay down much longer.

◀ A curtain of fish underneath the keels of our two diving boats. Apparently, they were waiting for us in case we killed something, so that they could take the leavings. From below, the surface looked like a shining silver mirror. *Photo : Alexander McKee*

Chapter 5

ROCK OF THE CROW

Reginald Vallintine had begun diving around Giglio as an instructor the previous year, in May, 1961. Although an experienced snorkel diver and member of the British spearfishing team (which gave him all the basic skills), he had only limited time underwater with the aqualung. I recall he told me (with a grin) that he had only done about thirty sea dives when he took on the job of instructor—a marvellous chance not to be thrown away and a decision amply justified by his record since. This makes all the more remarkable, however, the way he coped with what happened at Corvo, helped by Roger Hale of my own branch.

One of the first things Reg did was to look at the local charts for clues to good, scenic dive spots with plenty of wildlife. The lone rock of Corvo, lying off a headland midway between Campese and Capel Rosso, seemed a likely place, but the Italian crew of *Sea Laird*, Costanso and Valdivio, seemed reluctant to go there. Sea monsters, strong currents and rip tides. Finally, Reg discovered the real reason. Two German divers had vanished there without trace or obvious cause in August, 1959, less than two years before.

Vallintine took parties of underwater tourists there from 23 May onwards, finding dramatic scenery—great rocks, large bushes of black gorgonia coral and the delicate pink *rose-de-mer*. From 150 feet downwards, the divers met many lobsters and moray eels. On 21 July Reg was leading Ted Derrick of London Branch on an advanced dive to great depths and had reached 170 feet, where he was searching the cliff for lobsters. Looking down into still greater depths, towards the sand at the base of the cliff, Vallintine noticed two irregular white patches far below. There was something not quite right about them, as if they did not belong there. Without actually intending it, Reg and Ted found themselves at 200 feet—and still 20 feet above the white patterns on the sand. But now there was no doubt: the patterns were made by two collections of bones.

Vallintine and his partner checked each other for signs of nitrogen narcosis—often revealed by wild, glaring eyes behind the masks, or by irrational behaviour. Satisfied that they were still in their right minds, they sank down to the sand at 220 feet.

The gloomy, ill-omened cliffs opposite Scoglio del Corvo, the Rock of the Crow.
Photo: Alexander McKee

The sight before them was unforgettable. Two skeletons, the bones bound together by their weightbelts and the straps of their twin-cylinder aqualungs, with flippers still on their feet, were lying on the sand.

They had found the two Germans.

The bodies were lying on a sloping seabed, one behind the other, as if they had been going deeper when death suddenly took them. The higher of the two bodies had beside it on the sand the loaded speargun which the diver had been carrying; it was already covered in marine growth.

This skeleton still had large pieces of flesh and muscle attached to the bones which had held the body together. The lower body was much less well preserved and, consequently, the remains were more scattered. Neither man had a head.

There was no time to make a detailed examination. The nitrogen in the bodies of the two living divers was high and the air in their cylinders low. They had to return to the surface far above.

Their first action was to put into the nearest village, which was Campese, and telephone the police. Within an hour, a police boat arrived and Vallintine was asked if he would be prepared to recover the remains. The police stressed that it was essential that what was left of the bodies should be kept separate; the men had relatives—indeed, their wives had been in the boat while they dived, waiting for them to come back; and had waited, and waited, until it was achingly plain that something catastrophic had happened down below and that neither of them would ever return to this world.

On 24 July Vallintine began his attempt to recover the two Germans, helped by Roger Hale of Southsea Branch who had now joined him as assistant instructor. To keep the remains of Karl Ponnerier, 31, separate from those of his young companion, Erik Eisenschmidt, 19, two marked sacks were prepared. Lines were to be attached to them at the surface, and the lines were to be paid out from a boat as Vallintine and Hale swam the sacks down to the bodies. The bottom ends of the ropes would be tied round the dead men's aqualungs. Meanwhile, in another boat there would be two coffins.

This was the macabre scene above, augmented by a police boat and other official craft, when Vallintine and Hale made their first dive at about noon. They found themselves being forced to swim hard against a strong current which was running in mid-water, and by the time they emerged into a still layer lower down, they had been swept so far off course that there was no sign of the dead men.

After waiting until teatime for the nitrogen level in their bodies to drop, they tried again—and found the Germans lying under a great overhanging rockface which Reg did not recall from the earlier dive when the discovery had been made. This time, too, they were unlucky: the ropes got tangled in the overhang above and it was impossible (in the short time available) to pull them down to the corpses.

Two deep dives in one day meant only one deep dive late the next day. This time, Vallintine swam the sacks to the bottom while Hale hung above him, keeping the lines clear of the cliff face. At the end of this dive, the sacks were within sight of the bodies and the lines were buoyed at the surface. One more day, and two more dives, should see the operation completed.

On the morning of 26 July, Reg and Roger swam the sacks to the first body. Then, while Vallintine put the bones into the sack, Hale tied on the dead man's twin-cylinder aqualung.

Vallintine went down the slope towards the second body but only managed to get about half of the bones into the sack. By then, air was low and he had accumulated a good deal of nitrogen in his body.

It was teatime before his decompression meter told Reg that it would be all right to dive again (although not for long). He put the remaining bones into the sack, tied on the aqualung, and then, glancing down the slope into greater depths still, he saw yet more whitened objects lying on the sand.

Descending to 250 feet, Vallintine found bone fragments and a German Barakuda depth gauge. He thought these objects might have been pulled down the slope by fish. However, there was still no sign of the men's heads.

Slowly, Vallintine and Hale returned to the surface, the job done—or so they thought. But a hang-up developed at once. The Italian police hauling up the sacks met resistance; the lines came taut and would not move. Exasperated, Vallintine put on a fresh aqualung cylinder; only a single bottle this time—a set reserved for decompression, part of his safety procedure. At 150 feet he found the lines snagged under a rock ledge, and cleared them.

No sooner had he got back into the boat than the lines went taut again. As he had not taken off his aqualung, Vallintine went straight back in. There seemed to be nothing wrong with the lines—they hung clear of the rocks. Reg had to pull the lever activating the reserve, which would not last him long at these depths, and it was only as he reached 150 feet, with his air supply already becoming 'stiff', that he saw that one of the two sacks had snagged at the base of the rock 50 feet farther down. Reg reached this last sack, unsnagged it—and had no more air. He was 200 feet down.

Panic would have been fatal. Vallintine finned hard for the surface, and, the pressure lessening as he rose, managed to take three of four 'long wheezy breaths' from the bottle before reaching real air again. Another aqualung was ready for him to go down and decompress, by hanging on the anchor line. Meanwhile, the sacks were pulled up.

More than a month later, Vallintine was diving at Corvo with 'Bogie' Kane of the Institute of Oceanography. They went down to 180 feet, found the giant overhang, and dropped down the far side, past the place where the bodies had been; they alighted on the sand at 240 feet, among many tiny pieces of scattered bone which must have been pulled away from the bodies by fish. Leaving his partner to wait there, Vallintine went down still farther to another rock at 280 feet. Under it he found a German snorkel tube, heavily encrusted (which showed that it had been down there some time), and firmly wedged, a human skull. Still farther down were other white objects, but Reg felt that he had risked enough. At 280 feet, he must have been poisoned not only by the nitrogen content of the air he was breathing at such high pressure, but by the oxygen content, too, which

95

becomes toxic at this depth. He finned slowly back up the slope, rejoined his partner, and they both went up for a long decompression stop at 10 feet below the boat.

Both he and Hale had suffered considerably from nitrogen narcosis while recovering the remains, and Vallintine thought this might have been the cause of death for the two Germans. Against this, he would have expected one diver to be affected before the other, as the narcosis varies from man to man. It varies in other ways, too, he had discovered, being worse on an empty stomach than when diving soon after a meal. He concluded that, from their position on the sand, they appeared to have been in diving formation when they met their deaths; and that no one now would ever know why.

*   *   *

Reg's last dive to recover parts of the bodies had taken place almost exactly a year earlier, on 31 August, 1961. Now it was 28 August, 1962, three years after the tragedy, as we curved out past the *faraglione* standing sentinel on Campese Bay and went on to anchor alongside the rock of Corvo. That night, I noted in my log, telegram-style:

> For once, I was nervous. Ill-omened spot. Reg's vivid writing. I was still too heavy, although I had taken off one big weight of about 4–6 lbs. I sank down into the valley, following the others, taking pictures as I went. Then the film ran out, abruptly. Blast. Down at the base of the first ledge, at 130 feet, I saw one of the lads trying to cut open a sea urchin, although there were few fish to be seen. I thought he must have the 'raptures', so I stayed with him to see him all right. Afterwards, he insisted there had been plenty of fish for the urchin meat to attract. We swam along the base of the ledge at 130 feet for some time, then turned upwards behind Reg. The ascent of the rock face was like mountaineering, with flocks of fish instead of birds. Eerie, breath-taking.
>
> After we had gone up 50 feet or so, I noticed a high ridge on my right; and Reg's story clicked in my mind. I broke right abruptly out of formation to look over it. Yes, it was the place overhanging the death site. I swam out into space over it—like looking down from an aeroplane on a distant landscape.
>
> Back in the boat, Reg told me that there was another drop below the foot of the ridge I had noticed, and at the foot of this second drop had been the bodies. They were inexperienced in Germany, he said, and had no Mediterranean instructor. Went there in a boat

▲ Painting of a dancing couple from the Tomb of the Lioness at Tarquinia, sixth century BC. Typically, the girl is painted in white, the man in red, as if sunburned. *Photo : Valerioti*

Tombs in the cliff face at Norchia cut to resemble the façade of temples in the sixth to fourth century BC. *Photo : Alexander McKee* ▶

The Southsea team with their boat at Giglio in 1962. *Photo : John Towse* ▼

◀ Amphora recovered off Gig[lio]
in 1967. *Photo: John Towse*

Mensun Bound and Reg
Vallintine checking a char[t]
Giglio during the search in
to relocate the wreck site a[fter]
lapse of twenty years.
▼ *Photo: Alexander McKee*

with their wives. They went down, they never came back. Their wives waited for them to surface, until the waiting grew so long that they knew they would never surface now. It's so easy here to go too deep without realising it, down the death slope to 400 feet.

*   *   *

The following day, sobered but still enthusiastic, we went in search of wild-life again. Going north out of Giglio Porto, we turned into Lazzaretto Cove, where a lone rock broke the surface of the sea. As I followed our party down, some strange divers came suddenly into view. One had his camera in a big white metal case, the other had a Calypso. That one must be Victor de Sanctis.

I had already met de Sanctis twice underwater. So this was the third time we had met below. Sure enough, he gestured for me to pose at around 80 feet. But I had *my* camera this time, and we faced each other, nose to nose, $3\frac{1}{2}$ feet away, clicking at each other. I shot first.

Reg had promised a photogenic cavern, and so it may have been before the other divers got there. When I arrived I found the entrance small, so that with two bottles on my back I could barely get through, and the water so stirred up that photography was not on. Having done 25 minutes at depths down to 100 feet, I took a ten-minute breather and then went off for a snorkel dive around the headland. This proved to be psychologi-cally interesting.

As I rounded the point of the headland, I met another snorkeller, one of the girls. She was in a terrible flap. Tom was missing. Until now, it had not been clear that she cared about Tom. But now she set off at a tremendous rate, while I followed her, puffing like an old train. Every so often, she would stop, take the snorkel out of her mouth—and shout for Tom. I suppose we might have covered 500 yards and anyway were well out of sight of our boat, on the other side of the point, but there was still no reply to the girl's calls. She seemed frantic with anxiety.

Then Tom appeared out of nowhere, and the girl began to upbraid him for worrying her. They burst into a rapid quarrel, treading water, snorkels out, shouting at each other in their rage. I took a deep breath and went down to 10 feet or so, from where I could photograph apparently headless bodies with kicking fins.

To distract the furious girl, Tom showed me a large octopus down on the slope at somewhere between 25–30 feet. He had the lid of a large tin tactically laid down outside his front door, so once you had seen him, you could not lose him. I took deep breaths and went down three times for

(*Opposite*) Elfie snorkel diving. Unencumbered by an aqualung, the diver is much faster and more agile but cannot stay down nearly so long. (*Above*) Castello, the fortified town built on a high point of the island. *Photos: Alexander McKee*

photographs, taking two pictures at around six feet away and one closer in at the minimum focusing distance of three-and-a-half feet. The beast was well concealed behind a barricade of big stones at the entrance to his cavern. I could just see an indistinct shape sitting on a tentacle seemingly as thick as my wrist. A big one, this.

My photographs show clearly the fish which were circling just over the octopus, and I suppose they kept close because they were expecting me to kill him, perhaps leaving some morsels for them. I failed to oblige.

With an aqualung on one's back, one had plenty of time to experiment; but with only the breath in one's own lungs and 25 feet or so beneath the surface, one could not afford even a slight risk of being pinned down. Or, at least, I could not—I simply was not in the same class as a breath-holder with people such as Towse, Hale or Vallintine.

99

We were underwater tourists only. That afternoon we made our single land excursion during nearly two weeks on Giglio—to Castello, the walled town on top of the island, built as a refuge from Moorish raids. The illusion of tourism was enhanced underwater now by the fact that many of the lads took openwork shopping bags down with them. They swam along trailing these bags, stuffed to capacity with sea urchins, dead or alive, starfish, gorgonia, and samples of virtually everything else in sight.

Converted by their example, I made the morning dive of 30 August a 'shopping' expedition. This was to Cape Marino, south of Giglio Porto, and was led by Roger Hale because Reg had been slightly 'bent' the day before. In the afternoon I went along with a private oyster-collecting dive by the staff in the same area. I was invited because one of the Italian crew, Filippo, wanted me to take photographs of him in his new smart neoprene suit jacket bright with yellow tape. I captured the funniest photo of the day when, following Filippo, I saw him go straight through a shoal of the little black, fork-tailed fish known as demoiselles, turning them over and over in the backwash of his flippers. I think this was the expedition when Maurizio Sarra got so many oysters that he gave me some for tea.

Wildlife and photography occupied us the following day as well, again at Cape Marino. My afternoon dive, when we were anchored over an underwater island, was a memorable experience. I had only a single cylinder set so was reduced to 25 minutes at depths down to 100 feet; I was wearing a Ful-Vue mask, with glass sidepieces which make the wearer resemble a blinkered horse and hold a lot of air (a disadvantage), but which allow vision to both sides as well as to the front.

Terrific panorama, like from front seat of a fighter. Our formation went on down towards a desert at 100 feet, and as we were approaching 80 feet, Reg pointed to eleven o'clock. And there they were—a silver squadron of Dentex, booming along like Heinkels, sunshine glinting from their hides against the grey gloom.

They were a little lower than us, and apparently going round us, in a detour. Very big, very fast. I broke left out of our formation and went down on them, much slowed by the drag of my big camera case. I came tearing downwards over the last crag before the rocks fell almost sheer to the desert, and they were still going away and down; I was not catching up, just holding them.

They almost lured me down the death slope, but without a depth gauge I dared not pursue them farther down. At the speed the chase was going, I could have killed myself inside a minute. I expect they know what our limit is. These were the type of fish (possibly the same ones) which the Southsea group saw a few days ago on the *secca*, and of which Maurizio Sarra got close-up colour pictures for *Mondo Sommerso*. How did he do it?

I came up out of the depths, over the hill, with enormous horizons shown by the three-piece mask. Definitely a flying feeling, the landscape reeling past, rocking gently, or wheeling round as I turned. Then, nearing the surface on the shoulder of the underwater hill, I suddenly felt cold water flowing past me; then I saw it. You could, by climbing slightly, *see* the cold layer as a moving stream—little ripples and eddies of silver pouring down the mountainside. You could put your hand into it and feel a distinct boundary.

*   *   *

Next day, 1 September, was to be rather special. So special, that for once I thought it worth wearing a wet suit jacket. I didn't want to be 'narked' unnecessarily or shivering from cold when my observations might be important.

This was to be a deep dive on an interesting, intact wreck for de Sanctis to photograph. Reg put the anchor down on top of the wreck at about 150 feet. Then told me to lead the party. He's a good chap at giving you confidence, for I certainly lapped that up, the two Londoners being present (both 1st Class divers and I no class at all). Go straight down the anchor cable, as fast as possible, was his order. I did so, not much troubled by ear-clearing. At one point, Londoner Pete passed me and got the lead; then had trouble with his 1st Class ear just as I finished clearing mine; and I zoomed down past him, turned near our anchor cable, and alighted on the wreck.

Piles of amphorae, mostly shipshape, mostly intact, buried deep in sand; just the necks sticking up in orderly rows. And a few 'pits' among the cargo, where 'souvenirs' had been removed. That wreck must have been over 100 feet long.

De Sanctis loomed up almost at once with the Calypso which would soon be mine, but I was not much use to him as a model. My neoprene jacket having been pressed to the thinness of tissue paper by the depth of water, I was too heavy and, bumping on the bottom, stirred up a little 'smoke'. When I had used up more of my air, I would become lighter for the ascent.

I went away from our boat anchor, down the slope. I re-set my watch, five minutes having elapsed already. Then I lay down and quietly searched among the amphorae for bits of ship, or crew mementoes, or cargo other than pottery jars. I found a pottery sherd,

Le Scole: Rows of amphorae (third century AD) lying stacked in the hold of a Roman wreck at 165 feet. The broken amphora lying on top is evidence of looting. *Photo: Roger Hale*

then an iron box affair open at both ends. I ought to have brought it up, and was dying to do so, but Reg had warned not to take anything as this exceptionally well-preserved cargo was due to be properly excavated by the Italians. I broke off a little of the flaking iron at one end to establish that it really was iron.

My brain was very slow at this depth, and the sharp edge had been taken off my sense of self-preservation; but there was no sign of the 'narks' and I was sufficiently in command to watch my watch to check how I was doing. I noted that ten minutes had now elapsed on the bottom. I was breathing slowly and thought I had a lot of air in hand, having—thank God—a twin-set. I was still lying there quietly, sifting and examining in the sand, when the small Londoner came down the slope to me and beckoned officiously: 'UP'. Then I saw that everyone else had gone, and that I was alone on the wreck.

Un-narked by narcosis but slightly narked in another sense, I headed up. Our anchor was at about 155 feet, and as I had gone down the hill quite a bit, I had probably been at 165 feet. Not having a depth gauge is a nuisance, and the British decompression tables sewn on to one sleeve of my jacket gave the stop times from only 130 feet. I stopped at 10 feet and hung there for 10 minutes, timing it exactly with my watch. Then I chased over to Reg (who was wearing his decompression meter) to ask if it was OK to surface now. It was.

I assume this cargo ship hit Le Scole rock, heeled while sinking, spilled some deck cargo overboard; and went down the very steep rock slope to the sand at its foot. Pretty obviously, there was at least the bottom half, possibly even two-thirds of the hull, of a large Roman freighter, intact under the sand. But already there were signs, particularly what looked like a bomb-crater amidships, that the cargo was being removed wholesale and indiscriminately; probably for sale (I heard that amphorae were then selling at the equivalent of £150 each in New York).

All the amphorae in the top layer (which was the only layer visible) were of identical type. One party of divers decided to raise one jar as a souvenir and take it home. The amphora they chose to lift was unusual, in that the stopper was still in place. They drove this in with a spear, preparatory to getting the sand out and so lightening the jar for the lift. But what came out was not sand. It appeared to be grain. This was normally a bulk cargo, and to carry it in separate jars would be an unbusinesslike waste of shipping space. The contents may perhaps have been some special seed rather than grain, but now we shall never know. However, the amphora itself was of a well-known type, from the third century AD. That is, late Roman, about 1,600 years old.

This wreck, lying just off the entrance to Giglio Porto, had been discovered by Reg Vallintine on 16 June, 1961. Every day, since the start of the season in May, he had been taking out his tourists on exploratory dives in what was then almost virgin territory. And almost every day they found traces of an ancient past—tops, handles, necks, bases and sides of the old jars. And all of them broken, incomplete. On this particular day he had with him Sigi and Heinz from the Munich Underwater Club, both experienced divers. After anchoring at a promising spot, the three men put on twin-sets and slipped over the side into a visibility of close on 100 feet. Clouds of the little rock bream parted to allow the three divers through while the larger sargi, taking fright, slid down into clefts in the rock and disappeared.

Great rock reefs sloped steeply down below them. Following a rock ledge

Angela with the amphora just after it was brought up from the Roman wreck off the rock of Le Scole. *Photo: Alexander McKee*

down to 140 feet, they found a gently shelving sand slope at its foot. As they swam down the slope the weed and sea growth thinned out and disappeared. Then, ahead of them, at the distant limit of visibility, an unnatural contour began to take shape. They swam closer and the shape became an enormous mound studded with tiny tubes. They suddenly realised what it was: the wreck of a great Roman ship. The 'tubes' were the necks of amphorae buried in the mound! There were hundreds of them. None of them ever forgot that first moment of discovery. Pointing madly, and trying to shout through their mouthpieces to attract each other's attention, they finned around the wreck. Every single amphora was intact and covered in red, white and brown growths. Tiny pink and blue fish swam in and out of the encrusted necks; from one neck a purple moray observed them, opening and closing its jaws. Overwhelmed by euphoria, they felt like the finders of Atlantis.

During the succeeding months, Reg took many tourists and some visiting professional divers to this wreck. In September it was announced in *Mondo Sommerso* as a new discovery by someone else (who had been shown the wreck by Vallintine). Later, it was the subject of an article by Maurizio Sarra published in *L'Aventure Sous-Marine*, the French diving magazine, with an early reference to amphorae as 'the jerrycans of antiquity'.

When I saw that Roman ship, little more than a year after its actual discovery, the name Le Scole had become briefly famous among continental divers, a 'must' on the underwater tourist's itinerary; and already the looting had begun, fuelled by the thought that if you didn't take it, someone else would. Some photographs exist, including an excellent monochrome by Roger Hale, showing clearly how the amphorae lay in rows almost on their sides, implying a great angle of heel for the hull underneath. If the implication was true, then almost one complete side of the vessel must have lain there below the sand. I took no photographs because de Sanctis told me that he thought my big case would not stand up to the pressure. The glass porthole was certainly large. However, I do know now that my open-ended 'box' affair was really a mould of an iron object which had dissolved into the natural concrete formed on the outsides by the chemical process involved in its dissolution. But all I had as a record was a freely drawn sketch made after I reached the surface.

*　　　*　　　*

We had dived to 165 feet on Le Scole in the morning. De Sanctis was returning to the mainland by the afternoon boat and handed his Calypso to me. I had intended to buy such a camera in Italy anyway (but had found them unobtainable on my journey). This Calypso was now second-hand but had been tested to great depths by one of the best people in that field. I did my first test of it that afternoon, diving to 75 feet off Cape Marino. Due to the hasty transfer, I loaded the film wrongly and got nothing. And next day was the last diving day. After that, I had to go home, too.

So on Sunday, 2 September, I kept on getting into the water, cadging part-empty bottles from other people who had surfaced with the reserve still unused. In the morning there was one last deep dive to the 'Spanish galleon' at 140 feet off Capel Rosso, followed a few minutes later by a short dive in the shallows to shoot a complete colour film. Then I reloaded with black and white and did another short dive in the shallows at between 10 and 20 feet; and exposed all 36 frames. I put in a new black and white for the afternoon's dive to 125 feet; the last time I would see the wreck on Punta del Morto and have the chance to do anything about this unidentified site.

The dive at Capel Rosso was not very happy. I only had a single cylinder, and for the first time at Giglio had ear trouble. My left ear clicked satisfactorily each time I blew hard, but the right was stubborn and the ache in it would not let me go farther down. I kept pressing down, then pulling up to a more comfortable altitude, as though on a roller-coaster, heading up-current after the others. With anguish, I saw them disappear behind the crest of the rocks that led to the galleon, until finally the only traces of them were streams of bubbles expanding upwards towards the surface. Over on my right, someone else was hovering high up, also probably unable to clear.

I must have been falling gradually and the ear clearing itself, and equalising the inside pressure with the water pressure around me, without any violent effort from me, for, while I was rationalising the position, ready to give up and just take pictures in the upper layer, I suddenly saw the galleon's mast below me on the sand at the foot of the cliff, 40 or 50 feet down. I swooshed down on to it like an eagle after prey. I wanted one of those dinner plates.

An item like that should be identifiable, and this wreck—or collection of superimposed wrecks, more likely—was mysterious and puzzling. How could a real galleon's mast still be standing? Was the ancient pottery higher up the slope really Roman? I searched around for key pieces to unlock the puzzle. The light was too dim for pictures, so I hunted around in the sand. I uncovered the deck in several places—it really did seem to be a deck, and if so, then the implications were tremendous. Everything looked grey in this light, even the deck planking; the fish too, were grey ghosts, unmoving even when my finger was inches away from them. There was no sign of the plates which I had seen stacked together, edges up, on my previous visit here. I noticed a curious white stone at the foot of the mast. I picked up a bit of broken pottery; and saw more of some hollow, metal, heavily-encrusted tubes which I had noted before. I had thought perhaps they were musket barrels (an idea suggested by the lead shot which was also present). This time I selected a specimen to bring up.

Once more I found the small Londoner tapping me on the shoulder and motioning UP! This time, it was just as well, for a few seconds later, the air in my single cylinder ran out and I couldn't locate the reserve lever among all the tangle of straps around my spine. This continental system seemed less safe than the British practice of carrying a pressure gauge which tells you exactly how much air you have left at any time.

In the boat, I examined my 'musket'. It was in the shape of a hollow barrel, but hexagonal, one-and-a-half inches in diameter. Too big for a musket but right for a swivel gun. The encrustation on it included sea shells. Only later did I discover what it was: a 'concretion'. That is, a natural concrete which has formed round an iron object which has been so long underwater that it has dissolved by chemical action into the surrounding natural crust. In principle, it demonstrated the same process as the open-ended 'box' I had seen and recorded on the Le Scole Roman wreck. In effect, these were the moulds of former iron objects.

For the last deep dive of the holiday, we moved from Capel Rosso, the southernmost headland of Giglio, to Punta del Morto, the most northerly. This was the Jumble Sale/Bazaar site, expendable because everything was broken and there could be no hull remains. No one knew what ship this was, where it came from, or when it had sailed the Tyrrhenian. I had already removed an amphora top and a base of the pointed 'shipping' type of jar. But that might not be quite good enough. I determined to make sure. I had not been too clever the first time, but this dive was to be my twenty-first in 11 days. And I had the Calypso to record what I did—a dream camera, so easy and so certain in operation, so small, with so little drag.

I loaded a black and white film (much faster than the slow colour films then available) and went in for a 40-minute dive, to make a total of 85 minutes underwater for the day. My log records that I went

Over the rocks and down the gulley to the remembered jumble lying on the very steep slope in the winding gulley below that at 125 feet. No Londoner this time to tell me to come up, and a big twin-set on my back. Reg kept with the three inexperienced Swiss boys, and let me go to it. I went. I selected two different, flat amphora bases and knocked off the unnecessarily large areas on the spot with a stone. (Reason: the possibly fatal drag.) The others went up with Reg, having only singles, and I stayed on down, turning over the amphorae and taking pictures of them at f3·5. It grew a bit misty, so I rose up above it, mistakenly thought the light brighter, and stopped down to f5·6.

Then some biggish fish, I think sar, began diving on the disturbed amphorae—presumably there were succulent worms exposed now—and they kept on doing it, two to three feet in front of my nose. Mistakenly, I indulged in frantic clicking, as each shot seemed better than the last; and anyway this was the last film on the last dive. I might as well use it up.

The rest had long gone up, when at length I decided to call it a day, and ploughed back up the cliff face with my amphorae bases. Up on top, there was no sign of anyone, so I lay on a rock 10 feet under to decompress in lazy fashion, taking pictures meanwhile of fish and *Sea Laird*'s bottom. Four lung dives in one day, two of them deep (140 feet and 125 feet) must have built up the nitrogen saturation quite a bit, so I determined to use up all my air in the shallows,

Fish feeding on a sea urchin which had been cut up. The force with which these tiny fish slammed into the dismembered urchin was awe-inspiring. *Photo : Alexander McKee*

having left, as I thought, a good margin. No future in needing 15 minutes' decompression and having air on your back for only five minutes. Two choices only then: stay down and drown; go up and get bent.

Then I saw bubbles over the other edge of the cliff, round the corner from the wreck, and up came Reg in a cloud of demoiselles, holding an amphora top with handles. I closed on him, but my film stopped after one or two. I was presented with amazing, easy masterpieces, and I had used up some of my material on duplication. Reg then joined me on the shallow rock, decompressing and feeding fish, including some gloriously coloured ones: some had green and red lateral stripes, others had yellow and brown vertical stripes.

That evening, as we packed and relaxed, rumours spread (relayed by people who had been watching the Italian television news), that Maurizio Sarra had been attacked by a shark and was believed to be seriously injured. Reg Vallintine hazarded that, knowing Maurizio's style of photography, he might have irritated the shark by trying to make it pose for him in some new, spectacular fashion; for that really was the way Maurizio worked. Remembering those impossible, incredible colour pictures of a herd of huge dentex at speed, I could believe it.

In Pisa the next day, on my way home, I bought an Italian paper which confirmed the news. Both Maurizio's legs were gone, one of his eyes was gone, he had had 308 stitches. The incident had happened off Terracina, south of Rome, where Sarra had been exploring just after his visit to Giglio. The paper referred to the atrocious wounds inflicted by this 'tiger of the sea'. I went into the nearest church and prayed.

The afternoon papers, which came out just before I left for the airport, carried the death notice.

He was 28, and author of a book entitled *My Friend, the Shark*. One report quoted Maurizio as having said: 'I was meant to be born in the sea.'

Chapter 6

WHAT'S THE ULLAGE OF AN AMPHORA?

We were the first that ever burst
Into that silent sea.

Samuel Taylor Coleridge, *The Rime of the Ancient Mariner*

After that summer, I saw no more of the wrecks around Giglio until 1982. Although my belief in their importance—and alarm at their probable destruction—never wavered, it was impossible for me, with a large and growing family and a living to earn, to try to organise any kind of rescue expedition. What did emerge was a growing concern for the Campese site above all others.

To start with, I collected all the information, drawings and photographs of the Giglio and Giannutri sites, regardless of whether they were wrecks or so-called 'dump' areas, which I and all the other members of Southsea Branch had amassed in 1962. Secondly, I kept in touch with those members of the Branch who continued to go back to Giglio, collected the information as it came in and discussed it with them all. John Towse, for instance, was returning to Giglio as late as 1967, and could confirm that the Campese site still existed, although some looting had taken place. Reg Vallintine left Giglio after the 1963 season to set up a diving school off the North African coast, but Roger Hale of Southsea, who had been his assistant for some years, became chief instructor at Giglio in succession to him in 1964. He also was convinced of the importance of Campese and was particularly careful to record, where possible, what had been recovered from this site. He was able to supply sketches and often photographs of seven particularly interesting artefacts: a large dish, a jug, a goblet, a possible oil lamp, a lead anchor stock (one of three seen), and two amphorae, one of very large capacity. Apart from the anchor stocks, not one item was the same. This was extraordinary. I could think of no parallel.

Coupled with this, was the alarming news that, by 1964, nothing whatsoever remained of the late Roman ship 165 feet down off the rock of Le Scole. The depth had not deterred the looters from plundering it to destruction. Quite certainly, there had been a lot of ship hull underneath. I now bitterly regretted taking nothing whatever from this site.

It was clear that the Campese wreck was not Roman. Reg Vallintine had had some of the items looked at by experts, who identified them as Etruscan and Greek, dating from around 700 BC, and he had published this information in *London Diver* of April, 1962. I looked up the back issues of this magazine and added to it the information obtained by Southsea divers—Roger Hale, Alan Lee, Jack and Pat Millgate, P. Robyns and John Towse. Altogether the material filled an album with 98 pages of typescript, drawings and photographs, covering a dozen definite or possible wreck sites. These 98 pages I reduced to 24 for an article in the Southsea Branch magazine, *Solent World*, which I edited. This included eight drawings by Hale of artefacts from Campese which, following Vallintine, I said carried Etruscan and Greek items of about 700 BC. I then sent copies to influential people such as Miss Joan du Plat Taylor of the London Institute of Archaeology. From Hale's drawings, she was able to identify two amphorae as being neither Etruscan nor Greek but Phoenician; which made the Campese site yet more exciting and enigmatic. The cargo was even more mixed than we had realised. As for the ship which had carried it—was she Etruscan, Greek or Phoenician? She had sunk in Etruscan

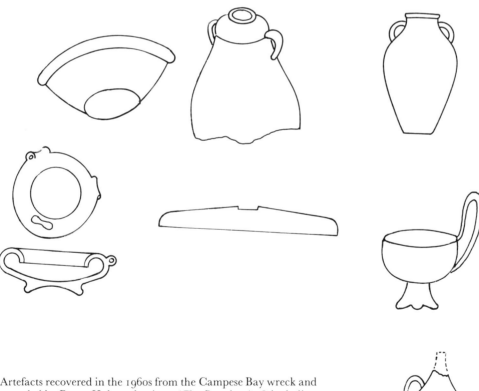

Artefacts recovered in the 1960s from the Campese Bay wreck and recorded by Roger Hale at the time: (*Top Row, l to r*) 18-inch diameter dish; 24-inch diameter Phoenician amphora; 30-inch high Phoenician amphora (both amphorae match with finds from the Phoenician colony at Motya in Sicily). (*Centre, l to r*) 10-inch diameter oil lamp (in plan and in section); 6-feet long lead anchor stock (one of three seen); 3-inch diameter goblet. (*Bottom r*) 4-inch diameter jug. *Drawn by Maurice Young*

waters, certainly, but that did not rule out entirely the Greeks or the Phoenicians as owners. This was a mystery, but a mystery which might be solved. I had dug in the sand and found that there were buried remains, but how extensive were they? And how thorough would the inevitable looters be?

Strictly speaking, the amphorae drawn by Hale might be Punic rather than Phoenician—from the Phoenician colony of Carthage rather than the Lebanon proper—and Miss Taylor stated that there seemed to be links with the Carthaginian colony of Motya in Sicily. That might make trading sense.

The amphorae bases and neck which I had recovered from the 'cascade' of shattered pottery on the slope off Punta del Morto proved that this also was a non-Roman wreck and very old. Miss Taylor was able to say that the pottery was of fourth to third century BC and its origin was Marseilles—then a Greek colony in what is now Provence in Southern France. That made excellent sense, for the wreck was on the headland facing any ship coming south from Provence. So this trading vessel had gone down some 2,300 years ago. But as ship and contents had shattered on rock, the remains were nothing like as rich—and certainly not as strange—as those of the Campese wreck, partly buried in sand.

I promptly published this new information in an issue of *Solent World* in 1966. In 1967 I wrote to Professor Lamboglia, listing all the Giglio and Giannutri wrecks known to me, adding that, 'The most important of the above seemed to me to be the wreck on the *secca* in Campese Bay.' The following year, 1968, saw the publication of my first book on underwater archaeology, *History Under the Sea*, in which I devoted a complete chapter to what I now knew about the wrecks of Giglio and Giannutri, stating that the Campese wreck contained Etruscan, Greek and Phoenician pottery dated to about 700 BC, and describing this site as 'The most interesting wreck of them all'.

For twenty years she remained in my mind as a dream, perhaps to be fulfilled one day. But meanwhile there were other dreams, more immediately practical, close at hand.

*   *   *

Not least among my reasons for doing no more than this about the far-off Etruscan site was that I was midway through a fascinating investigation of a 'Church bells under the sea' legend in Hayling Bay, a few miles from my home. Now, for the first time in history, it was possible for ordinary people to go down and find out if there was any truth in such stories. We did indeed find submerged ruins on the site—but no church bells.

The important dating evidence from Campese and Punta del Morto, re-photographed in 1981 to help the Oxford team. *Photo: Phil Burner*

The other great undersea challenge off my home coast was the lost wreck of the *Mary Rose*, sunk in battle with the French in 1545. Virtually nothing was known about her, except that she had been the first English battleship to carry complete batteries of heavy siege guns, then a novelty even in land warfare. I thought she might have sunk in an area where a soft seabed would preserve much of the hull and contents. I had already, early in 1962—months before going to Giglio—begun the long task of researching her and finding out where to search.

It is hard now to recapture what I felt then—in the late 1950s and early 1960s—of that sense of opportunity which, if not taken, would never recur. Only one group of divers would make the great discoveries; the group who went first with insight and determination and never gave up.

Many of us felt like that, and it was never better shown than at the World Underwater Congress held in London by the British Sub-Aqua Club in October, 1962, a month or so after I came back from Giglio. There had been nothing like it before, and there never will be anything like it again. We had all seen Cousteau on television, and the charming Hans and Lotte Hass. Here they were in the flesh, Cousteau with his exciting concept of 'Homo Aquaticus'—of man living under the sea—which caught the headlines. But here also, in their own fields of study, were men equally eminent—Sir Alister Hardy to talk about the sea itself, Sir Mortimer Wheeler to chair the archaeology session in which George Bass was a lecturer. And for the highly technical deep diving experiments then taking place or projected were Jacques Piccard, Ed Link and the controversial Swiss team of Buhlmann and Keller (who contested the general belief that narcosis was caused by nitrogen). Presiding over the Conference was Lord Mountbatten of Burma, standing in for the Duke of Edinburgh. Lord Mountbatten had done a good deal of diving himself while he was in the Navy.

The organiser was Peter Small of the BS-AC, who at the conference teamed up with Hannes Keller and was invited to take part with him later in the first dangerous experimental dive in the sea to 1,000 feet, using gas mixtures devised by Buhlmann. One thousand feet was reached and Keller survived. Small did not, nor did a cover diver who tried to rescue him.

In 1962, 1,000 feet was sensational; utterly impossible on compressed air. Marred by tragedy as it was, nevertheless the experiment marked a revolutionary advance in techniques. Changes equally as great were simultaneously occurring in other underwater spheres, notably in archaeology and the excavation of wrecks.

*   *   *

It's as near as dammit true that, until the era of the aqualung was well launched—around 1950, say—the lost ships of history had remained undisturbed since the day they had gone down.

But one has to put in a quibble about depth. Many wrecked ships are not sunk at all. Technically, they are 'stranded'. I could remember some from my earliest childhood. There was the trawler—how dirty it was with grease and oil, and how it smelt—which I boarded where it lay, high and dry on a beach in Northern Ireland. It was intact and undamaged, and my brother and I spent many hours exploring all over it. And up on the beach, half buried in the sands of Whitecliffe Bay in the Isle of Wight, was one half of a torpedo boat destroyer to which violent things had been done while it still floated. The story went (I don't vouch for it because my age when I first climbed over this wreck was four years at most) that two 'tribal' class vessels, the *Zulu* and the *Nubian*, had collided; both had been torn in two, and the parts had later been reassembled as one ship only, called so they said, the *Zubian*. It seemed a jolly good tale to explain that half of a warship which served my brother and myself as a beach playground after swimming.

There was another I remember from my childhood in the Isle of Wight—a dark hulk heaved up on the rock ledges off Bembridge. The *Empress Queen* had struck in 1916 but was visible above water for many years, certainly into the 1920s; then gradually she disappeared from sight. But not altogether from human ken, for I explored her once when diving off Bembridge in the 1960s. There was still a good deal of her left, only just under the surface.

These, then, are from the first category of shipwreck—vessels which were stranded, not sunk. From them, and also from ships submerged in shallow waters, items of value are normally recovered at the easiest possible time— just after the accident. The most famous treasure ships of all, the Spanish 'Silver Fleets' (so-called because that was a main cargo), when wrecked became the target of strenuous salvage efforts, employing native divers. Almost 2,000 years earlier, the Romans also used divers to recover cargoes from ships sunk in the notoriously dangerous port of Ostia, the maritime centre for Rome.

The divers probably relied on breath-holding, although possibly diving bells may have been in use. At the time, the lost cargoes were documented and usually well known. Even if plans of the sunken hulls were not immediately available, the general construction methods were known and the layouts familiar. The type of life endured aboard these ships would also be common knowledge then. And how they were sailed and worked, where they went, and when, and why, and who owned them.

And the names of these vessels would also be known. Some of them, no doubt, were as famous in their day as the great four-funnelled liners which I used to watch steaming past Bembridge—*Mauretania*, *Aquitania*, *Berengaria*. The great battleships, too (familiar to me from Naval children's parties)—the *Iron Duke* class, the *Queen Elizabeth* class, the *Revenge* class, the *Nelson* and the *Rodney*. And the graceful battlecruisers—the *Tiger*, the *Repulse*, the *Renown*, the *Hood*. Some had fought at Jutland, some went to the breakers, some went to the bottom in the Second World War. Because we are so close to these ships, we know all about them and what their fate was to be; even where some of them lie now, and the names of their dead.

For the ships of antiquity—from the times of the Romans, the Greeks, the Phoenicians, the Etruscans—we have no names. We have paintings on cups or vases, some paintings on tomb walls, a few carvings on stone blocks. But no names, no detail, even of those ships which were stranded or sunk in shallow water, let alone those which went down at the foot of precipitous cliffs or vanished out of sight of land into depths we still cannot reach.

Fishermen, especially those dredging deep in the hope of harvesting a crop of sponges, might pick up an amphora or even part of a statue—probably from the top layer of a largely buried wreck—but no one can conceivably have seen any of those ships again, except perhaps briefly by breath-holding, before the invention of reliable deep-diving apparatus. The first discoverers of the *Mary Rose* in 1836 were the Deane brothers of Whitstable in Kent; inventors of an 'open helmet' system; they began their work in the 1820s and found that the device would operate down to 120 feet, with the possibility of reaching 180 feet. They used ordinary compressed air, just as an aqualung diver does, although it was supplied in a different way. The helmet diver therefore faced exactly the same problems with bends, nitrogen narcosis and oxygen poisoning, plus an extra hazard: the possibility, if he exerted himself too much, of a lethal build-up of bad air inside his helmet.*

Improved pumps to supply sufficient air at great depths enabled the helmet diver to reach 200 and then 300 feet. At first, the effects on the diver's body of going too deep were either not understood at all, or only partially guessed at. In the Mediterranean and the Aegean, the Greek and Turkish sponge divers were compelled by the pressure of poverty to dive too deep for too long too often, even when they did sense the hazards. A great many were crippled or killed by bends. But it was some of these men who saw, for the first time in 2,000 years, the lost ships of the ancient world. To be precise, what they must have found were the upper cargo layers of ships which had been loaded with solid, long-lasting materials.

*   *   *

It was the turn of the century, the year 1900. Two caiques from Syme, driven off course by a gale, were sheltering by the island of Antikythera in the Aegean. Diving for sponges was the business of the Greeks who crewed them. Rather than waste time, their leader, Captain Dimitrios Kondos, decided to do a series of dives close in to the ugly cliffs where the water was calmer. A current ran there from the headland, carrying

*Ordinary atmospheric air consists of 78·05 per cent nitrogen, 21 per cent oxygen, ·93 per cent argon, ·03 per cent carbon dioxide, together with minute amounts of hydrogen, neon, helium, kryton and xenon. When breathed under pressure, these gases have differing effects on the human body. By switching the proportions in an artificial 'mixture', for instance, by using helium to replace the nitrogen, the 'narks' may be avoided—at the cost of distorting the human voice and making the diver very cold. These processes are too complicated and costly to be used in amateur diving.

food for sponges. The first diver he put into the sea was called Elias Stadiatis. He went down to 30 fathoms—180 feet—and Kondos decided to give him five minutes at that depth before pulling him up. But Stadiatis did not wait for that. He came up rapidly, climbed the ladder, and when they got his helmet off, began to babble about seeing dead naked women, their limbs scarred by disease . . . and horses . . . people . . . men and horses.

Kondos then dived himself and landed on a sandy ledge which sloped from 30 fathoms to 35 fathoms, and then dropped steeply into impossible depths. On the sand ledge was a sight so incredible that without proof, he knew, no one would believe him. There lay piled up a great heap of bronze and marble statues, as if the contents of some national art museum had been poured out lavishly on to the ocean floor. He looked for something loose and light, and found it in a man's hand, made of green metal, hollow, and filled with sand.

Almost certainly, this was a cargo of classical Greek art, looted by the conquering Romans in the first century BC, and on its way to Rome in a Roman ship. Probably the transaction was legal. The clear comparison is with the 'Elgin Marbles'—classical Greek statuary removed by Lord Elgin with the permission of the Turkish conquerors of Greece. Much of his 1801–1803 haul reached the British Museum in due course; but other cargoes were lost at sea, just as this one had been.

Intact pot from a still-secret wreck site near Giglio. *Photo: Roger Hale*

Kondos reported his discovery to the Greek government, with the broken bronze hand as evidence, and a State-financed salvage expedition resulted. Technically, it was prodigious—statues being recovered from depths in excess of 200 feet. But its direction was by non-divers from the surface, and these directors were antiquaries or archaeologists, people primarily interested in what we now call the 'goodies'. In any case, it is only lately that there has been any general awareness of the possibility that hulls may survive, wholly or in part, under the sea for any length of time. In 1900, no one thought in terms of the discovery of a wrecked transport vehicle; they thought exclusively in terms of a collection of antique treasures. What was done, with the best of intentions on the available evidence, was an act of official plunder, not dissimilar in excellence of motive to the 'salvage' of the Parthenon frieze by the Earl of Elgin.

Of course, the wreck of Antikythera cannot actually have been the first ship of antiquity to be sighted by the helmet divers; it is merely the first that we know about. Piles of old jars in association, perhaps, with lead anchor stocks, must have been noticed sometimes by sponge divers; and the sponges on the jars removed, and perhaps the lead stocks themselves. But how many such wreck mounds were sighted we do not know; still less can we know if many of the divers realised that these mounds represented wrecked ships, some remains of which must lie buried beneath. The question was still being argued in 1962 among the aqualung divers.

The next reported discovery by Greek sponge divers was three miles out to sea off Mahdia in Tunisia, at a depth of 127 feet. The year was 1907. Not coincidentally, this site, too, contained classical Greek statues (it was the sale of some of these on the local black market that alerted the authorities to the fact that someone had found a valuable wreck). An excavation of sorts followed—once again, commercial divers directed from the surface by academics. Basically it was treasure hunting once more.

There was a lull during the First World War, then another reported discovery by Greek sponge divers off Cape Artemision—the scene of a great naval battle in 480 BC between Greeks and Persians, but unconnected with it. The year of discovery was 1926 and the depth was in excess of 125 feet. This third site also produced classical art work: magnificent bronzes. These could be dated, but not the ship which was carrying them. The original sponge divers had given way to an expedition organised by antiquarians who, on being stopped by the police, were succeeded by a government-sponsored expedition, which represented official treasure hunting on the Elgin model.

Naturally, three treasure wrecks in a row could not be coincidence. The finds represented not a cross-section of classical ship losses but wreck sites which, in the opinion of the sponge divers, were possibly of commercial value—unlike any amphorae wrecks they might have seen—and which became known because authority concurred in their estimate of the value to museum collections. Academics became lyrical in their prophecies of what might lie under the sea: the bottom of the Mediterranean was clearly the greatest treasure storehouse in the world.

All these wrecks were deep, and where they lay on a slope, the working depth varied (the depths I have given are indications only). The time the divers were able to spend underwater was not very great. But the toll was high. At Antikythera two men were crippled, one killed; at Mahdia, three men were crippled; at Artemision one man died from the bends.

The invention of the aqualung introduced the age of popular diving. The time was after the Second World War, in the late 1940s. The place, initially, was the south of France—along the coasts of Provence where goggle diving had flourished before the war. The most Romanised part of France, where there had to be countless Roman wrecks; and indeed, much older ships. The adjoining Italian coastline is identical—the present frontier artificial—but in the time of the Etruscans it was occupied by another strange people, the Ligurians, who also spoke a language which was not Indo-European, and whose territory to the south adjoined Etruria. These rocky shores, perhaps the most beautiful in the world, looked out over some of the oldest of sea routes: from Greece and the East on the one hand, to France and Spain, and even England, on the other. And although the Mediterranean seems warm and kind, it can blow a fury with only a minute or two's warning, and while doing so, the wind can rage round the compass. Safety can become danger in no time at all. For the historically minded diver, it was to prove a fruitful place.

The aqualung changed the situation completely, because it was simple to use and to maintain (unlike the pure-oxygen sets worn by military and naval 'frogmen' for war purposes, which emit no tell-tale bubbles). Nor did it require the cumbersome backup of the helmet diver: pump-operator, lifeline-tender, and so on. If you wished, you could dive off the shore alone (although it might take several trips on foot to cart the gear from the car down to the water's edge).

The sponge divers were few in numbers, whereas the aqualungers were a multitude. The sponge divers were professionals, whereas the aqualungers were doctors, dentists, architects, bricklayers, stevedores, clerks, historians, business people, pastors, submariners, butchers—you name it—who went under water in their own time, when they could afford it, unpaid and amateur. The sponge divers had to earn their bread and ouzo underwater, so they went where the sponges were, and when there, had no time to stand and stare, whereas the aqualungers were free first to wonder, and then to explore, and to choose their field of exploration according to their interests and tastes. Among the aqualungers themselves there was a sharp division—between those who had lived all their lives on the coast and those less fortunate who lived hundreds of miles from the sea. The former had far more opportunities for diving and so gaining experience, besides knowing a great deal more about the sea itself than those who saw it rarely. Not surprisingly, it was divers from the local clubs on the coast who made most of the early discoveries.

The discoveries themselves were in turn sharply divided into two categories: the many nameless and unreported wrecks on the one hand, and, on the other, the few famous sites, which became well-known because archaeological work was done on them and the media found people only too willing to talk.

Virtually all were amphorae-carriers, freighters with cargoes of wine and fish and fruit. Virtually all were first seen by aqualungers. There was one linking exception: an amphorae wreck at 130 feet off Albenga in Liguria (now the Italian Riviera). The first discoverers were fishermen who trawled up amphorae in their nets in 1930 and during 1945–1947, dated to the first century BC. The first divers were helmet men working for a famous Italian salvage company but directed (from the surface) by an Italian archaeologist, Professor Nino Lamboglia, in 1950. He used a grab to cut a trench across the wreck mound, and the grab broke many of the objects on which its jaws closed. Most of the finds were of amphorae, but there were a few pottery bowls, and some broken timber from the hull, including fragments of lead sheathing, and parts of three bronze helmets. Lamboglia came back in 1957 with a team of four aqualung divers operating from a small boat, and made a survey of the site which showed a typical wreck mound (like a prehistoric barrow) with the grab-dug trench cutting across part of it.

Elsewhere, aqualung divers also visited sites first found by the helmet men—Cousteau's team went to Mahdia in 1948 and a local club did excellent survey work there in 1954–1955. Cousteau's men also visited the other statue-site at Antikythera in 1953. Therefore, these two wrecks became famous in the 1950s and 1960s, while Artemision was forgotten.

Four French sites became well-known: Antheor (1948 onwards), the great Cousteau dig at Grand Congloué (1952 onwards), Titan off the Ile du Levant (1956 and 1958), and Dramont (1956–1959). And there was one wreck in Italian waters: Spargi off Sardinia (1958). All were first or second century BC amphorae-carriers. In some, ship timbers were exposed and samples taken, but as no one knew how to conserve them, the timbers

John Towse with a Le Scole amphora (*left*) and two necks from an unidentified wreck ▶ off Giannutri. *Photo: Alexander McKee*

speedily shrank, curled and distorted. Most were deep or very deep (150 feet or more in the case of Grand Congloué).

There was one very shallow site (only 21 feet down and fully visible from the surface) which failed to be recognised (as a wreck) for many years. The site consisted of 14 rocks 250 yards off St Tropez on the French Riviera. At first, they were just 'those old rocks'. Then it was found that the rock was marble (which is, of course, old). The local fishermen's tale was that they were old millstones which had been 'thrown into the sea' long ago. They were eventually identified and raised (in the early 1950s). The heaviest weighed 38 metric tons, which would defy the efforts of the mightiest Olympic athlete to throw anywhere. These 'rocks' proved to be the bases for columns and had been cut from the marble quarries at Carrara in Italy; probably they were intended for use in the construction of the Temple of Narbonne in the second century AD.

There were no traces left of the actual ship which had carried the marbles of St Tropez. In such shallow water wave action during gales would have dispersed and destroyed virtually all of it. But one still has to insert a mental question mark, because the amateur divers of that time and place tended to be more expert at spearing fish than in recognising wreck sites. Mussolini had not been surpassed as the finest underwater archaeologist in the Mediterranean area. To expose two large pleasure vessels of Nero's at Nemi, he had drained the lake in which they had sunk, and then recovered the hulls for exhibition. Most knowledge of Roman shipbuilding still came from these two state barges from the first century AD, most probably sunk in the time of Nero or Claudius, and recovered by Mussolini in a campaign begun in 1928. The war in which he subsequently involved Italy put paid to the ships, museum and all. Both had been large—one 239 feet by 78 feet, the smaller 234 feet by 66 feet wide. They had been plundered as long ago as 1446, so a controversy had arisen as to whether the expense of their recovery had been worthwhile. Italian and American archaeological opinion thought it had, but British archaeologists took an opposing view, which is still current. 'Three fine bronze animal heads and a wooden hulk seem a poor return for such expenditure.' The raising of the *Mary Rose* almost exactly half a century later was to be greeted in identical terms.

This attitude is not unlike that of the treasure-hunting divers who destroyed, occasionally with explosives, almost all the classical wrecks found in the Mediterranean. This happened to the Dramont wreck in 1957, which got into the books because some of the smashed amphorae were given to Fernand Benoit of the Musée Borely at Marseilles. But the majority never achieved fame; indeed, the looters may have deliberately kept quiet. Many hundreds of wrecks were involved—off the Planier islands, Maire island, La Ciotat, Cap Roux, Antibes, Fos, the Hyères islands, St Tropez, Fréjus, Porguerelles, Cagnes-sur-Mer, Nice. Some of the finds were of Etruscan amphorae, and one of them, off a headland at Nice, was certainly an Etruscan ship, lying at very considerable depths, from 150 to 260 feet. Known to have been brought up from this site after it was discovered in 1955 were buccheri (vases of black clay, typically Etruscan), some delicate, painted pottery which was either Etruscan or Corinthian, and at least 170 amphorae datable to the middle of the sixth century BC—around 550 BC, that is. When I went to Giglio in 1962 I did not know of this: how many wrecks had really been found, how valuable they were, or how they were in process of destruction. I was aware only of the famous ones—those I had been able to read about in translations from foreign books, mostly French. I was not always impressed by the archaeological work recorded there. Nor, for that matter, were the people who carried it out.

The atmosphere, tensions and relationships of that time are well illustrated by an article Dilys Powell wrote for the *Sunday Times* which had sponsored the first British underwater expedition abroad in 1954, with the backing of the British School of Archaeology in Athens. The diving expedition was led by Richard Garnett of Rupert Hart-Davis, the publishers, who was also a leading light of the British Underwater Explorers Club, founded in 1953, the same year as the British Sub-Aqua Club. The expedition was to Chios, an island in the Aegean.

At first the company was entirely archaeological. 'Is it true,' someone asked over the beans, potatoes and onions which were the main dish at midday, 'is it true that the divers have to eat four pounds of meat a day?' 'The divers': in isolation antagonisms grow tall and shady. No society is more pugnacious than the academic: the ferocities of learning are contagious and persistent, and even today, though it is eighteen years since, an idler, I lived in the world of archaeology, I have not lost my prejudices. Mention certain names, certain theories, and I bristle.

However, once they got to know each other, the two parties fused amicably, perhaps because the director of excavations was an early enthusiast for combined land and sea operations, and in spite of the fact that few of the divers had archaeological or scholastic qualifications. They were mostly:

Active young men or good-looking young women who had been drawn to Emporio by nothing more than a liking for adventure and a desire to dive and who, once there, found themselves working under direction.

The archaeologists had a case, too, for not all divers are of the mild, intelligent sort described by Dilys Powell. An informed analysis of the diving community in the late 1950s appeared in the Spanish diving magazine *Mundo Subacuatico* and was reprinted in the British diving magazine *Triton* in 1960.

> Since the first days of its existence the CIAS (Centro de Investigationes y Actividades Subacuaticas, Barcelona) has opposed the spirit of records and competition which predominates in certain sectors of underwater activities. This spirit is completely contrary to the true essence of underwater exploration. Confusion exists about the relation of diving to other activities of a sporting nature. DIVING IS NOT A SPORT. It is investigation, adventure, discovery, but not a sport. We are not interested in heroes or supermen; rather we believe in the quiet work of the team, in the close collaboration between scholar and diver. We must root out this boastfulness which tends to make diving like a vulgar motor race. On the contrary it will suit us to revive among divers a true interest in the sea, for archaeology, for marine biology and for the many aspects and problems which oceanography offers.
>
> The aqualung is a priceless tool for the study and exploration of the Sixth Continent. We must not waste the enormous possibilities it offers. Let us make war, then, on records, rivalry and boastfulness. Let us encourage interest in Study, in Science, in a word—in the sea.

The writer was making a true definition of a diver (professional or amateur) as a man or woman who studied the sea and understood something of it. Not, for instance, as necessarily a ship expert—but a person who understood what was likely to happen to wrecked ships because he was familiar with the principles of the environment into which it fell. Not a sailor, who knows more about the winds and waves than he does of what is in the sea (but nevertheless has his vital place in underwater archaeology because of his understanding of how ships work and the problems faced by their captains). No one person can possibly amass all the knowledge—it does require a team.

In the pioneering 1950s this was not realised let alone accepted; indeed, people from the power-hungry disciplines probably still would not accept it today, even after the passing of thirty years.

*   *   *

In my opinion, there were two significant breakthroughs in wreck archaeology, which at the time I followed with interest. One was off the coast of Sweden, in the Baltic, the other was off the coast of Turkey, in the Aegean. Remember, there were no rules then—and most of the precedents seemed to me to be almost uniformly awful, rather than examples to follow.

The Baltic breakthrough was initially the work of one man: Anders Franzén. He reasoned, correctly, that because there was no 'shipworm' in the brackish waters of that inland sea, old wooden wrecks must still survive, virtually intact (provided that they lay deep enough to avoid damage from storms and ice). On this basis, in 1950 he prepared his wreck-finding programme; in 1953 he began to search for the ship at the top of his list, the galleon *Wasa* sunk in 1628 off Stockholm in 110 feet. In 1956 he found her. And in 1961, after years of work by Swedish naval divers, she was raised by the Neptune Salvage Company. It was an achievement totally eclipsing anything done in the Mediterranean. The real significance of the *Wasa* project is not normally understood. What Franzén had said was: There is a great gap in naval history—we know virtually nothing about the galleon type of warship, for instance—but I think one particular example, the *Wasa*, is likely to be well preserved; I will find her; and then raise such a 'hullaballoo' that we'll find the money to bring her to the surface and restore her. It sounds so simple to say, but actually to do it is another matter. Witness the Mediterranean work up until quite recently—a few samples of broken bottom timbers, quickly allowed to dry out, distort and crumble to dust in some museum basement. And not as the result of a planned search for a particular ship, but usually mere accidental discoveries, haphazardly made, haphazardly handled.

The archaeologists complained bitterly about the *Wasa* project, because, at the time of the salvage, the Salvage Company was in control. They thought the archaeology suffered (there was some reason in what they said, but no practical alternative at the time).

The breakthrough off the Turkish coast was also initially the work of one man—an American journalist fascinated by the sea, Peter Throck-morton. For the two years 1958 and 1959, he lived, dived and worked with the team of Turkish sponge divers led by Captain Kemal Aras. It was epic research—and highly dangerous. As a result, he learned of some twenty important ancient wrecks, and from a vague clue realised that one wreck in particular which Captain Kemal described, must be incredibly old—for it contained copper, and the copper was corroded. Like Anders Franzén at around the same time, he too made a fuss. And the result was an expedition sent out by the University of Pennsylvania in 1960. It was international in composition. The director was George F. Bass, an American archaeologist specialising in the place and probable period of the wreck—1200 BC—who had learnt to dive in order to control the work actually on the bottom. This was a great advance on classicists directing helmet divers from the surface. The technical adviser was Throckmorton, whose knowledge of the sea and of ships—and of the Turkish divers—was considerable. The conservation of the finds, and the record keeping, were in the hands of Joan du Plat Taylor of the London Institute of Archaeology, who never did learn to dive. Frederic Dumas, of the Cousteau team, was chief diver—he had very firm ideas of his own as to how ancient wrecks should be dealt with, based on many years' experience. There were also other Frenchmen, Americans and Britons, as well as Turks and Germans, but the first three on the expedition list—Bass, Throckmorton and Taylor—I got to know soon afterwards (as I did Franzén also). This was neither coincidence nor accident: I happened to admire their work, and asked their advice.

Their work at Gelidonya off the Turkish coast proved to be a landmark. Not perfect—Bass told me he rated the work at 80 per cent only—but it was methodical and brought to a conclusion. An important factor was the size of the ship—only about 25–30 feet long, the size of an ordinary motor boat. The cargo was utterly different from anything met with before: a load of metal, perhaps from the Cyprus mines. And it was the oldest by far of any wreck so far discovered. (Throckmorton, again, was to find one even older in 1975, off Dokos, near Hydra in the Saronic Gulf; but this turned to archaeological tragedy, some of which I was to witness.)

Bass next turned to a somewhat larger vessel, also discovered by Throckmorton in Turkish waters, and this again made a great contrast to the usual amphorae wrecks. Although the cargo was amphorae, the date was much later—the seventh century AD. Part of the hull of this Byzantine merchantman lay under the sand at 120 feet, and a reconstruction was attempted. But it was made by an archaeological student, not a ship expert. However, the excavation, which lasted from 1961 to 1964, was a great advance on anything that had gone before.

*   *   *

These, then, were some of the landmarks in history under water from the beginnings at Antikythera in 1900 to the time of the discoveries at Giglio around 1960. The *Wasa* was to influence my search for the *Mary Rose* and, as a historian myself, I fully appreciated the real point of George Bass's work at Gelidonya. Bass was a specialist in the period, and so was able to suggest that the Gelidonya vessel, which was carrying a scrap metal cargo of raw copper ingots, bronze ingots, and possibly tin, was Syrian and returning from Cyprus around 1200 BC. For complicated reasons, this tended to place Homer very much nearer to the times about which he wrote—the Siege of Troy, the voyage of Odysseus—and in consequence possibly more accurate than had been generally believed. Previously, his references to Phoenician merchants had, in the opinion of scholars, placed him later than 1200 BC, for the sailors of Syria, Canaan and Phoenicia were not supposed to have been operating then. But here was just such a ship as Homer described, and roughly datable. Even the details of cargo stowage (on top of brushwood) made sense of a much misunderstood and mistranslated fact described by Homer who, clearly, really did know how heavy metal cargoes were actually stowed in the times of which he wrote. The scholars who had mistranslated had, obviously, known nothing whatever about the loading of merchant ships (it is highly unlikely that they would); but, nevertheless, an appropriate expert—that is to say, a man who did know the practical side of shipping, should have been consulted. Or so I thought.

What I was at the time requires some explanation, particularly as it led me to make various judgements concerning the wrecks at Giglio and underwater archaeology generally, which in turn led to action being taken. My father was a doctor in the British Navy, so I grew up with warships. When he was stationed at Malta in the late 1920s (and I was seven or eight years old) my parents took me round various historical sites, and I can well remember my indignation because, although we stayed in Naples for some time, I was never taken to see Pompeii. That set me on the archaeological-historical road, as a pastime; I did not think of earning a living at all. From the age of 12 I wanted to be a fighter pilot, but when the war came in 1939, I eventually joined the infantry (London Scottish,

Amphora neck—a casual find, probably not from a wreck.
Photo: Roger Hale

then Gordon Highlanders), and when I went off to Normandy in 1944, it was with a small British unit attached to the headquarters of the First Canadian Army. I did not see much close-up action, only two actual battles, both in 1945—Emmerich and Arnhem—and a few very small affairs; but it was all useful experience for the self-taught military historian I was to become.

After the war I had various Army jobs in Germany, finishing up with four years in Hamburg as writer-producer for the British Forces Network, working mostly on what in radio are called 'features' but in TV 'documentaries'. Here I experimented with the new style of 'feature' programme, using quotations from eye-witnesses, from documents, from recorded orders and reports. I found this much the most effective way of presenting the facts, and when I returned to Britain and eventually began writing books of military history, this was the method I used. I realised that it could also be employed for many long-ago battles or campaigns, where sufficient documentation existed, and it was while researching the history of the Spanish Armada that I discovered just how many fields of knowledge contribute to a true understanding of ships and the sea. There are all sorts of ship experts—naval architects, shipwrights, and nautical historians—whom one ought to consult.

During the time I was writing feature programmes for the BBC, I took another job, to which I have already referred, as part-time editor of the house magazine published by a group of coal (and later oil) companies operating in South-East England, with wharves and depots along the coast from Dover to Poole. They had some ships of their own, and close links to a company which owned fleets of coastal colliers and oil tankers. It was my job, over a dozen years or so, to explain the workings of all these companies in the Group to other companies within it, not necessarily doing the same job. The world of coastal shipping and cargo distribution is more complicated and specialist than may appear. To cover all the stories available, I had to do a lot of travelling and interviewing; and occasionally sailed in some ships of the fleets, ranging from oil tanker to dredger or tug.

Naturally, this did not make me an expert on any aspect of coastal shipping, let alone all of them. I simply learned a bit about merchant shipping and cargo handling (and developed considerable respect for the much neglected men of the British merchant navy); and how to recognise someone who knew what he was talking about, from a lifetime in the job.

*   *   *

When I came back from Giglio in September 1962, aware that all the

Metal detector contact found by the author in 1982 at the foot of the south face, tagged for the next team to excavate.
Photo: Alexander McKee

The seaward face of the *secca* ▶ falls away steeply to over 200 feet in marvellous visibility of perhaps 100 feet. The Etruscan ship may have struck the top of the reef and then drifted downwards to around 150–160 feet. Taken in 1982.
Photo: Alexander McKee

The author (right) with Chris ▶ Storey after an excavation shift at 135 feet, 1983.

▲ Mike Russell digging in an area which was to produce planking and a thick layer of pitch, 1983. *Photo : Alexander McKee*

Waiting for the inflatable boat to return from the site to the little harbour by the Medici
▼ Tower, much more crowded than it was in 1962. *Photo : Alexander McKee*

sites—confirmed or merely suspected—were doomed to destruction by looting within a few years, I tried to work out by my own deduction, and by enquiries among people who were really expert, how ancient cargoes might have been handled; whether the so-called 'dump sites' really were so, and whether the usual description of amphorae as the 'jerrycans of the ancient world' was justified. The article which resulted was published in *Diver* for June–July 1963 as *What's the Ullage of an Amphora?* It may be worth quoting at length, because it shows what people were thinking at the time; not only my own views, but those of the people I was arguing against. Everything is very different now, because everything is known. But the 1960s were a time for physical exploration and theoretical speculation, and this is its chief interest. My starting point was to suggest that we should forget the scholars for a moment and consider instead how modern professionals operated. They were, of course, business men first and foremost; they actually had to earn their living in the market place.

What is the modern equivalent of an amphora? The chorus-answer is: 'Jerrycan!' With one lone voice muttering in the background, 'beer bottles and bean tins'.

But any visit to a modern wharf would suggest a different answer. For centuries, liquids have been carried in wooden casks bound with iron; the old smugglers' 'tubs' which sometimes held 'baccy for the parson' instead of 'brandy for the squire'. They lasted so long, because they represented a practical compromise between the conflicting demands of shipping economy and ease of handling. A 'tub' could be man-handled—just—if it was really necessary; but usually it was rolled along to the warehouse after being lifted out of the hold by a crane or ship's derrick. If it was not to be stored locally, the lift would be direct to a vehicle, to avoid waste of man-power. Similarly, to avoid waste of crane-power, a net, holding a great many casks at a time, would be employed.

An amphora could not, of course, be rolled along the ground without damage (at least, I doubt it), and probably on occasions they were carried out of a ship on men's backs; but the general picture at a Roman or Greek port was probably very similar to that of a European port today. I have contemporary paintings and sketches showing the discharging of the old sailing colliers on the south coast, and while some show a line of men carrying baskets of coal on their shoulders (obviously to a dump situated on the quay), others depict quite a different scene—the brig run bows first onto an open beach, and the crew discharging the cargo with derrick and winch direct to horse-drawn carts queuing up on the sand, much the more economical method. I think we may presume that the Romans knew just as much about Time and Motion studies as our grandfathers did; and many of their ships were much larger.

Starting with this stubborn belief that no one was going to be fool enough to be unnecessarily lavish even with slave man-power, I made enquiries; and discovered that, in parts of the Mediterranean area today, amphorae are still in use, and that they are in fact discharged in grape-like clusters, slung together, by ship's derrick or dockside crane. Instead of the net used for wooden casks, a line is usually passed through the handles, and sometimes a second line is looped round the bases.

Going on from there, I found that the commonly accepted method of stowing amphorae on shipboard—in racks with holes in them for the bases—is not the only one. In the smaller craft at any rate, no racks are used. The amphorae are placed on the bottom boards, on their sides, with the bases interlocking to give solidity to the cargo and prevent it shifting in rough weather. How they were stored in the larger Roman ships, I do not know; but, certainly, the idea that an amphora with a very slender base was a 'shipping amphora', designed to fit into a cargo rack, cannot be the whole story. I made several dives to the Punta del Morto wreck at Giglio and deliberately took three bases from the cargo of smashed amphorae—three bases of completely different type, one thin and slender, the other two broad, but not the same design. In short, three types of amphorae from one wreck, and only one the so-called 'shipping amphora' type. The idea behind this deliberate selection was that, if one type could be dated, that would date the other two also, and, incidentally, the wreck. Most of the amphorae types simply are not listed. Yet identification is vital, for these finds mean something; three different types in one wreck, and in another wreck, amphorae of one type only. There is a clue here to the cargoes, ports of origin and destination, and perhaps much else; if only we had the basic information.

A point which seems most to have surprised diver-archaeologists is the number of date stamps and shippers' marks found on the stoppers, or bungs (such as that found by Southsea divers in a Le Scole amphora), and also on the handles. But a modern cask carries, if anything, rather more. At the discharging port alone, the cooper employed by the warehouse company will 'scribe' each cask with a code number, denoting the ship from which it was discharged, as well as the 'bung', or customer's number. A consignment of amphorae might have had to travel 2,000 miles, both by road and sea, and possibly be trans-shipped as well. Of course they had to be fully and properly marked, as a guide to the various people who would handle them en route—labourers, foremen, and so on. Otherwise, you could have an elementary disaster, such as stacking in the wrong order; the consignment for the first port of call underneath that for the last port of call, for instance. Then, as a check against pilfering, it would have to be possible to refer back to see who handled what, where, and when.

The contents would have to be checked, too, not less than twice. As amphorae come in so many different sizes, this may seem difficult, but I doubt that the Romans found it so. Again, there is guidance from the modern equivalent. The wooden casks also differ in shape and size but have their contents gauged accurately enough. The different types have distinctive names—'pipe', 'butt', 'hogshead'. Sherry is usually carried in a 'butt', port in a 'pipe'. This rams home again the point that, if we knew more about amphorae types, we could probably say with reasonable certainty what the cargo of any given wreck was. Undoubtedly, each Roman or Greek warehouse had a skilled workman, equipped with special tools, to check their contents.

Nowadays, a cooper does this job, measuring the containers with a 'flogger', or 'flagging iron', to find the ullaged contents. One of them defined ullage for me by saying that, roughly, the 'ull' represents what should be in the cask, and the 'age' what really is there. This particular man had an array of weird-looking instruments designed for the task, and, as a matter of routine, he could check more than a hundred casks a day. But the cooper and his skills will soon be obsolete, too, because, more than half a century after the introduction of power-cranes, technology has at last caught up and doomed the wooden cask to the museums, along with the amphorae. The new-type container for wines and spirits, introduced in 1962, is a rectangular steel box many times the size of the largest cask. Not even a gang of gorillas could lift such a weight. The giant containers are discharged by mobile crane direct from the ship's hold to specially-designed road vehicles; and the transition, from the slave-based economy of the ancient world to the mechanised twentieth century, is complete at last.

I wrote this late in 1962, having personally witnessed the introduction of the new methods by the company for whom I edited the house magazine.

Intact amphora from the Le Scole wreck. *Photo : Roger Hale* ▶

For the same reason, I was never in any doubt as to what most of the Giglio remains really were.

Just as existing methods help us to understand the practical problems of the amphorae trade, and their probable solutions, so they enable us to make a reasonably informed guess at the answers to the popular question: When is a Roman wreck not a Roman wreck? Or, more precisely, when can an amphorae mound be explained away as an undersea rubbish dump?

Some people narrow it down to a roughly ship-shape mound, with amphorae necks sticking out of the sand in regimented rows. Anything at all untidy they dismiss as mere rubble, dumped in the sea to get rid of it. Others, however, argue that this represents a ship which burst its sides on hitting the bottom. There is no quick proof either way, so what are the probabilities from a practical point of view?

Let us assume that a merchant has accumulated a large number of broken, cracked, or otherwise unserviceable amphorae, and that they are taking up valuable storage space. If he is a bad business man, he begins to scratch his head and wonder just who will be likely to buy them from him. If he is a good business man, he can think at once of at least three possible customers, and will immediately send a slave round to ask for quotations. Building contractors, roadmakers, wharf constructors, anyone engaged on levelling and preparing sites—those are the obvious customers, then and now. There's lolly in rubble.

But let's suppose that the great Roman Depression has arrived and the tycoon can't find a customer. Well, he hires a labourer with a cart to dump the stuff on the nearest tip or, failing that, into the sea off the harbour wall. Instead of making a profit, it sets him back a bit; but not very much.

The one thing that never occurs to him is to hire a ship (plus the crew and dock labour involved) to take the lot miles away from the harbour and dump it overboard. If you have the slightest doubt about this, ring the nearest shipping company and get a quotation for the hire of a 1,000-tonner for 24 hours. You won't have much change out of a year's salary. And, as there were no old Roman steam engines, our ancient tycoon is faced with the very real possibility, if the wind is foul, of having to hire the ship for several days, possibly even a week (if a mistral hits him halfway through). If the Romans really did carry on like this, then the reason for the decline and fall of their empire is evident. It went bankrupt.

Of course one should be suspicious of scattered amphorae in harbours and roadsteads, where they might really have been junked overboard by the crews of ships; but never dismiss them, for ships do sink in these places, too. I should be inclined to take notice even of a single amphora off a coastline, since the possible explanations include: deck cargo junked from a ship in trouble (which may not have got out of trouble and may be lying nearby); deck cargo fallen from a sinking ship as it went down; or 'amphorae pirates' at work on a wreck farther down the slope.

I was certain that most of the supposed 'dump sites' were wrecks, of great but varying importance; with Campese top of the list, partly because she was Etruscan, partly because I hoped that a significant amount of cargo, and possibly hull also, might survive looting. Once the surface amphorae had been removed there would be little to signal the casual swimmer that there was anything underneath. The great depth—and consequent limitation of bottom time—would in any case tend to discourage what might well be futile digging.

Inside the *Mary Rose* Ship Hall in 1983: John Towse, Alan Lee, Alexander McKee and John Baldry. Towse, Lee and McKee were all at Giglio in 1962, and with Baldry carried out the first diving operation of the *Mary Rose* project in 1965, two-and-a-half years later. *Photo: Portsmouth News*

As the years went by, I acquired much theoretical and practical experience of the potentialities of ship burial. In April, 1965, five of us from Southsea Branch had set out to make the first underwater search for the *Mary Rose*, and four out of the five—Roger Hale, Alan Lee, John Towse and myself—had all dived the Campese wreck in 1962. This time the discovery—if there was one—would not be accidental. We were searching for a known shipwreck, but there were four different locations given by four different historians, and all were wrong. The *Mary Rose* proved to be totally buried and invisible at a quite different site, half a mile away from the best guess by an historian and four miles distant from that indicated by the worst expert.

Both the search and the resulting excavation were immensely more difficult than anything encountered in the Mediterranean. There was the sheer size and complexity of the ship, and its great depth of burial. Originally, the site had been covered in five to six feet of semi-liquid mud. In the closing stages of the excavation, when that overburden had first been cleared away and then the soil which had filled the ship, one could swim down 16–18 feet inside the seabed, inside the hull, a shattering demonstration of the preservative properties and potential of ship burial. I had believed that it would be so, but it was still impressive actually to see it.

It was this final stage of the *Mary Rose* project, in 1980 and 1981, which, by a chance meeting, was to launch a preliminary reconnaissance of the Etruscan wreck in Campese Bay and, if that proved successful, the mounting of a properly financed and equipped excavation. Of course, I did not expect another *Mary Rose*, a liftable ship. But I did hope that there might be a cargo layer several feet thick above the bottom timbers of a collapsed hull and below a foot or so of sand cover.

Chapter 7

THROUGH HIGH
PROVENCE

The Return to Giglio, 1982

Newcastle, Maine.
January 26, 1981.

Dear Alexander,

It's a long time since we corresponded. The bearer of this letter, Mensun Bound, will explain to you face to face the vicissitudes of my recent years which I hope will excuse my being a bad correspondent.

I am very proud for you and the success of the *Mary Rose* project. A wonderful exhibit of bulldog determination which would have pleased a Drake or a Hawkins.

I write, then, both to introduce you to Mensun Bound and to assure you that he has my complete confidence; and to solicit your help and moral support in a grand venture which Mensun will explain to you at first hand.

Peter Throckmorton

The young couple who had been given this letter for me arrived at my home by the sea at Hayling Island, next door to Portsmouth, having driven down from Oxford. They told me later that they had felt as if they were bearding an ogre in his castle. I am not in the least like that, but I had in the past made myself unpopular by proving a number of archaeologists and ship experts wrong, after they had written me off behind my back as a madman looking in an unlikely place for a ship which they were all aware had been broken up with gunpowder more than 120 years before.

Peter Throckmorton's 'vicissitudes' had come to a climax in the summer of 1975, when he had made a greater and far older discovery even than that of the Gelidonya wreck of around 1300–1200 BC, which George Bass had later excavated off the Turkish coast. His affairs had been going well and he had bought a house on the island of Hydra, three hours' sea travel from Athens in the Saronic Gulf. He invited my wife and myself to join him if, as planned, we were in Greece that year. He had virtually no backing and financed his archaeological work by his writings. I was in the same boat, but at least I was operating in the waters of my own country,

135

whereas Throckmorton was an American in Greece, at a time when, politically, both Britain and America were unpopular at government level. Theoretically, underwater archaeology was impossible in Greece. In an attempt to preserve whatever underwater heritage there might be from looting and dispersal, the Greek archaeological authorities tightly controlled permits for aqualung diving (but at the same time the Greek tourist authorities wished to attract foreigners and allowed diving schools to be set up, including a German-run one on Hydra).

Nevertheless, a small group of Greek enthusiasts had established the Hellenic Institute of Marine Archaeology, with Peter Throckmorton as Technical Adviser. During the negotiations for a permit to survey the seabed around Hydra, Peter was assembling a first-rate team of specialists, to include a naval architect, a draughtsman and a photographer as well as archaeologists. The idea was to run an Ocean Science Seminar from Peter's 50 ft schooner *Stormie Seas*, with a good and varied team of lecturers. They would look at the Gulf of Hydra from all aspects—oceanographic, archaeological, cultural. If they found an abandoned village, they would ask, why? If there was a pile of pots in the sea, then similarly, why? And there were 20 or 30 ancient wreck sites shallow enough to look at without aqualungs. They would check these for signs of interference.

By August, after a season in the Gulf, looking hard, they had become sensitive to seeing things. The 20 or 30 possible ancient wreck sites certainly had been looted; and some had been destroyed. The law was not really working to protect them. Then, on 26 August, while returning to the surface, Throckmorton noticed a pile of ballast stones and asked a girl archaeologist, Leslie Whale, to take a close look and get a sample pot for him. The pot she selected was in a concreted mass, just like the finds from the Gelidonya wreck. Peter reported this immediately to his Greek boss and two days later he raised 25 pieces of pottery. All the pieces were Early Bronze Age II, and seven were definitely Cycladic. Possibly there were two wrecks, and the dating range was between 2700 BC to 2200 BC, at least a thousand years older than the ship off Cape Gelidonya. Once again, Peter Throckmorton had found the world's oldest known wreck.

That should have been the signal for a precise excavation by Throckmorton's excellent and thoroughly experienced team, which would have told us a good deal about the earliest seafarers and their cargoes. But, as I read the signs, it was precisely the great importance of the find which ruined Peter's discovery at Dokos. A different and largely unqualified team took over and everyone else—including Throckmorton and his specialists—was forbidden to dive the site. It was during this depressing and, I suspect, destructive episode in the chequered history of archaeology underwater that my wife and I arrived in Athens.

It was to be an unfortunate time for me, too. A few weeks later, I left Hydra on a stretcher carried by one American and three Australians, and thereafter spent 19 days in an Athens hospital. The only consolation was my convalescence in Peter's workplace at Kastella near Piraeus, convenient for strolling round the three galley harbours dating from the classical period; no ordinary tourist would spot their sparse remains, but with Peter as my guide they became vivid. And having recreated the classical harbour before my eyes, he went on to show me exactly how the Battle of Salamis was fought and why Xerxes was defeated. I had read a number of accounts of this clash—one of the 'fifteen decisive battles of the world', according to a nineteenth-century historian, Creasy. But I confess I had never properly understood it. I did now, with Throckmorton to show me the battlefield in stages which marched with the Persian advance.

*   *   *

When Mensun Bound and Jo Yellowlees called on me early in 1981 with a letter of introduction from Peter regarding the 'grand venture' Mensun was promoting, I thought back to Dokos and the prehistoric wreck from the Cyclades, and the Athenian interlude when Peter had shown me Salamis.

Mensun explained that he was from Lincoln College, Oxford, and had worked on the *Mary Rose* the previous year; but he was actually a Falkland Islander and his concern was the remains of many nineteenth-century clipper ships and other traders which had got into trouble rounding the Horn and ended up beached in the Falklands. Many of them were quite well preserved, and one, the SS *Great Britain*, had been removed already and taken to her home town of Bristol. I nodded, for I knew all this. I had seen over the *Great Britain* just after she had come to Bristol and had heard Peter Throckmorton lecture there in 1971 and mention these very ships. I well remembered him saying that, potentially, as museum exhibits, they were all profit-earners; but raising the money to save them in the first place was the snag.

When I learned, in conversation with Mensun, that he was a pottery expert who had worked underwater on a number of Mediterranean sites, such as the *c.* 50 BC Roman wreck of Madraque de Giens and also with George Bass, I realised that here was someone who might help to turn the Campese dream into reality. As the Etruscan site seemed to me to be so much more important than the derelicts in the Falklands, I told Mensun about it and then took him into my office-cum-library where I kept my ship-files and also the key items which had served to identify this or that wreck—at one end of the time-scale the sailing battleship *Royal*

George, sunk at Spithead in 1782, at the other the broken pottery of Punta del Morto, Giglio (fourth or third century BC), and also the amphora handle from Campese which I had labelled back in 1962:

CAMPESE BAY

(Secca)

140–160 ft

ETRUSCAN & GREEK

700 BC

When, in 1965, I had published the known facts about the wreck, I had discovered that it also contained Phoenician (or Punic) ware; I had republished this information locally in 1966 and internationally in 1968. If the dating was correct, then this presumably Etruscan ship, although much more modern than either Dokos or Gelidonya, was still some 200 years older than the warships which clashed at Salamis and belonged to a mysterious people much less known about than the Greeks who left a large literature behind them.

The data I had collected on the Giglio wrecks, consisting of many hundreds of pages of typescript and photographs, plus drawings, were not then immediately available (I had loaned my albums to Vallintine in London). However, once in my library, Mensun pointed almost at once to the handle from Campese Bay, and asked to examine it, ignoring the Punta del Morto pieces. I was impressed that he had been able to pick out what was to my mind by far the most important of the Giglio sites, merely by the evidence of a single handle (with no pot attached) stacked on a top shelf. Further, he was an experienced diver and had youth on his side. Also, unlike Peter Throckmorton and to a much lesser extent myself, he had not sustained war injuries which are felt more as one grows older.

Mensun wrote to me in March, still mainly interested in the Falkland Island hulls, but also in a Roman wreck off the Isle of Wight which I had mentioned I was looking for. I pointed him towards Campese Bay by writing to him on 28 May, 1981:

> I'd loaned my original notebooks to Reg Vallintine, who is writing a book, but I find that I published a very brief summary of the rescue work he and Roger Hale did on the Campese Bay wreck which I called 'Etruscan', in *History Under the Sea* . . .
>
> Although the other wrecks around Giglio were looted to destruction, Reg Vallintine has always had hopes that this one, the most important of them all, probably, may have survived because the wreckage is inconspicuous and he and the British divers there tried to keep the exact location secret . . . He has always hoped to interest

138

an underwater archaeologist in this site, and I suspect would very much like to take part in an excavation, possibly running the diving side, for which, of course, he is extremely well qualified. It might be worth a mention to George Bass or somebody similar.

Another important point was that Vallintine spoke Italian and Mensun, from his work in Italy, also had a grasp of that language.

In July, Mensun had the time to reply to my letter 'pushing' the Campese site.

> I was very interested by what you had to say about the Giglio wreck, and will write Mr Vallintine immediately following this. I also have a couple of sites tucked away in my mind in the Med, but from what has already been removed from the site, the Giglio wreck promises to be more important than my own, and the dates suggested by the museum (*c*. 700 BC) are exactly consistent with my own period of greater expertise (although I must say from the evidence of the amphora alone, I am tempted to think this date a little high) . . . I am sure you will wish to be involved if anything should develop.

And that was it as far as I was then concerned. It was now up to Mensun to meet Reg Vallintine and see his material as well as my notebooks which Reg had on loan. Then came the much more difficult task of actually launching a project to make an initial survey of the site, to sound out its potentialities. Bound would have to obtain approval from the University of Oxford, which would mean submitting his plans to thorough and complex scrutiny; only when this was obtained could he apply to the Italian archaeological authorities for a permit (and they were known to be less ready than they had been in the past to allow foreigners to work on their sites); and, finally, there would be the job of raising funds. Considering the importance of the site, I thought this might not be too difficult; but as I well knew, raising money when you still have to prove something can be sticky, whereas an attractive certainty becomes a big band wagon, successfully running over all obstacles.

*   *   *

I was in a strange mood when I set off for Giglio on 29 August, 1982 — twenty years, almost exactly, had passed since my previous visit. The expedition was, of course, bound to contain a distinct element of hazard: I had now been diving for twenty-four years, and had no doubts about that. The site was deep and there was no back-up at all; no decompression chamber nearer than Rome. What was strange was that this element of risk had become attractive, because my eldest daughter was almost certainly dying of cancer. I had to look within myself and think, what shall I do? If I go away now, I may never see her again and so will have to live with that forever. On the other hand, I may die, too, and so join her quickly—if there is in fact a life after this. In youth, I used to believe there was. Now, I was not so sure.

On the other hand, Giglio was not at the end of the world. One could keep in touch by telephone and be back in half a day. And the Etruscan wreck was something which had been on my mind for twenty years. I am extremely selective about wrecks; very few seem to me worth the enormous expenditure of time, effort and money required for their investigation. Notable exceptions were the *Mary Rose* and the wreck in Campese Bay. The *Mary Rose* because she was a 'key' vessel in the development of the battleship and was, furthermore, likely to be so well preserved that a great deal of the hull and contents should be left, including several hundred mariners and soldiers with their clothes, weapons and possessions. The Campese wreck because she was Etruscan and therefore intriguing, and because of the weird nature of her cargo as so far discovered—almost every piece different. The reason I concentrated on Henry VIII's ship rather than Tarquin's, was that the Tudor flagship was almost literally on my doorstep—within half-a-dozen miles of my home. Further, as a war historian I felt qualified to deal with her. Whereas Campese was more than a thousand miles away, in another country whose language I did not speak, and containing a cargo quite outside my spheres of knowledge. What I wanted was for some specialist in the period to excavate the site—which was why I had mentioned the matter to Professor Lamboglia back in the 'Sixties—and to take part myself, if possible. And now it was actually happening because, in the first instance, Mensun Bound had called on me about something quite different, and I had put him in touch with Reg Vallintine, the wreck's discoverer.

The way I had visualised it, Vallintine would run the diving and also liaise with the local Italians, with whom he was popular. But, twenty years later, it was not working out like that. Reg had just left an important job with the British Sub-Aqua Club to set up a new diving school in London. He would not have time to spend all September in Giglio, which was the period planned for the expedition. Worse, he might not even be in the country then, for he had a commitment abroad with his pupils. The appalling thought then occurred—how would we find the wreck? None of the university people had seen the site. I was the only one with any knowledge of it, and then I had been taken there by Reg with no thought that I would ever actually have to locate it for myself!

Reg sent me a small-scale map which identified the particular under-

The cross on the rocks opposite the wreck site, commemorating two Italian divers who died by the 'Grouper Hole' in 1959. *Photo: Alexander McKee*

water island we wanted as the Secca I Pignocchi, with a note that it was opposite the 'cross on rocks where Italian spearfishermen disappeared'. The *secca* was a long reef, so where exactly along it was the wreck—down at 150 feet, remember, where no search could be carried out for much more than minutes? I contacted John Towse, who had last seen the wreck in 1967; he thought it was about halfway along the most southerly reef. Roger Hale was in America, so there was no time to ask him. I thought that probably I could find it—given time. But it could take two weeks, I suspected. The entire project would be halted.

Mensun himself was out in Sicily, working on another project, and would not return to England until the end of August. Meanwhile the main burden of dealing with problems like this and many, many more fell to Dr Paddy Phillips and his wife Colleen, from Wolfson College. The expedition would have to be self-contained; everything from tents to boats, from compressors to diving gear and food, would go out in a van lent by Perry's of Aylesbury. I had volunteered to help drive this vehicle to Italy, together with Jenny Haworth and Paul Bramley, both of St Anne's College, Oxford. As passengers in the van would be Melanie Reichelt of St Hilda's College and, when he returned from Sicily, Mensun Bound accompanied by Jo Yellowlees. Other people would travel independently and meet us on Giglio—including David Corps and Hamish Hay, both from Oxford colleges; and 'Big Mike', an English teacher working in Palermo.

None of this would ever show on television, where diving is always dramatically easy. In real life, it's not like that. The diving itself is comparatively soft compared to the what-goes-with-it (both before and after). And a university expedition at long range involves a great deal more effort. I was spared most of that, but nevertheless the time from leaving my home at Hayling Island for Oxford and actually arriving at the camp site at Campese was eight days—24 August to 4 September.

For me, the journey was a mixture of memories. Just so, we had driven through central London in 1944, but to the docks for embarkation, with the V1s puttering in overhead, a ton of explosive in each. This time we were to embark at Dover on the car ferry for Calais. In July, 1944, the Germans were in Calais—we could see their searchlights as our convoy lumbered through the Straits of Dover in darkness. But it was precisely because I had taken part in that long-ago invasion—and was used to driving on the right—that by unanimous vote I was the one to drive off from Calais quay just after midnight. Next morning, we were still driving, motoring through Châlons sur Marne, by Laon and Rheims, from Artois to Champagne.

We stopped at 10 a.m. and tried to sleep for a few hours in the van. That night, trying to save money by avoiding the tolls on the Autoroute to the Sun by going along minor country roads in darkness and rain, we got well lost and decided to take the motorway after all. At Lyon we gave up being miserly in favour of an actual bed in a cheap hotel—ah, the luxury of not lying on kitbags or trying to doze in the corner of a driving cab while somebody else took the wheel! The weather was still exactly like England—cold, damp, raining.

September 1 began as a grey autumn morning; then, as we drove south on the autoroute, the sky began to show patches of blue and, was it imagination, or was it really getting warmer? Past Grenoble, where roadworks narrowed the traffic lanes, I touched wing-mirrors with a French lorry, which delayed us a bit, but the horrific stories about continental driving proved quite unfounded. Crossing the Alpes Maritimes on a road which peaked at 3,500 feet, we had to move into the crawler lane, for we had a heavy load—two inflatable boats and their engines, a compressor, 18 aqualung cylinders, weightbelts, army tents, diving gear, and personal equipment, rations and the means to cook them. Cloud clung to the pine forests on the mountain tops, but we drove into brilliant sunshine at Sisteron (not far from Avignon in Provence), a breathtakingly beautiful

Not much sleep in the back! Jo Yellowlees and Melanie Reichelt on top of a mass of camping, cooking, and diving gear—plus two inflatable boats, an engine and a compressor. *Photo: Alexander McKee*

site above a river gorge, with a bridge below and a castle above. I liked Provence at once. Almost, I could have spent the rest of my life there.

The fields and the rocks glowed in a kindly golden light as we drove by the river Durance to the bridge of Mirabeau and past Aix-en-Provence. On the way I noticed that Vaucluse was signed, and recalled a Cousteau adventure told in *The Silent World*. That night we rolled into Fréjus and, in spite of the town being given over to a pop festival, found somewhere to park the van and a cheap place to sleep.

We had now arrived at what I thought of as the Cousteau Coast—all the early sites from *The Silent World* are there. Just south of Aix are Marseilles and Toulon—and between them, Grand Congloué. South of Fréjus were other ancient wreck sites—Titan, Dramont, Antheor. In Fréjus itself the 'Marbles of St Tropez'—the cargo of the Roman merchant ship which had been raised in 1951—had been on public display since their transfer in 1968.

We rolled out of Fréjus at 8 a.m. on 2 September, glimpsing a Roman aqueduct and amphitheatre on yet another grey, colourless morning.

143

When Cannes and the Lerin Isles appeared I had my first view of the sea. In spite of its connections with Cousteau, that, too, was grey.

However, as we drove round the coastal road following the steep hill contours, past Monte Carlo and into Mentone, the palm trees and the vivid pink bougainvillea made plain that, at other times of year, this could indeed be the Côte d'Azur, the azure coast. By the time we reached Italy, just down the road, we were convinced. The sun came out, brilliant and warm, and from the border post at Ventimiglia we could see both Rivieras, the French behind us and the Italian ahead.

The road we were now on was a very ancient route. It was the Via Aurelia—the Roman road to Rome—and we were in Liguria, the country of a people who had been almost as enigmatic as the Etruscans. And there was a road sign pointing off seaward to Albenga! One more ancient wreck site from the first books on the early aqualung adventurers.

Just past Albenga, I took over the driving—and soon wished I hadn't. But there was no stopping to allow for my cowardice, for we were on the autostrada leading through Genoa and past Rapallo. This new motorway was horrific. Man had asserted his power over nature by driving tunnels through the coastal mountains and spanning by viaducts the deep gorges in between—through which at this moment a strong wind was raging. I drove into tunnel after dark tunnel, to emerge into blinding Riviera sunlight on a curving roadway raised hundreds of feet high above the bottom of each gorge, with a roaring wind catching our high-sided van and trying to blow me sideways over the edge and into the gorge. I loathe heights. I feared this even more. And then into the darkness of the next tunnel we rushed, and out again into blinding light on a curving roadway hundreds of feet high and a wind pushing the van towards the edge. It was a fast road, too—one could hardly crawl. When would it end? How much more of this was there?

It ended somewhere in Genoa. No, it ended *over* Genoa, for there was some fantastic Italian variant of Spaghetti Junction, going up in circles high over the city like a giant roller coaster, with the wind still roaring and urging me over the edge, and the sun blinding bright on the windscreen. It was like a funfair helter-skelter, but at full motorway scale and no safety measures. If anything is likely to keep foreigners out of Italy, this is it. Even Attila would have quailed before it. I was shaking so much that I could spare only a few brief sideways glances down at Rapallo as we passed, on the edge of the dark blue Ligurian Sea.

We entered Tuscany by moonlight, and were signed off the motorway between Pisa and Livorno; with Florence signed further inland. Thereafter

◀ The border post between France and Italy near Ventimiglia. *Photo: Alexander McKee* we followed the coastal road towards Cecina Mare, the Tyrrhenian Sea lying calm and still under the moon on our right hand. It was late before we found accommodation. Around midnight, before going to bed, I could not resist the temptation of warm, clear water, so went down to the beach with mask and flippers. The water was warm enough, but the bottom was sand and the visibility less than two feet. However, there had been an Etruscan settlement here; and there were still Etruscans around—the two women who served us breakfast could have come straight out of an Etruscan tomb decoration. Obviously, they were of mixed race, but many are depicted with an Eastern cast of features, particularly around the eyes; very, very distinctive, and instantly recognisable to the present day, but mysterious still.

We left Cecina Mare at nine o'clock and, by the time we rolled into the ferry base of Porto San Stefano at 10·45, I was wishing I had changed into shorts first thing that morning. What it would be like after mid-day didn't bear thinking about. There was a ferry due in shortly, but no room for vehicles until much later that day, we were told, so I got on board with just my cameras and small kit, to make contact with the advance party already on Giglio. I knew none of them by sight, but we soon identified each other. There were the Australian couple, Paddy Phillips and his wife Colleen, the one a doctor of medicine, the other of psychology. Paddy I had known as a voice on the telephone, but I had met none of the others—Mike Wright, a biochemist, 'Big' Mike Wanstall, the English

The *Giglio Espresso* waiting at Porto San Stefano to take us over to Giglio. The water, crystal-clear in 1962, was oil-covered and polluted twenty years later. *Photo: Alexander McKee*

teacher from Palermo, and Hamish Hay, a medical student. They were living in a pensione on the waterfront at Giglio Porto. Reg Vallintine, I was happy to learn, had arrived after all and was dug in at the Pensione Bahamas, a much grander building now than in 1962, but still under the same kindly manageress. When the van arrived with the tents, we would all move over from the port, on the eastern side of the island, to a camp site overlooking Campese Bay on the north-west coast. Meanwhile, I just had to get into that water, so I went off with Mike Wright to find a snorkel site. We found a wreck in 36 feet—but it was only a rowing boat, sunk recently.

In the evening I used a public call box to telephone home, the first of many calls to find out how my daughter was. She was better, out of hospital, and seemed to be improving.

We moved next morning, 4 September, to Campese. The camp site was a series of terraces cut along a rocky hillside directly overlooking the Secca I Pignocchi. On the rocks below were the memorial cross and plaque to the two Italian divers who had disappeared off there in 1959. The way down to the sea was steep, rocky, uneven, difficult when carrying heavy loads, so the compressor, the bottles and the big inflatable boat were left on a ledge at the base of the cliff. The engine, the petrol tank, the weight-belts, the demand valves, the metal detector, and our own personal diving gear were all that had to be carried back up again. In addition, the tents had to be erected and the camp set up.

Nothing had been done the day before because the van had been delayed—and anyway we had taken longer over the journey than had been planned. Reg, who had arrived before us, only had a couple of days more on Giglio; after that he had to go back to London to run his business. Having studied how to find the site again, and knowing better than most how difficult it would be, I stressed that the one vital thing we had to do was get Reg into the water and the search underway. And this we did. We anchored on the *secca*, then Reg and Mensun went deep and searched northwards without finding the wreck. But on the way back, Reg recognised the 'Grouper Hole' which, at 70 feet or so, overlooks the slope down to the site. I was swimming above them, covering their search on snorkel only, and taking photographs of the tremendous compressed air curtains created by their bubbles coming up from the depths, expanding as they came. The visibility was so clear that I could actually see the two divers go into the cavern. When they emerged they rose up the rock face to around 20–25 feet and began to decompress. I went down and made a couple of passes, photographing Reg feeding the fish, using a Nikonos III, the Japanese successor to the French Calypso.

That evening, Reg got out his charts and old logbook from the 1960s.

The first entry, for 2 August, 1961, confirmed the depth—amphorae and large blocks found on a mixed sand and rock bottom at 150 feet. The next two dives went even deeper—160 feet; then two more dives at 150 feet (including one to obtain an amphora for the local museum), followed by a yet deeper descent to 180 feet. In 1962, the depths had varied quite a lot—140 to 200 feet. I was interested to see my own dives briefly recorded:

25 August 1962. 150 ft. McKee, de Sanctis, a.m.
p.m. Shallow one. McKee.

In 1963, Reg had gone down to 215 feet to check for signs of wreckage below the average 150–160 feet, but there had been nothing showing. He seemed to recall finding some sherds in rock crevices farther up the slope at 130 feet. But clearly, if there was anything still on view after a lapse of twenty years, then the 150–160 ft depth band was most likely to contain it.

Next day, 5 September, 1982, I spent 26 minutes on snorkel covering Reg and Mensun at depth. I was still using a depth gauge marked patriotically in feet, but everyone else had gone metric. Consequently, Reg reported that he had found a big timber in the sand at 45 metres and at 32 metres three thin sherds on the high plateau. Forty-five metres is roughly 150 feet (remembering that depth gauges are not all that accurate and do not always agree precisely with each other, even when the calibration systems are the same).

Then I put on a bottle and went down with David Corps of Green College, Oxford. The visibility was quite incredible. I went to a kind of table-shaped rock on top of the *secca*, and then down an almost vertical rock face for 60–70 feet the other side, thinking the grouper hole was below this landmark. It wasn't, so keeping the right altitude for the grouper hole, I turned left along the face until I saw the line which Reg had put down, linking the grouper hole to the wreck site. I probed the sand in the gulley below the cavern to a depth of six inches but found nothing. I then went down to 105 feet where we could look out over the upper part of the wreck site at around 135 feet.

I had had an ordinary diving medical earlier in the year, but Paddy, as expedition doctor, had to give me another examination. A very fit 64-year-old, was his verdict, but stay above 30 metres (around 100 feet) to begin with. I had said (I believed truthfully) that my only conscious weakness was in walking down the cliff carrying loads, which I assumed was due to my having broken my left leg in 1959 and having had a metal plate inserted; perhaps something had gone wrong with the plate? I think what bothered the medicos was, not, could I get myself out of trouble if diving alone, but was I physically capable of the very great exertion

Reg and Mensun preparing to dive at Campese during the preliminary search for the wreck site in 1982. *Photo : Alexander McKee*

which might be needed if I was diving with a partner and had to rescue that other person? At the time, frankly, I did not know. My actual worry was different—that we were going deep and had no decompression chamber. I was confident underwater but I do like back-up on the surface in the appropriate form—rescue boat in fast water or a cure for the bends in deep water.

That evening we had a gruesome lesson in what lay in wait for us if we were unwary. We went to visit a German diver, Heinz Oylschar, who had been 'bent' a few years previously. He had a wonderful summer house in Giglio Porto but was a cripple. With a steely determination I was to see matched by a Southsea diver that year, he was fighting his disability— but even on crutches, so far he could take only one or two steps. We were very quiet and sobered as we watched him. He told us that he had got the bends while making a second dive in one day, a dive he felt uneasy about; but a companion had pleaded with him and, too easy-going for his own good, Heinz had done what instinct told him not to do.

The reason for our visit was Mensun's research into some of the artefacts which had disappeared in the 1960s. He and Jo Yellowlees had already spent a good deal of time tracking down some of the items known to have been removed, and were to spend more. By far the most dramatic, and possibly the most important, was that missing helmet. In 1962, I had been told about it by a London diver, but Reg believed that it had actually been taken away by a diver from Munich. Heinz had nothing definite to tell us, however. He thought it was just possible that the man was a Bavarian who had moved to Hamburg. All this was twenty years ago—the trail was cold.

All that surfaced from his conversation with Reg was the possibility of a ship battle in Campese Bay. Vallintine had found traces of burning and had assumed a pirate attack. Was the helmet, I wondered, evidence of defensive armour in an unquiet time—or just another unexpected item in a strange, diverse cargo? Or (assuming there really had been a sea battle), had the helmet been worn by an attacker? It certainly wouldn't have been carried for fun. Arguing from the steel helmet of my own day, heavy, cumbersome and off-putting, very often not worn in battle (in spite of the news reels), I was more than intrigued. Later, I was to discover that bronze helmets had been found in other wrecks—Albenga, for instance— but in a fragmentary or crushed state (probably because of the archaeological methods employed).

Had the Campese site been left untouched, what an exciting place it would have been! The discovery of the century, undoubtedly, if examined carefully from the beginning. In discussion with Mensun and others, I had given my bold opinion (before leaving England) that it was 60 to

A bronze Corinthian helmet of a type similar to that found by the German diver in the 1960s. *Photo: Scala, Firenze* ▶

▼ Our all-too-clearly labelled van at Châlons-sur-Marne: (*l to r*) Jo Yellowlees, Melanie Reichelt, Paul Bramley, Jenny Haworth, Mensun Bound. *Photo: Alexander McKee*

40 that the site had been so inconspicuous, once the surface material was mostly removed, that the wreck would have escaped serious looting since the 'Sixties. I suspect that this opinion may have played a part in obtaining a positive decision.

What we now learned from an Italian diver, however, shook my confidence. Our loaned van was brazenly labelled:

OXFORD UNIVERSITY
ARCHAEOLOGICAL EXPEDITION
GIGLIO ISLAND
ETRUSCAN WRECK

which I thought unwise, unless we wanted to attract looters. I had suggested that we cover up the line about the 'ETRUSCAN WRECK' before we left the mainland of Italy. I remembered the delighted shout of an Italian policeman at a motorway toll point: 'Etrusci!'

I had been super-cautious with the *Mary Rose* and was firmly convinced that I was right. But in this instance I was wrong, at first. The Italians, we learned, were laughing their heads off at the mad English who had come all the way to Italy to excavate a wreck which everyone knew had been pillaged to extinction years ago! A NATO ship, we were told, had sat over the site for months, sending teams of divers down daily and bringing up all sorts of objects. There could be nothing left. We were wasting our time, and might as well go back to England.

It sounded a depressingly likely tale, when coupled with the fate of the little museum of rescued artefacts which Vallintine had built up with the co-operation of the authorities. The contents had been dispersed and the museum no longer existed.

And next day was Reg's last dive with us before he had to go home. He reported that there was a boulder beyond the plateau at 40 metres (130 feet) which made a good mark for the wreck. There was a 'beam' there and 'many sherds'. Sherds. Broken bits. And that night a thunderstorm hit us, raining and roaring and blowing through the tents. No diving tomorrow.

Chapter 8

A TEABAG AND TWO WEETABIX

Digging and Detecting, 1982

By morning the rain and wind had given way to a blindingly hot sun. At lunchtime, the waves were subsiding and the team decided to launch the inflatable from the rocks with eight divers aboard. I did not like the look of the horizon one little bit. When you've lived by the sea for most of your life, your subconscious has been well programmed with warning signs—type of cloud, quality of the light, the very atmosphere, even the background noise of waves on the shore. All these subtly combine to hint at danger. But this was not a subtle occasion—we were clearly in for a bad electrical storm, and soon. Had I been a computer, all my lights would have been winking crimson.

The others did not have this background. Also, they were very anxious to get on with the job, and were, I think, unused to being stopped by the elements. As I was not a member of the university, I was in a delicate position. I could only suggest that it might not be a good idea to launch just now. Then, when they proved adamant, I ventured that eight divers and their gear in a boat about 14 feet long might perhaps be too much. Why not send out two teams of four, one after the other, rather than all eight at once? They finally decided on a British compromise of six.

So they launched with six and got about 50 yards out. What happened next I had seen before and was to see again in British waters—but never so fast. Within two or three minutes, literally, the wind went right round and blew in the opposite direction, meanwhile ascending the Beaufort Scale like a Porsche taking off from the traffic lights. From southerly breeze to northerly gale pounding the rocks, in little more time that it takes to tell.

The inflatable, powered by a big outboard motor, survived. But what chance would a sailing ship have had in a wind change like that, if caught just offshore? The sea was now boiling over the Secca I Pignocchi a quarter of a mile out. In Etruscan times it would have been an even more deadly hazard. Today its highest point is about ten feet below the surface, but there have been changes of land and sea levels in the past. Around Giglio, the sea is believed to have been about 12 feet lower than it is now. The *secca* would have been a splendid ship trap in those conditions for any

◄ Inflating the rubber boat below the camp site at Campese. *Photo: Alexander McKee*

▼ Launching the boat off the rocks. The wreck site lies only 200 yards out. *Photo: Alexander McKee*

vessel coming into or leaving Campese—or even crossing the bay farther out. One did not need pirates to explain a vessel lost there.

After the vicious storm, the air became exceptionally clear and brought into sight for the first time, against a crimson sunset over now-still water, the small, high island of Montecristo and the longer bulk of the Isle of Elba farther north. It was hard to think of it as a main industrial centre in Etruscan times, shrouded with dirt and smoke. Much easier to associate the smaller isle with the fictional tale of the Count of Monte Cristo. Just out of sight was Corsica, first a rival to the Etruscans, then part of their trading area.

At that time, although it is nowhere described in ancient documents, Giglio must have presented much the same industrial picture as Elba. None of the histories I had read, or was to read, had any note of it either, but the locals knew. In a small guidebook I came across a mention that,

> . . . not far away (from Campese) is the Ortana valley where the Etruscans, who lived in Giglio before the Romans, extracted and smelted iron (or rather haematite), making use of the island's then rich patrimony of woodland.

Down in Giglio Porto one could buy large cards with the colourful mineral samples attached, rather as the vari-coloured sands at Alum Bay in the Isle of Wight used to be marketed. Both were very interesting areas, geologically, because the earth's crust had folded at these places, to reveal strata which are normally deep down inside the earth.

That evening we drove up to Castello, the old fortified town on the summit of Giglio. It was spitting with rain, but nevertheless we went for a long walk through the granite-paved alleyways and lanes, enclosed within the formidable walls rebuilt in 1623 by the Grand Duke of Florence. The whole town was virtually a living museum of that time. The only modern touches were the television aerials above the fortifications, a couple of discos, a boutique or two. Otherwise, one was in the seventeenth century.

I found a public telephone and rang home. My daughter had gone back to Brighton. Her condition? Up and down.

*   *   *

The crude geography of the wreck site was an almost vertical cliff face down some 60–70 feet to the grouper hole. This had been the abode of an enormous rock fish in the 1960s; huge because he was old; old because he was wary. The cleft in which he took refuge narrowed and was difficult for a diver to enter. From here the rock face bounded downwards, but not so steeply, with many undercut crevices and often a sandy floor, until it opened out at the foot of the cliffs on to a slightly sloping plateau at around 90 feet. The plateau was rock, covered with patches of sand and eel grass. Its edge lay on the 100 ft contour, and lying there one could look out and down where a much steeper slope began, flowing round on both sides of a large rock at around 135 ft. The bottom down there was of sand and mud, with some rocks.

The wreck, remember, must have struck at an unknown point above, then sunk, possibly spilling cargo, perhaps even striking the cliffs, before finishing its submerged flight on or below that large rock, hitting in a cloud of disturbed sand and mud. So much was easy to guess. What we did not know was the path and trajectory of that last weird flight of the stricken Etruscan ship, her cargo and perhaps her crew. Therefore we would have to search all of the plateau.

On 8 September I was appointed supervisor of the shallow part of the site, starting at 85 feet and going down to 100 feet. I decided to begin by laying down an 80 foot base-line at the upper edge of the plateau, close to the base of the cliffs; and then another six feet farther down; and then probe the path between the two lines. That way, one could search success-ive parallel tracks across the plateau. I went down with Hamish Hay and, while he sketched the plateau roughly as a guide to future action, I found two rocks at the 90 foot level to which I was able to tie the ends of the base-line. I had intended to supplement Hamish's sketch plan with over-view photographs, but visibility had dropped sharply due to the gale.

Next day I was off-colour and did not dive, but had a reliable team of four. I asked Hamish to correct the sketch he had made, as he was not satisfied with it. I asked Melanie to probe down below the grouper cave. To Colleen and Jo I gave the task of probing paths along the base-line, starting one at each end and working towards each other, to avoid stirring up 'soup'. I stressed that we needed a firm geological and arch-aeological picture of that seabed. For example, what is the 'grass' attached to? Is it bedrock? Or an amphora? Or a sherd? Or a sea shell? We were not too familiar with Mediteranean seabeds, so we had to start by asking all the obvious questions.

Hamish came up pleased. Yesterday's sketch had not been good, but he had got it right this time. Melanie, Jo and Colleen reported that probing was slow and difficult work. There was sand cover over bedrock sometimes to knife depth. As far as the weed (or 'grass') was concerned, they had not established what it was attached to. Mel had found two sherds while

Melanie and Jo watching Hamish Hay fitting the demand valve to an aqualung cylinder. ▶
Photo: Alexander McKee

probing a path below the base-line (we only had one at this stage), Jo had a negative report and Col one sherd while probing along the other side above the base line. All were from an area of deep sand and poseidon grass near to the base of the cliffs.

An extra work-load had been thrown on the other members of the team. There had been a gale and rain during the night, torches had been seen flashing among the rain-swept waves and we had thought perhaps a rescue was taking place. Nothing of the sort, for when we had come down the cliff in the morning, we found that a number of our aqualung cylinders had disappeared. The flashing torches at sea must have been from swimmers actively raiding the beaches, and disappearing with our bottles. From now on, once our cylinders had been filled (in itself a tiresome, extended chore each night), they had to be carried up that rocky cliff in the dark. I was not asked to do this work, fortunately, for I would have been a liability. Apart from the diving, we all had reports to write each night, and we took turns, two at a time, at the daily dish-washing and cooking. Those on cook duty had to prepare meals partly from the rations we had brought with us, partly by purchase at the camp 'supermarket'. Breakfast was easy. A teabag and two Weetabix, then go and dive to 100 feet or more. Lunch we kept plain and simple—a couple of tomatoes and a bit of cheese, perhaps. It was in the preparation of the evening meal, the only one not to be followed by diving, that real artistry was always shown by

The camp site halfway up the hill at Campese. *Photo: Alexander McKee*

the cooks; and I thoroughly enjoyed every single one of them.

The rocks immediately below the camp were of course topless, while farther to the left they were bottomless as well; but there in the centre were the Brits, clad from head to toe in rubber suits, sweating profusely. To start with, as I hate being over-hot, I had worn only swimming trunks and a neoprene hood; but the gales seemed to have lowered the water temperature and as I was getting cold at the end of each stint, I took to wearing a suit jacket (with no trousers). The business of kitting-up in a crowded inflatable was a bit of a come-down; I was used to hard-boats— trawlers and such-like—and latterly a 360-ton ship. Protection of camera gear and spectacles is straightforward then, but on Giglio my flash unit got accidentally kicked to death early on. Apart from these minor nuisances, the diving was paradise. Even if you did get slightly chilled below, the blow-furnace sun above soon warmed you up in the boat. But apart from a reasonably-sized octopus I noticed once, there had been a great change in twenty years—I saw no large fish at all. Anything over two-and-a-half inches long ranked as a monster now. Similarly, the forests of pinna shells at depth had disappeared. Well, almost.

On 10 September, continuing the survey of the plateau, I set Hamish and Col to probing with thin rods (less potentially destructive than knives). The result was one piece of thin, rolled lead. Possibly significant in that Roman ships certainly, and possibly Etruscan ones, too, were sheathed with thin strips of lead as a protection against teredo and other marine borers. Jo and I followed and set to work a couple of feet away from each other digging in a gulley dense with poseidon grass. I sensed an unusual object hidden by the grass. Following its contours with my hand, I realised that it was actually a pinna clam growing vertically. That must mean a considerable depth of sand cover. I had to dig it out, finding that the lower six inches was buried. Having dug, I then examined the fill in the gulley. It was a dense mass of tangled grass and sand. The only way to remove it was to cut with a knife. Clearly, all this organic matter must be later than the time of the wreck. There could be significant items lower down, possibly in long-dead matter.

Next day, probing another strip of sand and grass, my fingers came on a curve which could only be a shellfish or a sherd. I removed the grass from around the item, which was three-quarters buried in sand and lying on its side. I dug around it and revealed a complete amphora base, similar (I thought) to one from the Punta del Morto wreck, several centuries later than the Etruscan wreck. Still, this was the first significant piece to be found. Mere sherds are not very informative.

We decided that the most efficient way of dealing with the rather unproductive plateau was to use a metal detector which the expedition had on loan from Professor E. T. Hall. It was larger, more complex and also more versatile than those designed for 'treasure hunting', based on the wartime mine detector. With this we might get something more significant than sherds. I was familiar with the ordinary metal detector, both for land and a model modified for underwater use. My original team of *Mary Rose* divers, backed by an early supporter of that project, had just used them successfully to probe buried wrecks off the Isle of Wight. Of one wreck, only a single, small timber showed; a test dig on that might be inconclusive and would certainly take more time than we had to spare. The metal detector, however, obtained several separate but strong contacts. I chose one of these to dig and, almost at once, two iron objects closely resembling *Mary Rose*-type wrought-iron breech-loading guns appeared. In fact, they proved to be iron pumps, probably nineteenth century. What the instrument had done was to short-circuit the reconnaissance process and immediately eliminate this wreck from the work programme as being unimportant.

Now a pump—or an iron gun—is a large object requiring only the crudest of detectors. With the Etruscan ship any metal objects were likely to be smaller than that, and on the plateau, because of the underlying rock, very much smaller—even tiny. And yet they might be the vital clues we wanted. One of the many strong points of the Hall instrument was that its sensitivity could be varied. It was also much easier for novices to misuse, as, to begin with, the instrument had to be zeroed in.

We first used the detector on 12 September and, at once, things started to go wrong. I teamed up with Hamish Hay, with whom I worked well. But this was 'one of those days'. I swam down the line to the anchor and found that it had dragged. The wind was acting on the boat above and the anchor was sailing along among the underwater peaks. I tried to snag it against one of the cliffs, but the boat was determined to drift into deeper water. Up top, no one can have realised what was happening so, as soon as the hook was hanging over impossible depths, I went up, stated shortly what the situation was, and hung on to the side of the inflatable, buffeted by the wash, as it motored back to the start point and this time put out a lot more line.

Then Hamish and I went down with the detector to 100 feet and swept back and up the slope to 90 feet then 80 feet. We got only a few small niggles and in places thick with poseidon grass which it was impossible to mark for digging later with the small rods we had. So we had to dig at once or not at all. Hamish carried out this heavy work and consequently finished his air sooner than I did. So he signalled me that he had to go up.

Because we were religiously diving in pairs, I broke off the detecting to see him up to a safe height, signalled 'Bye-bye', and then went down again to around 90 feet, mainly because I was becoming excited by the capabilities of the instrument but also because another diver had come down on his own. To my mind, he was perfectly safe (and so was Hamish), but the rules we were using said pairs.

I switched on the metal detector and soon got a big contact over a rectangular block. I got much too interested in this and ran my air almost out. At 30 feet that would have been no problem, but at 90 feet it was a different matter. At depth, one breathes in far more air and therefore the supply is exhausted far more quickly. Instead of swimming back the long way, up the cliffs, I pulled up fast in a curve, sucking three or four half-breaths out of the bottle, and even so, clearly wasn't going to make the shot rope. Nothing for it but to go straight up for the surface, vertically, just as I had done on this wreck in 1962. But now I was twenty years older and in addition was much slowed by the bulk and drag of the large metal detector. But I had no bother at all. I finned hard, breathing *out*

160

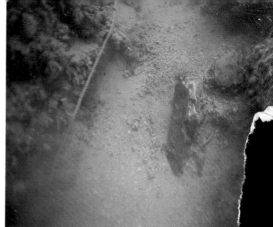

▲ Campese Bay from the heights above. The wreck site is near the group of boats anchored on the *secca*. *Photo: Alexander McKee*

Timber appears in area X-X-Ray as the excavation goes deeper. 1983. *Photo: Alexander McKee* ▶

Professor Hall's metal detector ▶ being brought up from the depths after use. 1983. *Photo: Alexander McKee*

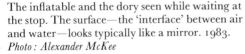

▲ The inflatable and the dory seen while waiting at the stop. The surface—the 'interface' between air and water—looks typically like a mirror. 1983. *Photo : Alexander McKee*

▲ The broken sherds of many shipwrecks on a single reeftop in Greece. Deeper down are wrecks where the cargo is still intact, protected for the moment by Greek law. 1984. *Photo : Alexander McKee*

◄ This amphora held olives, not wine; and the stones have survived the passage of two-and-a-half thousand years. 1983. *Photo : Alexander McKee*

A spectacular bubble curtain rising from the exhalations of the divers far below. *Photo : Alexander McKee*

most of the time, except for one breath near the top. I surfaced near the boat with the detector safe in my hand, and no one realising that I had run out of air. My pleasure at the happy end to the emergency was that I had got myself out of trouble without asking anyone else to help, and that I had brought up the detector, too, without effort. This convinced me that I could, if necessary, still carry out the rescue of a companion if ever that should be required. I had thought I could, but it is always nice to be sure.

The next pair of divers raised the block around which I had got the strong contact, but it was not an ingot, merely stone. I have a suspicion that this was entirely my fault; that I had not held out the detector at full stretch of my arm and had in fact been detecting myself or rather, my metal cylinder and weightbelt.

After lunch I had another dive with Hamish, this time to 80 feet, just below the grouper cave, where in another cave there was supposed to be some burnt wood—the origin of the story that the ship had burned after being attacked by pirates. We found the substance all right, but it was not wood. We logged it as probably resin, which turned out to be a more important discovery than we realised at the time. We also found three pottery sherds in this cave, in association with the resinous substance.

Jo and Col made a dive with the metal detector, but the day's ill-luck dogged them, too. They forgot to zero the instrument before starting to sweep, so their dive was wasted. Jenny and Melanie were more successful. Operating on the deep site at 130 feet, they got a contact which was dug next day. My day was not over yet, however, for I had to help cook the evening meal; and, of course, the others had the exhausting chore of filling the bottles and carrying them up the cliff to the camp site after dark.

We were not being paid for this, rather the reverse. The university ruling was, and rightly, that members of the expedition should pay for their trip abroad just as if it was a package holiday and that at least the same rates would apply. Of course, the accommodation was spartan—sleeping on granite often is—and we were cramped and stuffy in the tents loaned by the army. The rations also were on the sparse side, but one could always supplement them from the camp shop. Not one of us, I imagine, would even have considered swopping this for the most luxurious package tour imaginable, such was the interest and the hope that each day we might find the evidence to prove that a full excavation would be justified in 1983.

*   *   *

Monday, 13 September, was far from being an unlucky day. In the morning I went into Giglio Porto to see the 'copper shields', still in store, which had been recovered from the Campese site in the 1960s. Mensun was still methodically trying to track down as many of the earlier finds as he could. He had been told that the contents of the museum had been dispersed, except for some 'rubbish' in this store. When he asked to see the rubbish, he found it the exact opposite. The 'shields' (they were far too crude, thick and heavy to be actual shields, although they were shield-shaped) he recognised as copper ingots, incomparably more important than amphorae because, together with iron and lead, they formed the industrial basis of the whole rich Etruscan culture. Clearly, the Campese ship's cargo was part of a major trading pattern. By the small quay in the old part of Campese, Mensun noticed the barely visible circular walls of what must have been a kiln or metal furnace long ago. Much of the area had been 'developed' since 1962, with the building of hotels, restaurants, boutiques, shops, apartments and the beginnings of a marina, so it was hard to imagine how the shoreline had looked in Etruscan times, particularly as the sea then would have been farther out and at a lower level. Its dominating architectural feature now, the Medici Tower, a small fort built against the threat of Moorish pirates, was comparatively modern.

I went out with the late morning shift, diving again with Hamish Hay for a further detector sweep of the plateau. While Hamish detected and dug, I snooped down to 100 feet, looking hard in the gulleys and under rocks, but came across only a single sherd (which proved to be neither Roman nor Punic). It was beginning to look as if this area was almost worked out. However, we had had to investigate because important clues to the wreck site might lie here. For instance, the ship might have struck a submerged cliff on the way down and broken in two—the parts becoming separated, one landing by the big rock around 130 feet, the other ending up, where? Or the hull might have up-ended or turned over in its final fall, and some cargo might have spilled far from the central wreckage. The moment a ship fills with water, the contents alter relationship according to their buoyancy; they are subjected to new physical laws, so predicting where part of an unknown cargo might end up is impossible. One has to search.

Now it was beginning to look as if the deep site did in fact represent the bulk of the remains. On this day, using the detector again, Paddy Phillips dug the contact found by Jenny and Melanie the day before at 130 feet. There was some bronze object, together with part of an amphora, and both had been completely buried and invisible on the surface.

Immediately after the late morning dive, without stopping for lunch, we rushed off with two Italian geologists to see the Etruscan mines around the southern headland of Campese Bay. Our boat passed the *faraglione*, the rock stack off the headland. This mountainous headland had the sea on one side and the Ortana valley on the other leading down to Campese. It seemed to have been an industrial area in Etruscan times, although it was wild and deserted now. We passed green rocks protruding from the sea—presumably they contained copper—and then drove into a small and quiet bay with no proper beach. After scrambling over awkward boulders, we climbed perhaps 15 feet upwards and there, in the cliff face, was a semi-circular cave opening, half filled up, which was in fact the entrance to a long-disused Etruscan mine. Clearly, the ores would have been shipped out of the bay from a landing place now deep in the sea, as access from the interior seemed difficult if not impossible.

We embarked again and the dinghy roared off southward to an area of even higher cliffs where ores, sparkling gold and yellow in the hot sun, shone from the rock faces above the sea. There were several mines here, but the lowest was the only one I climbed to. This one had wooden props supporting the entrance because it was being worked again. The Etruscans had the technology to extract lead, copper and iron, in that order, from the ores which lay here, but could not push their temperatures high enough to get anything from the iron pyrites which lay below, and so they abandoned the mine at that level. In modern times, however, it became

The opening 15 feet up the cliff that marked the entrance to a long-disused Etruscan mine. The former landing-place below is now deep under water. *Photo: Alexander McKee*

possible to extract sulphur, so in 1949 the Italians reopened this particular mine. When they did so, they found what was left of the Etruscans' mining tools still lying there, after 2,000 years or so.

We went on to a third, submerged mine but one could see what looked like rust stains on the faces of the rocks which here rose almost vertically out of the water. If sea level were lowered by 12 feet or so, there would be a flat beach to seaward of this mine entrance.

The local Giglians knew of these mines, and so did the Italian geologists who guided our tour; but, oddly, the archaeologists seemed not to have learnt that Elba had a rival within sight (on a clear day). There is no known reference in ancient documents, but that could well be because the relevant writings have not survived. To my mind, this was the most exciting, and certainly the most important result of our reconnaissance— the discovery, not just of ship remains but of a whole previously unknown industrial area which that ship served.

*　　　*　　　*

Next day the first metal detector pair were Hamish and Mel. They went down beyond the plateau to 130 feet where digging had begun and part-exposed two pottery objects ready for removal. Col and I went in next to find Hamish's detector contact which we had tagged yesterday. I dug this by hand-stirring—driving waves of water at the sand and sucking in fresh, clear water all the time so as to maintain vision. I could not reach the contact before it was time to do some site housekeeping—repositioning the deep site rope for more rapid ascent. In the afternoon I went down with Jenny for some more necessary ropework, and was followed by Jo and Col who got a strong contact where I had dug in the morning, but without being able to expose whatever the object was. The tangled organic matter below the sand made digging a long, wearisome process; and of course we had very little time at 80 feet or so.

They had even less time down on the deep site, but Mensun Bound and David Corps managed to bring up the two pottery objects found earlier by Hamish and Mel. The first was like a Mills bomb—the round hand grenade used by the British army. At least, it was the same shape and size, but it was painted in black glaze and was decorated with vertical incisions, which heightened the resemblance to the grenade. From the archaeological viewpoint, it was just as explosive. Mensun explained that this was a Corinthian aryballos—an unguent bowl of the 'football' type— used by athletes to rub themselves down with oil after exercise. There was no soap in ancient Greece. Far from being unknown, they were well documented and dated, for this type of fineware from Corinth was only marketed over a short period, being ousted by the rival Attic ware, manufactured near Athens. The other little pot was a Laconian beaker decorated in black, red and white—a costly drinking mug made in Sparta around the same time. Whereas an amphora might remain in use for a century or more, these two items indicated a date just before 550 BC—say, 550–525 BC. Sixth century rather than seventh, and some 2,500 years old.

We had now got a very close dating indeed for our ship, and Mensun had been proved right in his suggestion that the seventh century date, originally suggested by the local experts back in the early 1960s, had been a little high. What was even more reassuring was the proof that the looters had not, as rumoured, cleaned out the site completely. There could be much more underneath, including timber.

I now had only four days' diving left, although some of the others were staying until the end of the month. Next day I dived twice with Jo, partly metal detecting on the plateau and partly carrying out camouflage and decoy work to protect the site either from casual tourists, who could easily disturb the archaeological picture without realising what they were doing, or from plunderers out for treasure; and the items being found *were* treasure, quite literally. They had been expensive goods in their day, being shipped out of Greece in transit for some unknown market; they were worth a good deal now in modern money.

Paddy Phillips, working on the deep site below us, brought up a number of sherds with painted lions and birds on them, and also an amphora top; all from a layer about 18 inches down. I was beginning to fret a little at being confined to the plateau. Without being immodest, I had far more underwater excavation experience than anyone else there; indeed, I think Mensun was the only archaeologist present. There were classicists, of course, who knew the period infinitely better than I did; but, to make one valid point only, I thought artefacts should be brought up in bags or boxes, instead of clutched in the hand. Indeed, I had had to evict my camera gear from the strong plastic box which protected it from damage in the crowded inflatable, in order to make room for the more delicate items we were bringing back; this also hid the nature of what we were now finding from the naturally curious naturists and sunbathers who thronged the rocks on which we beached the boat, dragged it ashore, and unloaded it.

I had another worry that night, when I walked down to Campese to telephone home. Each time I dialled, there was either no answer or else the line was engaged. It was not necessarily my home number which was engaged, but some exchange between Giglio and Hayling Island. Everyone could be out. They could all be at the hospital. My daughter could be dying.

In these circumstances, even if there had been undue hazard in my diving deep, I doubt that I would have cared. In fact, because of my greater experience, I thought I was probably safer than the others, particularly in an emergency. Of course, my stiff and painful knee-joints made me awkward on land, in stumbling down the cliff with a load, or in jumping into the boat from the rocks. But once in the water, no longer pinned by gravity to the earth, I regained complete freedom of movement.

Thursday, 16 September. I took down the metal detector, while Jo carried a spare bottle for a decompression stop. Then I went straight to 125 feet and hovered over Mel and 'Big Mike' working at 130 feet. No doubt at all: This *was* the 1962 gulley. I remembered coming down past here, I remembered looking up the steep slope, the big rock, the distant cliffs pale in blue haze, the greyness at depth. Reluctantly, having taken my pictures, I went up to 100 feet and then to the foot of the cliffs, where I began to dig a detector contact. After five minutes, I saw straight lines. This contact was a lead weight buried between four and six inches in sand and tangled old roots. It was a fisherman's weight, obviously. A very *old* fisherman, at that. Several thousand years old, possibly. From the wreck? Or from some angler sitting up on the *secca*? Most ships and boats carry fishing tackle; I've even known diving boats do it.

Air running low, so up the slope, looking in crevices, while Jo detected— and got a contact. I dug—and found nothing in the minutes available. So I marked the spot with two rods and went up for decompression.

On the following day I went straight down to 145 feet, slowing slightly at the edge of the plateau before entering the grey area. I was convinced that slow, careful movements at depth reduce the effects of nitrogen narcosis, and was confident my efficiency would not fall off markedly. My photographs (when developed back in England) matched exactly what I put in my log. The dig, being mainly in sand, was not as tidy as a similar excavation in the clay surrounding the *Mary Rose*, which had a plasticene quality. The soil appeared to have been moved down the slope, making the gulley deeper than I remembered it. Totally exposed now, lying completely on the surface, was a large stone anchor stock, broadly similar to those from some other ancient wreck sites in the Mediterranean; a substantial coarseware pottery sherd from an apparently pot-bellied amphora; and two pieces of wood, one substantial, the other a fillet. I dropped down to these two latter, where they lay at the base of the rock. The larger timber appeared round at first sight, but had been so badly infested by teredo that its original contours had been lost. I thought it might very well be from the wreck but recently uncovered by the digging on that slope, for no timber would last 2,500 years if in continual contact with salt water; only if it had been buried for the greater part of that time. This was my

167

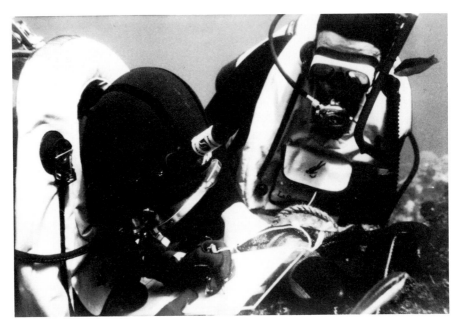

Writing underwater while carrying out a decompression stop on the rocks. *Photo: Alexander McKee*

own view. One could argue, and I think Mensun did, that it might be a 'collected' piece. However, there were no really strong currents to account for that.

Saturday, 18 September, was my last diving day. Jo and I detected to the south of the plateau, and got a contact buried somewhere under deep, tangled roots. I stopped in the middle of digging and let Jo reaffirm the contact. There was certainly a metal object underneath, but my time was up before I reached it.

But the deep team had another successful day. They brought up what Mensun said was a late Corinthian kylix—a drinking bowl—and some interesting bits and pieces, including part of an oinochoe—a pitcher. The expedition was now definitely a success. These finds would be proof positive to necessarily sceptical academics and fund-raisers that the site at Campese was truly important and well worth full excavation next year.

I became so hot packing my suitcase, that I had to go into the dark blue sea for a last snorkel. I took a few short breaths, then held it and dived. Between 15 and 20 feet down, the sticky warm water gave way to a deep cool layer, deliciously refreshing for as long as my breath lasted.

I was to fly back from Rome early next morning in a jumbo jet of Kenya

Airlines, having spent the night at Ostia. In a case of the bends, I remembered, the nearest decompression chamber was at Rome, a sobering thought for next year's expedition. From Campese, I had to travel by a road which rises 1,300 feet to Castello before sweeping down again to Giglio Porto. That alone—the reduction in pressure from going up the mountain—is exactly what one should *not* do with a bends case. You then wait for a small steamer, probably the *Giglio Espresso*, which takes an hour to convey you to Porto San Stefano on the Argentario peninsula. You then wait for a bus to take you to the railway station at Orbetello, where you wait for a fast train to the south on which there may or may not be any free seats; eventually, after travelling perhaps four hours and waiting possibly two hours more, you arrive in Rome. A pleasant enough journey if you are not in a hurry, but a death ride if you are.

We ought to do something about that next year—have our own decompression chamber, for instance.

*   *   *

From Heathrow airport I went to Oxford, picked up my car from outside Mensun's house and drove south. I reached Brighton in blinding rain. My daughter was back in hospital, weak but smiling. I dared not ask her any of the questions I wanted to put, because hope could still be so important to survival. I did not want to admit the smallest trace of fear.

The *Mary Rose* had not yet been raised. The announced time for the salvage had been 'late summer/early autumn 1982', but it was not until 12 October that, with some lucky weather and a great deal of breathless expertise from the professionals, the ship broke into daylight during what was certainly the longest running and probably the greatest cliff-hanger ever seen on TV anywhere. And it was seen all over the world. My daughter was able to watch the salvage on television, beaming with pleasure that, at last, the ship with which all my family had been associated from the beginning of the project was returning to Portsmouth dockyard where she had been built, after 437 years under the sea.

Three weeks later, my daughter Monica died.

Chapter 9

A CASE FOR THE CARABINIERI

Excavation, 1983

I had no intimation that things were beginning to go wrong until 18 May, 1983, when Mensun telephoned. He had a query about wide-angle lenses. What one did I recommend? Did I know of anyone who could loan a tent for six people? He was trying Atlas Copco for the loan of a compressor, such as I had had from them on the *Mary Rose*, to power an air-lift; but if that fell through, we had the alternative of using a dredge. He was going to Comex at Marseilles for the loan of a recompression chamber, but two divers would have to be trained to use it. I was not to assume that we would in fact have a recompression chamber and we would all have to be prepared to go without one. The BBC-TV team, which had earlier shown an interest in the project, were still planning to come out, and the producer, Roy Davis (whom I had met during the raising of the *Mary Rose*), was having diving lessons. As he would need to interview me to recreate the moment when I had introduced Mensun to the subject of the Campese wreck, it would be best if I came out a week or so before the BBC *Chronicle* team were due to arrive.

During the last months of 1982, I had kept in touch by telephone with planning progress, first with Mensun and then, when he left for Sicily, with Dr Paddy Phillips, who had it all buttoned up. We had talked over the plan Mensun would put to the fund-raisers. Basically, it would be two seasons' work. In 1983 we would excavate the entire contents of the hull, leaving nothing whatever for the plunderers to find except the hull timbers, which would not interest them. And then, in 1984, we would lift the hull itself, or whatever remained of it. The 1983 season was, of course, critical. Once we started recovering immensely valuable artefacts in numbers, potential looters would be swarming round like wolves, just waiting for us to pack up and go back to England.

Consequently, we had to have a long diving season, a large number of divers to keep shifts going all the time, adequate excavation machinery (and recompression facilities)—which meant a barge or old landing craft moored over the site throughout the season—and, naturally, a finds and conservation department, fully and properly staffed.

I had assumed that all this was going ahead—that sufficient funds had been raised to make it possible—but I had taken no part at all in the organisation and did not realise, until I heard the tone of Mensun's voice, that we were getting some of this but we were not likely to get all of it. I sensed that I was in for disappointment, but all of the bad news did not reach me until after I had arrived on Giglio. Mensun was only planning a short season of two months—June and July; there was to be no barge, only a small hired boat about a dozen feet long; and therefore no airlift, merely a dredge. And no recompression chamber, because Comex, who were willing to loan one, insisted, quite rightly, on the expedition providing a trained operator. Similarly, Atlas Copco would probably have loaned a big compressor, but there was no barge to mount it on.

So, once again, we were all going to have to accept a considerable degree of risk, but with more of us and under greater pressures. However, the project seemed so exciting that it was worth it. I am not sure that all the others quite realised that no decompression table is absolutely safe, even the conservative British Navy ones. Diving in the 1980s was utterly different from the 1960s. In the '60s we were wary, conscious that we did not know very much, and therefore alert for any dangers, expected or unexpected. But in the '80s many divers—not all—believed that it was all in the book and therefore tended to rely too much on their equipment.

There were, of course, compensations in the prospect of diving in deep blue, warm water under a bright, high sun. My first dive in 1983 had been on 22 January, in an investigation of a Viking legend. Sometimes the tidal pattern, which determined my dive plans, meant waiting to be picked up on the shores of Hayling Island at six o'clock on a winter's morning, and wading out to the dinghy in water so cold that it cut like a raw blade. The big boat we were using was good and fast, equipped with both radar and sonar, but its cabin was unheated. Although I had become fascinated with tracing the invasion paths and early harbours of all the many invaders of England over thousands of years, getting into cold, dark water early on a winter's morning was intimidating in a way that Giglio could never be. Only the black cormorants, perched on buoys and piles, watched us go out or come back. Perhaps the invaders had felt like this, before the raid.

The only thing we had to be thankful for was that no expert could tell us what to do or advise us to stick to the 'book'. We were not sport diving. We were going with eyes wide open where probably no one had been before us, just as we had done with the search for the *Mary Rose*, long before we had made her name famous. The other difference, of course, was that we were a tightly-knit group; most of us had been diving together for 15 to 25 years. We knew each other's strengths and weaknesses, and could communicate by more than a few bare signs. The university teams

171

were extremely good, but it takes time for instinctive understandings to build up between strangers.

When I flew out to Italy on 24 June, I was still looking forward to spending four weeks on what would undoubtedly be a meticulous excavation which would investigate every scrap of evidence. When chatting to Adele Wilkes, at the headquarters of the Mary Rose Trust a few weeks before, I had learnt that she was taking a fortnight's holiday to work on finds with the Giglio expedition (this was her job with us), and would be leaving for Pisa on the same morning that I was, but on a flight two hours earlier. We agreed to meet in Pisa and travel together the rest of the way, because I had done the complicated journey before. Alas, although I invariably knew where we wanted to go, no living seller of Italian travel tickets seemed to understand my pronunciation of Italian place names. (Later, by chatting up four charming Italian girls at Giglio, I learned that we Brits slurred all our words, whereas Italians gave every part of every word full value.) The Italians are supposed to be notoriously inefficient, but by some uncanny means or other, there was always a bus ready waiting for the train, and a ship waiting for the bus, and another bus waiting for the ship, so that, in brief, door to door, from leaving the south coast of England to arriving at a particular bay on an island halfway down the coast of Italy, took less than 14 hours.

Had I been on my own, I would have tried to make my way to the old camp site; for I knew no better. Adele, however, had learnt, more or less by accident, from someone coming back, that the expedition was not there this year. Instead, we should go to the football pitch in Campese . . . It all sounded rather like an initiative test in the army, to be carried out in a heatwave, encumbered with heavy suitcases. To circumnavigate the pitch would have taken forever, so we just plodded off along the seafront towards signs of habitation, I towing my suitcase behind me on a lead (Adele had christened it 'Fido'). Suddenly, as we broke cover by some buildings, a sweet-faced, dark-haired girl came rushing out of what seemed to be bushes in the garden of a villa, crying out my name (which was vividly emblazoned on my suitcase, for ease of recognition at baggage reclamation). The girl was Frances Rankine, responsible for drawing finds. We had arrived.

By the time we had sorted ourselves out, decided where we were going to sleep that night, and had something to eat at 'Toni's' bar down by the waterfront under the Medici Tower, we had come to realise that disaster had struck the expedition that morning. A couple of Italians, also sitting in the bar, were pointed out to me as villains, and I saw Christopher Storey (in charge of finds and treatment) get up and follow them at a distance to see where they went and perhaps get the number of their car. It was

The diving schooner *Florette* anchored in Campese Bay. *Photo: Alexander McKee*

late before Mensun turned up, very dejected. The site had been robbed of three or more valuable artefacts, he said. The team had excavated these the previous day, then covered them over for photography in the morning. There were two aryballoi and a large plate.

That morning, Mensun had got into conversation with an Italian diving team, who admitted diving the site and taking artefacts from it. He had asked for them back, mentioning that the Oxford expedition had the backing of the Italian authorities. The Italian divers had then shut up. At this point, Mensun thought that they had not done much damage and that only a warning was necessary (a tactic which had worked with many other diving teams). But when he had later dived the site with Joanna Yellowlees, he had found an enormous hole and valuable pieces missing.

In the afternoon, he had seen the Italian divers ashore, followed them to where they were staying and had taken their car number, which was a Florence registration.

What worried us most was that the whole expedition was extremely vulnerable. There was no barge moored over the site with people sleeping on board as a permanent guard. And there had been only three divers—Mensun, Jo and a physicist, Mike Russell; now that I had arrived there were four. This gap in the diving programme had occurred because one good team had finished their stint and gone home, and the next team would not arrive for a week or more, two on 1 July, half-a-dozen on 3 July. A single successful act of plunder like this might spark off many more.

173

We could not, with four divers and three shoreside technicians—Chris Storey, Frances and Adele—maintain a deterrent 'presence' on the site, or even keep it under constant observation. Whether or not a free-for-all pillaging of the Etruscan ship became the next act was now largely up to the Italian authorities. To say that this was not what I had imagined we were going to achieve this season is understatement. To cap it all, I learned that, because of a previous agreement, Mensun was packing up at Giglio altogether towards the end of July—in about five weeks' time— and going to another dig in Sicily.

Yet, a few days before, the expedition had made a discovery which seemed to assure the success of the season. Pete Shields was carrying out a routine excavation and had gone down six inches into the sand, when pottery began to appear—part of a large amphora about two feet long and two-thirds intact. This was the first large piece they had found, so Pete was excited. With Mensun, he carried it up to the boat.

The next few dives cleared enough sand to show that the amphora had been lying in a layer of pitch and that they had dug a crater in the pitch. So they carried on digging around the pitch and had got down about two feet, with visibility reduced to zero, when, as he fanned away more material, Pete felt his fingers touch something unusual. It was smooth and about the size of an orange. Then the object was loose and in his hands. It was an aryballos. A goat in black was painted on it. The handle was red at one end and it was smeared with pitch—and in the pitch, an orange pip from perhaps 2,500 years ago.

Pete carried on excavating—and there was another aryballos, smooth and intact. At that moment, the warning hammer being beaten in the boat above, began to sound as a signal to come up. As Pete emerged from the cloud of sand, Mensun could see that he was carrying not one, but two aryballoi.

Both divers were using great gouts of air, so excited were they, and waving their arms and making V-signs. Then discipline prevailed and they put the two finds in a plastic box. They ascended the shot line and began decompression, looking up at the surface but not able to go there. By putting a glass look-box into the water, the people in the boat were always able to check the condition of the divers hanging on the line below. They could see their excitement and knew something must have happened, so lowered a writing board. The divers wrote on it: 'We have made it', and drew an aryballos.

The little bowl found the previous year was not now the only one. The Campese wreck had at last lost its reputation, that 'every piece was different'. Two further aryballoi were uncovered on 23 June, the day before I arrived, but instead of being removed immediately, were left for photo-

Hand-digging at depth. *Photo:* ▶
Alexander McKee

▼ The two aryballoi which alone
seemed to make the 1983
expedition worthwhile. They
contained oil used by athletes to
clean themselves of sweat after
exertion. *Photo: Alexander McKee*

graphy. And then, this morning, Mensun and Jo had found only a great hole—surprisingly large since no really powerful machinery could have been used—the aryballoi gone, probably a third object also, with only a litter of broken fragments left and among them a metal probe, presumably left by the looters.

Next day, 25 June, I accompanied Mensun and Jo to the headquarters of the Carabinieri in Giglio Porto. The plunder of antiquities does not come under the jurisdiction of the ordinary police, but of this national paramilitary body which also carries out coastguard duties. It is in every sense an elite formation, but not always very popular. A rather young Marshal took Mensun's statement, sitting at an efficient-looking desk, clear of clutter (unlike mine). All the carabinieri were well turned out in a light shade of khaki drill with silver and red facings, armed with automatic pistols in left-side holsters. They also carried rifles (or carbines?) in their vehicles. The heat was tremendous, with virtually no draught inside the building, but these paramilitary policemen appeared crisply impervious to it.

The Marshal asked all the questions I understood a policeman should ask. Who saw this? Who said that? In what language? Our tedious translation chores, for the whole of this day, were undertaken quite free of charge by an Italian lady, Maria-Luisa, who was actually on holiday in Giglio from Rome. Indeed, later on it became clear that a number of Italian divers were interested in helping us actively with the project.

The Carabinieri then drove over to Campese, followed by ourselves in the van, located the light green car described by Mensun as belonging to the team of divers he suspected, and searched it. There were no artefacts in it—only a fitment which would enable a diver to excavate by channelling the highly compressed air from a spare aqualung cylinder. The men's apartment was searched also, but without result; I could see that their leader was vehemently arguing their innocence. One or two facts did emerge, but as the case may be *sub judice*, I shall not repeat them.

At eight o'clock that evening, the Carabinieri were still on duty. They came to the cellars in which we were living (underneath an apartment block by the sea), took Jo's statement, collected a sample artefact from the site, and also photographs of the type of artefact which had been stolen. Very hard-working and efficient, I thought. And sufficiently public, so that the news would be all round the island: 'The cops are cracking down on anyone who tries to loot the wreck.'

But what would happen when our expedition left the island next month? The *secca* itself is a very popular underwater site, with as many as four diving boats sitting above it at any one time. With the best will in the world, how was it possible to protect the Etruscan treasures, if we had to leave any unexcavated? Clearly, we were now in a rescue situation of extreme urgency.

The knowledge was not confined to Giglio. The story had leaked to the press and *La Nazione*, printed in Florence, had headlined the story of the valuable antiquities stolen from the 'Roman galley' at Campese. There are in Italy certain people actually able to make a living from professionally plundering antiquities from the sea; this would alert them all.

Diving began again on 26 June and I went down on an acclimatisation dive with Mike Russell. Basically, there was a very good system. From a small hard-boat about a dozen feet long, a shot line led very steeply down to the site, just above the large central rock. By hammering on a can or half-submerged metal tube, the time-keeper in the boat could signal to the divers: a series of bangs at intervals of a second or so meant, 'You have two minutes left—finish what you are doing now', while a continuous, savage hammering, sounding below like a clashing church bell, said, 'Come up! Come up! Come up!' Then, as the divers ascended the shot line, they found, at the two depths at which they must make decompression stops, spare air cylinders complete with demand valves. This was all back-up. Naturally, one was expected to time one's own dive and check depths also, plus, from time to time, the amount of air one had left. I went further: I wore a writing pad and wrote on it the exact time at which I left the surface, followed by the exact time I reached the bottom. There was room also for any working notes I wanted to make. In 1962, as a novice, I had left it all to Vallintine. Twenty years later, I left it to no one.

This time, for once, irritatingly, I had trouble making my left ear 'pop', so we went slowly to 80 feet (if you want to rupture an eardrum, you force it). At 100 feet, overlooking the site, there came a faint signal from above which seemed to be continuous, whereas we had been told to expect, although not so soon, a preliminary two-minutes' warning signal. We

Jo Yellowlees, Paul Bramley, Ric Wharton (who salvaged HMS *Edinburgh*'s gold), and Caroline Costello in the 'hard-boat' moored on site. The shot-line and spare cylinders were rigged from this dory. *Photo : Alexander McKee*

looked at each other and I shrugged my shoulders. We had done nothing yet. This reaction, also, was different from 1962. The first few years of diving are the best, and one should make the most of them, for then it is wonderful just to be underwater, alive and breathing and looking round at this amazing world you don't understand in the least. But after that, if you haven't achieved anything on a dive, then you have wasted your time.

I noted that last year's anchor stock had been moved off site to a higher position among the rocks and that there was nothing much to see on the site itself except the dredge and some marker poles. I moved out to overfly the site at 125 feet and to see for myself the crater the looters had dug. But I must have been over-weighted because, on checking my depth gauge, I noted that the needle was on the red line denoting 150 feet. The site looked black and forbidding, but I could not see the crater. I came back up the slope at once, then saw an interesting piece of timber in a significant place—the southern gulley by the large central rock. I spent half a minute inspecting this. It appeared, at first sight, to be a light frame—but only excavation would show.

Up above, not realising they had sent us the wrong signal, they had assumed we were in trouble and Mensun had come down to save us, unnecessarily, so there were apologies all round.

Next day I did a working decompression dive of 26 minutes (including stops) to 135 feet with Mike Russell. Our task was to clear timber in the gulley so that pot recovery could proceed in this area (which, to my mind, was a typical archaeological directive). I was very interested in the timber as such, for it might represent the only Etruscan hull remains ever recovered—but I would have to prove that it was connected with the pots. So I suggested to Mike that he dig above the rock in Z-Zulu area, while I took as my task the small piece of possible rib (technically, frame, if it was such) in the gulley, which was coded X-X Ray.

I began by taking pre-disturbance photographs of the area I was going to dig. I uncovered about a foot of the wood, clearing away the sand at the sides and underneath, to where at the lower end it disappeared into a kind of concretion. The piece was much longer than Mensun and I had thought it would be, about six inches in diameter but so massively infested by teredo on the upper sides that measurements would be misleading. The wood still retained some flexibility, but had to be handled very gently. It was closely associated with pottery—many coarseware sherds and stones to the south, in the small space between the timber and the side of the crevice. On the other side, between the wood and the central rock, I exposed about half of a broken amphora standing almost upright (Mensun lifted it a few days later, and judged it Samian—i.e. from the Greek island of Samos off what is now Turkey but was then the Greek colony of Ionia).

Mike Russell, working just up the slope above me, had uncovered what looked like an amphora lying on its side, and just above that some planking. I concluded my log entries that day with the note: 'If we have frames and planking we must either record or recover, as they may be vital evidence of ship structure and origin.' If we could identify the place where the wood came from, we could be pretty sure where the ship was built—whether indeed it was Etruscan and not perhaps Phoenician or Greek. The dimensions of ship timbers are also a simple guide to the size of the vessel. I had made a detailed examination of a broken-up wreck which a friend and I had found off Hayling Island in 1966 and noted the results in my log: 'Wreck is nineteenth century wooden-hulled sailing vessel of large dimensions, probably not less than 120 feet long.' Later, when we had found the bell and identified the ship, she turned out to be the composite barque *Caduceus*, 418 tons gross, length 124·1 ft, built Sunderland, 1857, sunk on passage with coals to Salerno, Italy, in 1881.

Next day a maestrale blew, and the day after that, too, so that diving was stopped. Then other people began to arrive. Dott. essa Paola Rendini, the archaeological superintendent for the Tuscan islands, visited us to see the finds so far. Then Reg Vallintine appeared, and Roy Davis, leading the BBC *Chronicle* camera team. In the first week of July, ten members of the university team joined us, all divers, together with Jane Pannell as head of conservation. Ric Wharton, the man who raised the gold from HMS *Edinburgh*, and a financial backer (as well as a diver), dropped in, followed a week later by his great rival, Henry Delauze, president of Comex. Both headed very large and impressively advanced diving organisations and what they had to say was very interesting. Dott. Francesco Nicosia, the archaeological superintendent for the whole of Tuscany, based on Florence, paid us a visit later, and also Prince Hans Adam of Liechtenstein.

Priority during this period had to be given to the filming because of the publicity and prestige bonus likely to result from a complete programme devoted to the wreck; and that, naturally, was likely to bring in financial and other support—but next year, not this year. Meanwhile, our time was running out. It was a dilemma I was familiar with from the *Mary Rose*, but never had it arisen in such pressing form.

During this time I tried to get in one deep dive a day—not always succeeding—and decided to concentrate on the timbers around the large rock, the top of which was at about 135 feet, the bottom in about 145 feet. If I did not do it, no one else might have the time. Bear in mind that I only had about 16–18 minutes actually working on the bottom; the rest of a 30–40 minute dive would be spent on the way down or decompressing

Dr Paola Rendini, archaeological superintendent for the Tuscan islands, with Mensun Bound. *Photo: Alexander McKee*

on the way up. I was deliberately working one minute less on the bottom than the others, and never doing more than one deep dive a day, because I knew from some of the best authorities in the world that, as you grow older, so does your susceptibility to bends increase.

Usually Mike Russell was working an adjoining area at the same time. What we separately uncovered was clearly related and I made a habit of photographing his dig area as well as mine and discussing with him what he had found. On our first dive on 27 June, we both found large parts of amphorae in association with timber; his wood was clearly planking, mine could be a frame—I wasn't sure. On 30 June, working an adjacent area, I found two pieces of planking, two pottery sherds and two small scraps of wood. The planking was badly infested by teredo on the upper surface, but not on the protected side. All these tiny bits of evidence tended to establish that the timber was not 'collected' but came from the Etruscan ship, which seemed to have struck the large rock and broken its hull at that point. Whether the break had been immediate, or occurred over a period of time, was not clear. I always liked the amassing of many scraps of evidence, as being more convincing than any single, dramatic item, but I was to get that, too.

I did not quite get it on 30 June, although I dug energetically on the possible frame. No more artefacts appeared, but as I worked down the slope, steadily clearing the wood to view, the massively infested upper part gave way to much smoother timber, apparently almost untouched. Significantly, I thought, there now appeared fragments of planking in association with the large timber. By the time I had to go up, the highest part of the timber was completely free and loose where it lay in the gulley, parallel to the rockface on its southern side. At its lowest part, farther down the very steep slope, a large black mass was appearing. Its relationship to the timber I could not then see because of a cloud of smoke flippered up by another diver (not Russell). In these tideless waters the clouds of disturbed sediments hung around for too long; one needed an airlift to remove them and keep vision clear all the time.

On 3 July, while Russell dug on the other side of the large rock, I began where I had left off and re-exposed the lower part of the timber which appeared to measure six by eight inches, very approximately, and could therefore be a frame from a ship, not a boat. I laid bare to view the lower visible end, which vanished into a mass of black pitch, presumably carried as part of the cargo. What was significant, however, was that the timber, the pitch and the side of the rock gulley were all now one conglomerate. No question of the wood having all drifted in there later. This was indeed Etruscan ship timber.

I missed out on 4 July, because the BBC and the newcomers between them monopolised the diving time, so that next day, I noted, I was in the terminal stages of malignant boredom, relieved only by an assignment to show the site to the two newcomers, Andy Smith and Piers Corneilson, and to clean it up a little. I took Andy and Piers down to the plateau and overflew the excavation at 130–140 feet. There was some confusion apparent. The marker rods were in disarray, the hose for the dredge was lying in the gulley where I had been excavating the possible frame, and that timber itself was now broken. I was becoming parochial about that piece of wood, I felt it was 'my' timber and resented anyone making the

The teredo-riddled end of the main timber broken off by a person or persons unknown.
Photo: Alexander McKee

area untidy. Anyway, I had not finished there. The amount of as yet undiscovered hull information, in that area and Russell's, might be critical.

On 6 July there was a good deal of filming on land. Doctor Nicosia arrived, greeting me with; 'Ah, Signor Mary Rose!' The role taken by the Italian archaeological authorities in the project was well covered by the cameras, but, alas, was not to appear in the finished product as shown to British audiences.

Next morning I was to have an underwater acting role with Jo Yellowlees at 145 feet, in area Victor-Juliet. This is not so glamorous as it sounds, because it is very difficult to tell one diver from another, even when you are down there yourself. Eventually, I was only able to recognise myself (at the second showing) because I was the one with the Nikonos III underwater camera, and even then I was only on screen nationally for some two-fifths of one second. For once, I was fully dressed underwater, my trousers being borrowed from Mike Russell and my jacket from the other BBC cameraman, David Swan.

The technical problems of excavating underwater in a way to combine both maximum speed and maximum care, are at least matched by those faced by the cameramen filming the operation. And they were greater at Giglio than they had been on the *Mary Rose*, thought David Swan:

> The main problem filming on this location was the depth. As the site lay between 130 and 160 feet down, we could spend only 15 minutes from leaving the surface before starting to come up again to decompress for 10 minutes in shallower water. This was a problem we shared with all the divers who were working on the excavation. Staying down much longer would have necessitated unduly long periods of decompression, so we stuck to this schedule where bottom time was at a premium and had to be used to best effect.
>
> An added limitation was that an interval of between eight to 16 hours was deemed necessary before a repeat dive for a similar duration could be made.
>
> To maximise filming time, John Beck and myself dived with the camera alternately to obtain usually just two deep dives a day. The one on the boat kept his hands dry to service and reload the camera for the other cameraman going down.
>
> Both of us cameramen had a dive partner loaned from the expedition to 'watch our backs' for safety and make sure that neither of us exceeded any time or depth limits. This left us wonderfully free to concentrate on filming, secure in the knowledge that the dive itself was in the safe care of our partners.

*　　*　　*

When Ric Wharton arrived in the middle of the filming period, on 4 July, he was brief in his comments to me. He had only lost one diver in six years out of seven or eight hundred who had worked for his company. The most dangerous diving was ours: amateurs going deep without much back-up.

That shook me slightly because, although I had judged our risks high, the diving involved in the salvage of the *Edinburgh*'s gold was on the very edge of the new North Sea technology. Very cold waters—not far from the Arctic Circle. Very deep waters—800 feet, if I recalled rightly. And therefore saturation diving involving the use of a new and artificial mixture of gases to be breathed at that tremendous depth. All that merely to get down there. Once there, to go into a big ship which had suffered severe torpedo damage, so that everything inside was a black chaos. And to go into that, depending on a thin line dragged behind you carrying the breathing mixture, vulnerable to the sharp edges of steel (severed steel, after it has been underwater for a while, cuts like a finely-honed razor, as I well knew from diving a U-Boat), and always, always exposed to the constant risk of a swift, noiseless cave-in or silent shift of high-piled debris in the tilted compartments one has entered; remembering that a ship that size would have you lost for the first two or three days, even if it was safely afloat and you were living in it. I thought I knew what Ric meant, however. Some of our divers had not been much below 30 feet or so before they came to Giglio and had had very little experience generally. They were very high quality people, but their diving had been limited. Ric Wharton's men were professionals.

Those with us at this time included two classicists (Alison Bonner and Paul Bramley), an archaeologist (Caroline Costello), a scientist (Andy Smith), a newly-qualified medical doctor (Ann Walker), and a brilliant student of biochemistry (Richard Skelt). The two latter became known affectionately to all as 'Doctor Bob' and 'Rico' respectively.

Just after Ric Wharton left for home, the President of Comex, Henri Delauze, arrived with his chief diver. Quite independently, without prompting, they repeated (but in a French accent) what Ric Wharton had said. Scuba diving in pairs to great depths twice a day is the most dangerous type of diving. No back-up. No oxygen. No decompression chamber. No surface demand. Comex used pairs, too, but they were differently equipped—one diver was on surface demand (that is, his air supply was supplied to him from the surface through an air-line), while the other diver used tanks (as we did) and was not tied to the surface. Comex was even bigger than Ric Wharton's outfit. Although based on Marseilles, it also operated worldwide, and especially in the North Sea.

However, what worried us all, team and visitors alike, far more than the risks to ourselves, was the archaeological disaster in store for the expedition in some three weeks' time, when the project would be wound up and the *secca* left open to the looters. I had already approached Mensun and suggested that he cancel his impending move to Marsala in Sicily to resume last year's search task there. He told me that Dr Nicosia had suggested the very same thing, but that he simply could not give up his commitments there without offending his hosts. Failing that, Henri Delauze suggested physically covering up the site by one of two means. The first was to lay anti-submarine nets over it—not perfect, because it was possible to cut them. The second alternative was to employ a dredger to dump sand or mud on top of the site. I said that we had actually used this method on the *Mary Rose* one winter, with the prime object of protecting delicate excavated areas from winter wave-action, big spring tides, and attack by marine organisms; and that it had worked well. Actually aiming the load had been quite easy—I had scored a bullseye into the trench!

Our anxieties were heightened by the nature of some of the finds now being made. We were getting more tiny fragments of lead sheathing and also arrowheads. A Bronze Age sea battle would have been fought close enough to see the enemy's face, but it would have begun, as now, with a fire-fight before the foes came to hand-to-hand conflict. In those circumstances, a comparatively high-sided merchantman might well have been defensible even against a war galley, particularly if the cargo vessel, in addition to its usually sparse crew, carried a small detachment of soldiers. I began to favour the missing bronze helmet in this context rather than as cargo or as some individual's exotic possession. What was heartening was that these comparatively tiny objects, hard to distinguish in the gloom of the depths as artefacts from the stones and shells also found in the sand, had not escaped the excavators. Although we were working against time, great care was being taken.

These dives were all very much the same. Blue, immense underwater vistas early in the morning, before everything had been disturbed; but if you were on a later shift, then a dark mist hanging over the site. And to signal the end of each shift, the hammering ringing down from above— DONG ... DONG ... DONG ... into the depths of the sea like some spectral bell, melancholy and menacing.

Then hanging on the shot at two different depths—five minutes on the lower, 10 minutes on the upper where the boat was only 15 feet away, but it was death to go there before your time was up.

And then the pay-off. Tired, dispirited and cold, hanging on to the shot—if you'd found nothing much. But elated, hardly able to wait to reach the surface—if you'd done well. And once ashore, striding out proudly back to billets as if you'd won a battle.

The five-minute wait at the first stop, an essential part of the decompression procedure.
Photo : Alexander McKee

For the indispensable shoreside technicians, it was not like that. They had hard, monotonous, highly-demanding work all day long and half the night in enervating heat. I was reading D. H. Lawrence's *Etruscan Places* in off-hours. Lawrence didn't think very much of archaeologists. 'Who wants object-lessons about vanished races? What one wants is contact,' he wrote. In his words one can feel the stunning heat coming off the fields, the Etruscan farmers in their big straw hats, burnt red-brown by the sun (the women must have been kept indoors, he suggests, for they are painted as pale creatures on the tomb walls). None of the scholarly books make you feel how their working lives must have been, only Lawrence; and he was absolutely right, for, except when I was diving, the heat varied from uncomfortable to unbearable right round the clock, apart from a brief space at about two in the morning.

The unreasonable, even childish, pride in making a find was a fresh sensation for me—and only partly because normally I am the Director and have to think 'long'. Whether or not a diver finds anything of import-ance on a particular dive is simply a matter of there being something there to find in the first place, which is partly a matter of luck and partly intelli-gent direction. But here, everything was intensified because we had so little time; unless some fairly drastic decision was taken soon, the story of the Campese wreck would certainly go down as the underwater archaeological disaster of the century. For sponge divers or sport divers to star in such a tale was one thing; for a highly-qualified scientific team it would be quite another matter. I could see myself pretending never to have heard of Campese.

The expedition was due to pack up about 26 July. My last diving day would be 20 July. On 10 July I went down to 145 feet to check the timber around the rock (now coded R-1) and then dug higher up the slope with Caroline Abbott. A massive, brittle, black substance, which I at first thought must be timber, was appearing—in fact, it proved to be a frozen layer of pitch as much as two feet thick. While I dug this I set Caroline to dig higher up and to my left, so that we would not obscure each other's visibility with the sediments we were stirring up. I noticed that she had exposed the top part of a lead ring which was standing almost vertically in the sand. Curiously, it was flat on one side, rounded on the other. We fanned around it gently, to expose by degrees anything else lying near it; but there was nothing. At length we had fanned away all the sand around it, and the ring fell over on its side. Up to this time, we had not touched it—merely sent mild waves of water around it to wash the sand away. Lead brailing rings (an item from the rigging) are quite common on ancient ships; but this one was strange.

I was becoming seriously worried about the timber. The upper part of the heavy piece I had excavated earlier and which had been broken off by someone, had now disappeared. One of the planks exposed by Mike Russell back in June had been taken up to the surface by Reg Vallintine; a lighter piece of planking was still down there. But it seemed to me that looters might well be raking around the site and disturbing timber in their search for valuable artefacts. To me, the timber represented three different parts of an Etruscan ship's hull and it was therefore equally important. I suggested to Mensun that I saw the 'frame' or whatever it was, certainly a main timber, where it entered the pitch; and recover it for surface photography and drawing. He agreed, but took the view that all timber should be taken down again to the site and buried under the sand, because there were no facilities locally for conserving wet wood.

So the next day I went down with Angus McDonald and, while he dug the 'frozen' river of pitch which lay under the sand, I settled into the gulley beside the large rock (R-1) and with my knife sawed away at the lower end of the main timber. At first, I thought I would not manage as the wood was firmly in the pitch. However, it proved to be badly teredoed and my saw-blade was soon through it. Even so, my right wrist began to throb. Once the wood had been detached, I got it into a polythene bag I had brought down with me for that purpose. The removal of this piece enabled me to dig where it had been and I uncovered at once part of an amphora top—the rim and one handle.

The timber proved to be infinitely more important, however. The tunnels bored by the teredoes blurred the measurements a little, but it was a substantial piece about $10\frac{1}{2}$ inches by $7\frac{1}{2}$ inches in section; and, moreover, it was bevelled, with the possible remains of a trenail (or wooden peg). I thought it might be a wale, a timber cut like a very thick plank, which is laid on the outboard side of the frames to give fore-and-aft strength, assuming a single-skinned hull. With double-skinned sides, planked inside and out, there can be internal wales also for further strengthening. The *Mary Rose* was built like that; but then she was a battle-ship, designed to take, as well as to give, heavy punishment. Merchant ships, however, are usually lightly-built and lightly-crewed, for obvious economic reasons. In a commercial cargo ship, such dimensions suggested to me a vessel not less than 60–80 feet in length and quite possibly as much as 120 feet. That is, not an island-hopping caique of the sort one still sees so often in the Aegean, but an ocean-going merchant ship capable of going out to the Azores—or even round to England. When Mensun saw the timber in air he became excited and agreed that it was a most important piece, from a ship, not a boat.

That day a very interesting find was made lower down the slope. It was a lead ingot with spaced-out lettering on it—I A V. One would expect the heavy ingots to represent almost the lowest level in the wreck, and I was already coming to the conclusion that the ship had broken. Yet another stone anchor stock had been uncovered near the large rock (R-1), but this did not necessarily indicate the bow area, because the use of stern anchors is widespread in the Mediterranean.

More and more, the frozen river of pitch was assuming greater importance as we probed its extent and thickness. On 12 July I joined Jo in digging the area where the looters had stolen the aryballoi. The area was extensive and consisted of jumbled pitch mixed with soft wood fragments and seashells. Next day I went down with Angus and dug under the pitch, finding that it was only four inches thick at that point and easy to break up with my knife blade. A barrel of pitch had been one of the finds in the *Mary Rose* and its preservative properties were remarkable. On 14 July I partnered Gavin Walker. His first task was to fasten a rope from the surface to a bag of pitch which had been broken up by other teams, and see it hauled to the surface. Then we went down the slope, below the large rock to around 150 feet, where we began to dig by a white line laid down by Mensun. I was able to cut a face uphill and note the stratification. The top layer of soil was white-brown sand. The next layer was black sand. There were few seashells and no artefacts at all. I then cut the face to the left and got another decisive negative.

Ashore, the bags of pitch were examined by Jane Pannell. She identified amber, a substance found almost entirely in an area of Russia just south of the Baltic. A sheepbone with carving on it was brought up, too.

On 16 and 17 July I worked in area Victor-Lima, again around 150 feet, just above a lower line of rocks (the central and largest being coded R-2). Again, I dug a face uphill, finding shells, a small piece of wood, and three coarse sherds on the first day, when I was with Richard Skelt. We were back in the area of the wreck. But the following morning the first team down reported that overnight an amphora had been looted and an important wooden object trapped in the pitch had been smashed (no doubt the thief had used force trying to free it). I dived late in the afternoon with Caroline Costello to an amphora part-dug by a previous pair. My depth gauge indicated that my wrist was in 148 feet of water, so my toes lower down the slope) must have reached 152 feet.

Caroline, an archaeologist from Ireland, selected the amphora and began to free it. This forced me away to the left, crowding me increasingly against a rock. I dug hard and reached bedrock—nothing more just there, so moved a trifle. The sand here gave way to a 'shadow' in the soil—and sand with small black bits in it. This was extremely important, as it seemed to be an organic layer of some kind. I could not hazard what it might have been: a sail, rope, some part of a vanished cargo? If this had been the *Mary Rose* I would have stopped and marked the area 'off limits' with a yellow sign, for careful investigation at a later stage. But I only had three days more and the expedition a little over a week. I went through the shadow and found four sherds and some stained seashells, some large. In a rescue situation there was not much else to be done, but I have no doubt that the 'shadow' represented a layer of decayed organic material. The amphora, when raised, proved to be full of olive stones.

Next day I went to the same area, Victor-Lima, with Richard. He had just done brilliantly in an examination and was so pleased with himself that I thought we might not get on. The very reverse proved true. He just wanted to belt down to the bottom as fast as possible and get on with the job, which was my own urge. Earlier, my habit of dozing or reading after lunch had given some people the idea I was infirm, so they continually gave 'Are you OK?' signals. At last I realised what women divers must feel like—well-intentioned people anxiously looking after their welfare when they don't need it.

The day before, I had become so interested in the problem presented by that 'shadow' layer that I had run my air low and the needle of the pressure gauge was halfway into the red before I noticed; however, there were bottles suspended at the stops, and I used one. Now, diving with Richard at 145 feet, and working on a face, I glanced at my gauge after being down only a few minutes—and it was showing 40 ATS (about half of what one needed for an ordinary ascent). It had been showing over 200 ATS on the surface, so a leak must have developed after I had submerged. I attracted Richard's attention, showed him the gauge, with needle about to enter the red, and left. Climbing up the slope, and directly above R-1, I noticed a plank with two apparent trenail (or peg) holes leaning against the shoreward side of the rock. That had not been there before—so perhaps it was more evidence of looters at work on the site (although a watch had been kept on it the previous night).

In these circumstances (of little air left in an already leaking bottle) the surface seemed rather far away. However, I reached the stops with no trouble, and breathed off the emergency bottles there, finally surfacing with absolutely no air whatever in my own cylinder. Two more days to go.

I decided on my next dive to examine the area disturbed by the latest piece of looting and to recover the trenailed plank. It was within feet of where Russell had exposed two different types of plank (both subsequently raised) and within a dozen feet or so of the main timber I had raised (which was also associated with planking). The renewed disturbance by strangers was particularly disquieting because we had begun to make finds which previously might have seemed to be in the realm of fantasy. There exists

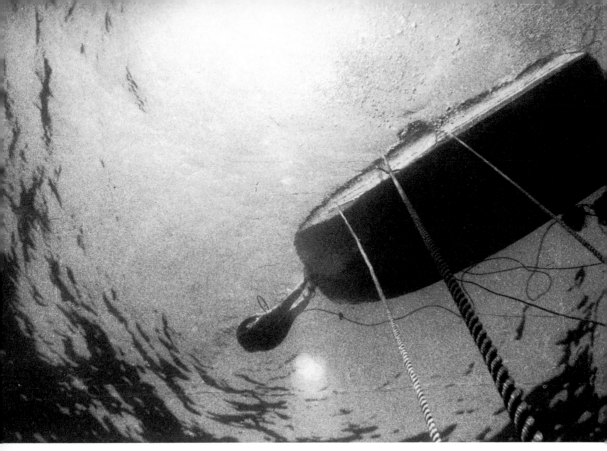

Waiting for 10 minutes at the second stop, with the bottom of the dory clearly visible above. *Photo: Alexander McKee*

at least one Etruscan picture (a bas-relief at Chiusi) showing a wooden writing tablet being used for note-taking; the shift which had dived that morning, just before my own, had found exactly such a tablet (which in use would have been wax-covered). A shift just after mine brought up something more fascinating. Gaiety and dancing, as well as dining, seem to have been an Etruscan passion; and many of the tomb paintings show dancers stamping it out to the music of flutes—very often double-flutes. Parts of a flute—or of several flutes—were the next find today. It was absolutely wonderful, bringing one much closer to the people of that time and place. Rope was also found.

That these discoveries coincided with further intrusions on to the site by looters who were obviously raking around for 'goodies', was appalling. They were likely to smash anything like this, as merely bits of old wood, while digging down in the hope of fine pottery. Next day, a team from the first boat out early in the morning found a definite piece of flute with the holes in it. There was a suggestion that the ship was carrying flutes as part of its cargo, some in an unfinished state. Or perhaps there was a flute-maker on board?

Later in the morning I dived with Caroline Abbott to recover the trenailed plank dug up and discarded by some unauthorised visitor. I put it gently into a polythene dustbin-liner, wrapped the material round the plank four times, and then moved it to a large open box for lifting. Simply picking up a piece of timber and clasping it to you while you swim back up the shot line and then hang around for 15 minutes on the stops, is positively guaranteed to inflict severe damage on wood which is water-logged and as soggy as wet cheese. In a few minutes you do more harm than nature has achieved in two-and-a-half thousand years. Having placed my 'parcel' ready for collection later, I went down the slope and carried on digging. The following day, 20 July, would be my last, so I needed to think carefully about what I would do.

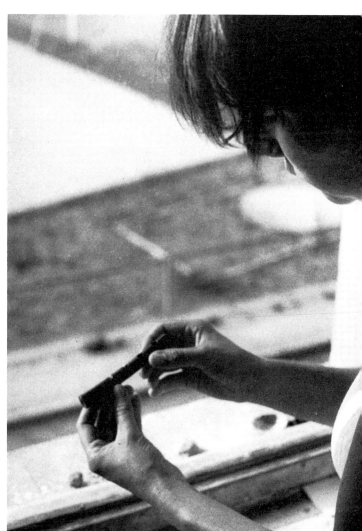

Frances Rankine with part of an Etruscan flute, a marvellously preserved find. *Photo: Alexander McKee*

My companion was Paul Bramley, whose job was to make a search with a metal detector. I thought I would clear up some unfinished business, first of all in the area where the looters had dug up the trenailed plank (which was also in Z-Zulu where Russell had uncovered two different types of plank close together) and within a few feet of a large and curious concretion which had not yet been raised. I had also photographed these previous finds, both in detail and showing their relationship to each other.

There was clear evidence of some hard digging by someone to get down through the sand, throwing up the timber which had been in the way. At the bottom of the 'excavation' there was more timber of the same type and, by extending the stranger's efforts a little, I was able to reach that large concretion and establish that it was lying over the planking. This only took a few minutes and convinced me that we had ship hull in this area, but badly broken (probably against R-1), and not merely some miscellaneous, collected wood. Simultaneously, of course, I had shown that the trenailed plank definitely came from this one dig in this one place and was also from ship hull—not a piece that had just drifted in there. One needs to be very sure in such cases, because otherwise an inverted pyramid of speculation can be based on a too-hasty assumption.

I then went down to X-X Ray, the gulley from which I had removed the main timber, to spend my last minutes at 145 feet. I found timber and pitch mixed, together with one piece of lead sheathing, three coarse sherds, two fine sherds, and six separate lumps of pitch which might contain objects. I came up the gulley for the last time, film finished, watching the great bubble-curtains of air expanding steadily as they rose to the surface from the divers still working farther down the slope. Down there, beyond the depths for which we were insured, there might yet be marvellous discoveries.

Chapter 10

THE MAESTRALE
STRIKES AGAIN

Rescue Campaign, 1983

When they reached the surface the timbers went to Jane Pannell who was in charge of conservation; and she put them in tanks with a fungicide added to the fresh water. I asked Frances Rankine to draw all four pieces as rapidly as possible, so that I could study them before I left Giglio on 21 July. Her job was not to produce 'artistic' drawings of the sort required by Sunday newspaper supplements, but, in effect, plans of each item. I wanted these eventually to show to knowledgeable friends back in Britain—in my own team of original *Mary Rose* divers were a shipwright and a ship draughtsman. I could hardly go back, say to them that we had uncovered part of the hull of an Etruscan ship—the first time this had ever been done—and then be unable to give more than a vague description.

Bearing in mind that some of the measurements were uncertain because of damage and deterioration, what we had was as follows: firstly, three planks of three different types and three different sizes. The heaviest, excavated by Russell and raised by Vallintine, was about eight-and-a-half inches broad and two inches thick; it was bevelled along one edge—that is, it was from a clinker construction composed of overlapping planks. The next heaviest was a plank made of yellow wood, about four-and-a-half inches broad and one-and-a-half inches thick; also excavated by Russell, it had a half-inch diameter hole in it which suggested a fastening of some kind (although I had never seen a trenail-hole quite like that); it was apparently of carvel construction—that is, where planks are joined edge to edge. The third and lightest plank was the piece uncovered by the robbers and raised by me. It might have been five inches broad but seemed to be only three-quarters of an inch thick. It had two holes in it, each approximately an inch in diameter. One of the holes was exactly like the holes bored in the planks of the *Mary Rose* by Tudor shipwrights to take the wooden pegs which would fasten them to the frames. The other, although much the same size, had either been bored at an angle, or was some natural knot-hole (although it did not look like it). Discussing this with Jane and Richard, the suggestion was made that this, too, was a hole for fastenings, but that the material could have been rope, not a wooden

The trenailed plank in a holding bath at the billets. *Photo: Alexander McKee*

peg or trenail. Richard had found rope on the site which might fit this theory.

So-called 'sewn boats' have survived from the mists of prehistory. The best-known in England are those found at Ferriby on the north bank of the Humber (possibly as old as 1500 BC), and at Brigg in Lincolnshire (600 BC). The latter, of course, was approximately contemporary with our Etruscan wreck. This plank also appeared to fit a carvel type of construction, rather than clinker. There is nothing remarkable about two methods of construction being used in the same vessel, the *Mary Rose* being a case in point. The main hull planks, very large and heavy, are butted edge to edge in carvel fashion, but the much lighter castling is clinker built, rather like a garden shed, with the thickness of the planks decreasing according to their height up the hull—a means of reducing topweight.

The measurements of the main, bevelled timber are uncertain, but it could have been $10\frac{1}{2}$ by $7\frac{1}{2}$ inches. It was therefore a fairly massive piece, suggesting a keel length of not less than 60–80 feet and overall length much greater. The only existing picture of an Etruscan ship known to me—from a tomb painting at Tarquinia, somewhat damaged and dated at around 460–450 BC—shows considerable fore and aft rake with a very deep hull. At the stern there are two steering oars (one on either side of the sternpost), and the usual boarding plank (common today on Greek caiques); but

194

also two masts. The vessel is quite unlike the much more frequent representations of Greek and Roman cargo ships, so once again, all we know about the Etruscans is that they were distinctively different from their neighbours.

Here at last, lying wrapped in polythene in Jane Pannell's tanks, and being drawn by Frances Rankine, was the first firm evidence of Etruscan ship construction ever to surface. And in the drawings lay the means to preserve and spread the knowledge.

*   *   *

From the beginning, the proliferation of finds had created problems. When I arrived in June, the team had a single basement room for everyone to sleep in together, and part of another room was in use to hold the finds. Some of these artefacts would have been rejected with scorn by a junk shop, while others were extremely valuable in material terms. When ten new divers joined us, Mensun hived some of them off to the camp site up the hill more than a mile away and the finds people were found space in an old workshop a mile or so up the Ortana valley, on the outskirts of an old Etruscan mining area. Then the remainder of us had to move from our not very adequate room to join the finds in their cellar. All this was temporary accommodation provided by the goodwill of local Italians. It was, after all, the height of the holiday season and Campese, after 20 years, was turning into a fashionable international holiday resort.

After a while we had to vacate the cellar altogether and Mensun, by going to the local mayor, obtained for us a few rooms in some derelict condemned houses a little way up the hill, on the far side of the football ground. To start with, there was no water, no electricity, the lavatory would not work, and we were warned to keep all doors shut to prevent the rats from coming into the building from the hillside. Gradually matters improved; we managed electric light in one room—which was the kitchen, and we got intermittent cold water to wash in and to flush the lavatory.

Then the finds started expanding again, creeping out of the finds room and into the bedroom. Before leaving England I had been reading up and studying pictures of Etruscan amphorae and other artefacts—and now I was actually sleeping with them at the bottom of my bed (and not thinking very much of it). The artefacts were followed by Mensun's large wall map of the site we were working which, of course, was added to continually day by day. To do this, 'Big Mike' Wanstall had to move Caroline Costello's bed and belongings to a corner. I watched with interest Caroline's simmering Irish temper day by day to the point where it boiled over. The divers as a whole were very hard worked. After diving there were various shift duties—to sit in the boat for a couple of hours without diving, simply timing the divers already down or doing standby; to take the aqualung cylinders to a local dive shop to be filled; to escort their own finds through the process of logging, recording and conserving; plus the usual duties of washer-up, drawer of water (in a queue for a single tap half a mile away), buyer of daily rations and cook. In very great heat. The only problem we did not have was rats. Until my last night.

That evening, the whole cheerful crowd of youngsters decided to organise a barbeque in the wilderness, high up the Ortana valley. I don't know how they managed it, but it was a great idea and in an appropriate place, surrounded by Etruscan mines. Before darkness came and the fire was lit, we climbed the seaward hill and I realised that we were looking down at one of those little coves where we had landed from the inflatable in 1982 to explore the old mine workings. The entire valley seemed deserted, but it must once have been a rich industrial area and the track we had climbed to get there must have been trodden out by the Etruscans exploiting the mineral deposits on the inland side of the valley.

Catching us off guard, that was the night a rat got into the kitchen and started jumping about, chased by a doctor. Despite these conditions, we were all keeping healthy and there was virtually no illness; just a few cuts and bruises and maybe a minor bend or two. According to the books of mediaeval history I had read, we should have been decimated by the Black Death weeks before.

We were all feeling much happier, because at last a decision to do something had been taken. The site was not to be covered up, and Mensun was still going to Sicily, but a big effort was to be made to raise money and recruit divers to carry on full-time working right through August; and to clean out all the worthwhile artefacts before the looters moved in freely. Four of the existing team had agreed to carry on for another month, so another ten divers per day were needed; the total number required being fourteen divers at any one time, so as to keep shifts going round the clock. We would have to start recruiting in England—and get immediate results; and we would also have to raise the money to pay their fares out to Italy and to buy the food they would need and to pay all the incidental costs—such as bottle filling.

There were two key people in England ready to organise the campaign—Claire Riley of BBC Radio Oxford and Colin Fox of Wantage who had been out as a diver earlier in the season. I agreed to spend a week or so of my time helping the campaign by appearing on radio and television and contacting friends in journalism who might be able to help publicise our appeal. Brenda Marsh, who had covered the raising of the *Mary Rose* for influential American publications, was one of these. And

Expedition members on a hill flanking the Ortana Valley and above the mines on the seaward side. *Photo: Alexander McKee*

I thought I might try Germany, too, again through a *Mary Rose* contact, Doris Heil. I had a number of friends in local journalism and radio, from Southampton to Sussex. It seemed to me that we had a jolly good story and might well be successful. I jotted down what I was going to say (if I could—some interviews, especially on television, are extremely brief), and I made up the amount of cash required out of my head—£10,000.

I left Giglio on 21 July, spending the night in Pisa. Immediately on arriving in Britain, I got in touch with Claire Riley and Colin Fox. After that, it was a bit of a blur. I managed a lecture and two interviews in Oxford and had to drive to London on three separate occasions, once to get up much too early to be interviewed on the BBC TV breakfast show. There were local radio appearances and various newspaper interviews, some on the telephone—these were the most hazardous, owing to the possibility of haste and misunderstanding. The radio interview format was the most satisfactory—one got half-an-hour or so, interspersed with music, and could dot the i's and cross the t's. TV was the most irritating—so little time and an exotic, complicated subject (although not so technically diverse as the *Mary Rose*, which had been a nightmare to compress into three minutes and 20 seconds or so). The press publicity was good, but the usual misquotes followed. I was known primarily as the originator of the *Mary Rose* project, and introduced as such. To explain precisely my connection with the Etruscan ship was more difficult. I short-handed the matter by saying that I had put the two key people together—Vallintine and Bound. But in one newsprint story this came out as a claim to have 'organised' the expedition which, bearing in mind the rats alone, was a distinction I was not anxious to achieve. I added that an excavation of the Campese wreck had been something I had wanted to see for twenty years, and this appeared as a claim that I was 'leading' the expedition, another distinction I did not covet.

I also met John Boardman, Lincoln Professor of Archaeology at Oxford and a leading authority on the Etruscans, who was continuing to play a considerable part behind the scenes and was actively promoting the attempt to extend this year's season for another month. Claire Riley and Colin Fox were also heavily engaged in the campaign, Claire almost continuously. The result of all these efforts was that we got both the divers and the money to send them out to Giglio and support them there. I telephoned round among my own team of experienced *Mary Rose* divers to see if any could afford to give up work and go out in August. The only one who was free was Brenda Bumstead, a teacher of chemistry living at Bembridge in the Isle of Wight. Her two children were teenage and capable of looking after themselves. Brenda was quite a girl.

The first time she had joined us was during a survey of a lost harbour off the Isle of Wight. Don Bullivant, an ex-sub mariner who had been part of the *Mary Rose* team for something like 15 years, was trying out his Mark IV model aquaplane. In principle, it is like a submersible primary glider, and is towed behind a boat with the diver lying on it behind a windscreen and operating control levers to vary his height above the ground. Because of the high speed, an enormous amount of seabed can be covered in a short time; and because the diver is not swimming but simply lying quiet, the air in the bottles lasts very much longer. The only drawback in British waters is poor visibility, which can change significantly during the course of a dive—from bad to worse (or vice versa). In this case it was for the worse.

Brenda had not used an aquaplane before, but she seemed a strong, confident girl, and got her turn. Also, these were her own waters and she had come out to join us in her own boat, both factors indicating competence. All went well for a while; then the aquaplane broke surface—without Brenda. Everyone went to action stations and the boat came creaming round. Nick Knights, who had had a sandwich in his mouth at the time, never completed the bite and cast the bread away. A minute or so later, Brenda popped up to the surface, smiling and unruffled. When someone enquired why she hadn't come up at once, Brenda called back, reasonably, that she had wanted to know what she had hit, so went for a swim round it to find out. The object was a sunken buoy, a dark object which, in poor visibility, had struck the aquaplane before Brenda could zoom up above it. She was quite right to stay down, of course—it might have been an interesting seabed feature. For these reasons, I thought that Brenda should have no trouble at Giglio. Nor did she. Her reaction was: '100 feet off Cowes—and pitch black!—seems deeper than 150 feet in the Med! Much, much deeper!'

Brenda had been diving for quite a long time, starting as a child.

> I got my first mask, snorkel and flippers for passing the 11-plus exam in 1952. My favourite uncle bought them. NOT dolls! I asked for a chemistry set as a child—and never got it. Chemistry was for boys! I only got my first chemistry set through the Open University when I was 33. I snorkelled in Lulworth Cove, off Corsica and off Arromanches. I took up lung diving in 1973 when the children were still quite small, and in 1974 moved to the Isle of Wight. In 1980 and 1981 I dived on the *Mary Rose*.

Brenda flew out on 10 August for nineteen days, and when she arrived on the quay at Giglio Porto, after a 14-hour journey, it was to find flags flying and a band marching up and down! Not another war, just a saint's day. She took the bus from Porto over to Campese, found the billets by the football pitch, and discovered that all the others were going to have a night out in Porto; so she dropped all her kit there and went back with them. Her first dive was to the plateau with Neil Blair from Aberdeen (whom she already knew from the *Mary Rose*). Then she started work in area H-Hotel. To begin with, there was nothing much—only little blobs of pitch from the digging higher up.

On 15 August she went out with the first boat, at 8·30 a.m., and in H-Hotel found more pitch but also a piece of wood and some small sherds. At 10·30 she was back on shore and, being one of the duty cooks, did the shopping for lunch—just pizza, bread and salad. The main shopping for the evening meal she decided to do later, after going out with the 2·30 boat. Back on shore at 4·30 she set out to shop seriously—and found all the shops closed. Absolutely nothing was open! It was another, national saint's day. However, the expedition did have some food stores in reserve, mainly packets of spaghetti bolognese, and Brenda suggested using up some of these.

Brenda Bumstead diving with the original *Mary Rose* team in search of a Viking wreck, April 1984. *Photo: Alexander McKee*

But somebody had opened a packet before, and made a mess of it, so they didn't want a repeat. Four of the senior people had already been invited out for a meal, so they weren't much interested anyway. The rest of us decided to go out for a meal. We'd been living in grotty conditions, so we thought: let's go out for a posh meal at the poshest place in Campese! It's a national holiday, anyway! The boys actually put on shirts and trousers for the first time (normally it was just shorts and skin); and I put on a skirt for the first—and only—time that I was out there. Even the waiters wore bow-ties. Everyone was fine that evening.

Next day was yet another saint's day, with dancing in the streets and a rowing boat race (Italians versus Italians). Cambridge weren't present, but Brenda thought that at least Oxford might have entered a team. But that day their problems started.

In the morning Scott, who was the youngest of us, aged 18, was ill. He had diarrhoea and was vomiting. Hugh Montgomery was the same—he was a medical student and our only 'Doctor'. They had both had ham with their pizza at the posh place the previous evening. So two of us were ill to start with. But on the following day Gavin was ill with flu and a high temperature. So three of us were ill now, and only four of us (from a total of 12) went out to dive.

The procedure was still the same. A small, hired hard-boat (a dory) was kept moored over the site all day. The line from it went down to the edge of the plateau where there was a rock with a hole in it, convenient for tying up the rope. That was somewhere around 100 feet. At the top end of the line, at two different but shallow depths, decompression bottles were rigged. The boat used for transporting the divers, and from which they dived, was an inflatable about 14 feet long. When, as on this morning, four divers went out, they would divide into two pairs. While the first pair went down, the remaining pair would divide into a time-keeper (who also banged the gong for them to come up) and a stand-by diver able to give assistance in the water. Usually, these two stationed themselves in the hard-boat, because the gong and the shot rope and the lookbox were in that. Then, when the first pair had come up, the second pair would dive, while the first divided into time-keeper and stand-by diver.

There were four of us: Neil Blair, the Scotsman who had worked on the *Mary Rose*; Tom, a London Cockney; Simon, who was training to be a pharmacist; and myself. Blair and Tom were to dive first; Simon was to time-keep, I to standby.

There were grey clouds in the distance, which we didn't take any notice of. Simon and I got into the dory, so we could look down the shot rope to see what the divers were doing. It was a flat calm.

The cloud got closer and it started raining. Still a flat calm, then a breeze, then a strong wind—and the sea state changed within seconds.

Simon made the decision to bring the divers up. He began to give the two-minute warning BANG BANG—BANG BANG—BANG BANG, but had only got 15 seconds into the hammering, when the sea state got so bad that we changed the signal to BANG-BANG-BANG-BANG-BANG-BANG! which meant 'COME UP IMMEDIATELY!'

The problem was, that the Deco bottles on the shotline were tied

'Come up!'—Richard banging the gong while the stand-by diver waits. *Photo: Alexander McKee*

to one side of the boat. The sea went up and down, but only one end of the boat could come up; which put the other end down. And the waves poured in.

Simon went to the end of the boat to untie the knot fastening the shotline; while I went to the other end, to balance it. Simon was being thrown back by the waves, and kept shouting, 'I can't undo the knot!' But I couldn't go over and help him, as it would have made matters worse.

Eventually a wave came over the boat and it started sinking. Simon fell out one way, I fell out the other. I couldn't see him. Only the divers on the way up could see both of us landing in the water at the same time. As they came up, they passed the boat coming down at about the six or seven metre mark.

It had been calm up to then, and completely calm on the bottom, so when they heard the hammering they looked at their watches and thought we had gone mad; but obeyed the rules and came up nevertheless.

When they got to the surface, we still had the Avon inflatable afloat. A rope which had tied the inflatable to the dory was still attached to the dory, which was sunk, so the Avon was supporting the dory which was hanging in the sea. Everything had tipped out of the dory, too.

Nevertheless, like perfect divers, Neil and Tom gave the OK signal, although everything had gone!

The waves were very high and debris from the dory, like floorboards and oars, was floating about. Brenda had not been wearing her mask, fins or snorkel, so they had gone, too; and without them a diver wearing a suit is awkward in the water. Brenda was wearing her ABLJ, a superior kind of lifejacket which inflates by compressed air even at very great depths. Unfortunately, the small air cylinder is situated in exactly the position to hinder getting out of the water and into an inflatable—it catches on the side at precisely the wrong moment. Even with fins on, and driving hard, it can be difficult; without the upward push given by the beating flippers, it can be impossible. However, for the moment, Brenda's buoyancy was a great help.

Neil Blair cut the rope linking the inflatable to the dory so that the dory wouldn't drag the Avon down. I'm pretty buoyant, so he used me to get some leverage to cut the rope. Simon and Tom got into the Avon. Tom, still wearing his set, came over to me, but I had said I was happy, so while the men were climbing into the Avon I went and collected two oars and some of the floorboards. I thought that was the best occupation for me, while they got their heavy gear off. Then they pulled me into the boat—because I had trouble getting in with the ABLJ on. And that was the end of diving for the day.

The divers had been down working at 150 feet, for which eight minutes is the NO STOP time. They were signalled up after seven minutes, passing their sinking boat on the way up.

The margin by which Neil and Tom had escaped a bend was that close. A matter of minutes. Had the sudden storm been delayed by only five minutes or so, and the divers worked on into decompression time—they would have been in great potential trouble, trying to stay at two required stop levels without a shotrope or spare bottles.

We didn't go into harbour, because the boats there were going up and down—we went straight up the beach and then helped Italians pull their boats up. Next day, after discussing what to do, we went out, found a lot of bits and pieces and brought them back up to the Avon. But the dory was halfway down the reef at 36 metres. How were we to bring that up? Dennis, an Irishman, arrived and I took him diving on the 18th to see the dory. We stayed several feet above it at about 110 feet. It was sitting right way up, looking completely unharmed, on a slight slope. NOT a wreck, but a perfectly good boat sitting happily on an eelgrass patch on the plateau. I was amazed at the good vis. That bad weather here didn't mean bad vis.

In Brenda's local dive spots—as in mine—visibility can occasionally be as much as 20 or even 25 feet, but the average is five feet and after a hard blow drops drastically to a few inches in shallow water and total blackness in deep water. Salvage in those conditions can be difficult if not perilous.

The fellers tied ropes to the dory's hull lengthwise (it was a cathedral hull), with four open-topped water-carriers—one at each corner— and then filled them with air. There was a fifth water-carrier on a longer rope in the centre, so it would surface first and spill air. It worked. Next day, 20 August, Dennis and I collected the gong and ropes which were still on the bottom. The dory was now back on site, with only one floorboard lost, plus the hooks for the deco bottles. But the gong was useless, full of water. A dull thud instead of a nice ringing tone.

So, two days after the maestrale, they were back in business. But sickness continued to plague them. On the 16th, Scott and Hugh had been struck by the vomiting and bowel trouble. On the 17th, Gavin went down with flu. Colin Burr arrived to join the team on the 20th, but went down with the stomach sickness next day, while Hugh, who had now recovered from his bowel trouble, went down with flu, and Martin dropped an Etruscan anchor on his foot. At the same time Richard was falling ill with flu. 'It was a hospital, not a diving expedition!' said Brenda.

However, she was still diving, on the 21st going farther down the slope to dig at 160 feet in U-Uniform, instead of the 150 feet at V-Victor.

Mensun Bound came, just for one day, and somebody in Campese asked us if we'd like an Etruscan amphora. We took the van to collect it, with Mensun to photograph it. This was when Martin dropped the anchor on his foot—he couldn't get a fin on for several days. Mensun said he wanted to move to another site, supposed to be Etruscan.

After one more day at Campese, during which Brenda found a large part of an Etruscan amphora, the whole diving team was moved to the new site, many miles away but somewhat shallower. I had, with Mensun, met the Italian who had discovered it; but its potentialities were unknown as, with potential plunderers everywhere, he had had to be very circumspect in his exploratory probes.

The idea of a move to this new site was so that we could get some money (for next season's work). 'Rico' and I put down a baseline and a movable search line to make it more organised. We had 10 divers now and used coat-hangers as probes. Four people didn't like this diversion, but on 25 August Martin came up saying he thought he'd found an amphora. He was wearing socks inside his fins to save his foot, but this time the amphora was worth the pain of the dive. We spent all next day digging out the amphora, which was brought up on the last two dives by 'Rico' and Neil.

This amphora appeared to be Etruscan, so diving continued at the new site.

About this time two of the shore staff also fell ill, Chris Storey and Jane Pannell. Jane had a lizard called Nigel. She had trained it to eat marmalade off her finger outside the house. He came to us every day on the steps when we had meals. She started him off on sugar and water, but what he really loved was marmalade.

We also had an Austrian baby called 'Boo Boo'. There was an empty room below and we got a squatter, an Austrian girl in her early twenties with a four-year-old son. She had been to India, Turkey, France as well as Italy. The boy joined us, had rides in the van, chattered in German. He learned English quicker than we

Surfacing towards the inflatable—and a surprise in store for someone. *Photo: Alexander McKee*

learned German. Angus babysat when Mum was out, but it was hard to explain to a four-year-old that it was OK for him to be on the steps or in the kitchen but not in the Finds Room. He was learning how to scrounge at four years old. Our boys damned the girl but they never damned the non-existent Dad. So there were two people we had to look after, Nigel the lizard and 'Boo Boo' the Austrian baby.

My last dive at the new site was on 27 August. I prodded around and found nothing. Hugh started diving again and came up with a bloody nose (sinus problems). On the old site we found two little pots but most of the stuff is now below 160 feet.

We were not able to dive below 160 feet using compressed air because our insurance did not cover us. Earlier, it is true, Mensun had used some Belgian divers who were on holiday on Giglio to go farther down the slope, because they were not bothered by insurance rules or people saying that it was 'suicidal'. So the Belgians were used below 160 feet and the Brits above. But one cannot always rely on friendly Belgians. Now it was perfectly possible (the North Sea experts told me), using North Sea techniques and helium mixtures, to go safely right down that slope to 215 feet—and many hundreds of feet farther down, if necessary. But that technique, with all the hardware involved, was very expensive. Certainly it could be made available. But only if one could be sure that the rewards (historical or material) were sufficient to justify it. And one could not prove that they were justified without going deep down that slope and actually digging.

This is the dilemma, now and in the future, of much underwater archaeology. And it was Mensun's problem for next year.

In crude terms, the 1983 excavation had been a success. One 'little pot' in terms of material value would probably have paid for the expedition (bearing in mind that most of us had paid our own way out there and contributed to the expedition in cash rather more than the value of our food and lodging). Some stalwarts had actually struggled out with their own heavy cylinders and weightbelts, in addition to normal diving gear and personal luggage.

But where did the pots (and other finds) go to? Did we bring them back to England? Patriotically, people felt that we should have done. Practically, we would never have got a permit from the Italians if we had proposed to possess the finds. Personally, I feel that the place for Etruscan artefacts is Etruria (modern day Tuscany). If you want to study them, you go to Italy, to Florence, to Tarquinia, to Rome. Of course, if we were very successful in recovering a wide and fascinating collection of artefacts from the cargo, from the crew and from the ship itself, then one hoped a mobile international exhibition might be organised at some time in the future, which might visit Britain, so that our own people could see what we had found.

To my mind, our results so far fell short of such success. But we did not yet know for certain what might still remain of ship and cargo down below that second line of rocks at around 160 feet. That was still well worth exploring as a priority.

Excavating by the base-line at about 150 feet. *Photo: Alexander McKee*

Chapter 11

1984—AND THE FUTURE

The programme on *The Wreck in Campese Bay* went out on BBC-2 on 28 February, 1984. It made first-rate television—the underwater sequences were particularly beautiful and striking—and attracted a lot of interest. For the 1984 season it had been hoped to have up to 50 divers and shore staff on the island, but the actual figure was around 22–25, with sometimes as few as a dozen, during the two months of June and July.

The 'new' Etruscan site, to which the team had been shifted in 1983, which had yielded a single amphora, proved completely barren in 1984. Perhaps that had been a chance find after all.

The original site in Campese Bay was worked again—and probably worked out—but not beyond the depth limits set by insurance, so there is still a question mark as to what may lie buried farther down a very steep slope. As it was, the recoveries were mainly of pottery sherds and a few scraps of wood. The only major find was structural—a length of timber about six feet long lying just below the rock where I had excavated a main timber in 1983, and above which the planking had been found. Mensun identified the new piece as part of the keel of the ship. The fastenings, he thought, had been a combination of trenails and lacing. Some people believed that this might be the upper half of the keel and that a lower part might exist deeper.

Jane Pannell was again in charge of the conservation of finds and also (because of a shortage of staff) had to do much of the recording. A Portsmouth girl, she had originally studied at Southampton College of Art where she had acquired an interest in restoration and conservation from her tutor, Malcolm Pepper. On leaving art school she went immediately to the British Museum where she worked as a conservator for four years, and then went off to Turkey to work with George Bass on the 11th century AD Arab wreck at Serce Limani.

The techniques Jane used at Giglio varied according to the material to be conserved. The aryballoi—the hand-painted oil-jars for athletes— were the most important. First, they had to be cleaned gently with a soft brush to remove surface dirt—taking care not to disturb the pigment. Then, like all the pottery, ornamented or otherwise, they were transferred

▲ Jane Pannell and Mensun recording finds at Giglio. In 1985 Jane went out to Turkey to work with George Bass on the Kas site, and found herself dealing with bronze knives and spears from a well-preserved wreck of about 1400 BC. *Photo: Alexander McKee*

◀ Intact amphora soaking in fresh water. *Photo: Alexander McKee*

to baths of fresh water, which was changed daily. This was to remove the salt which permeates pottery and can do damage on drying out if not removed.

There were the bronze items, the arrow heads and some unidentified objects they called 'nuggets'. These were stored in a solution of benzoltriazole, which stabilises the bronze and stops further corrosion.

The iron concretions were stabilised in a solution of sodium carbonate. The 'concretion' is simply the outer shell left when the iron has corroded. It is worth saving because it may be used as a mould to reproduce the exact shape of the iron object which was originally inside it, but which has since disappeared into this outer crust.

Some items were stored in a solution of thymol, which is a fungicide. They included amber, ivory, bone and wood. The bones found seemed to be those of sheep. One was squared off and had an indentation on one side, suggesting that it might have been a gaming piece rather than a pictorial carving. The ivory pieces resembled guitar plectrums.

Wood was probably the most fragile material, because the structure was completely full of water. On the other hand the writing tablet, which rather resembled a picture frame, was in quite good condition. This, too,

The sample of main timber raised by the author, in a holding bath. *Photo: Alexander McKee*

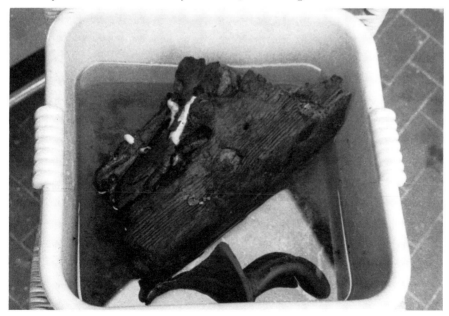

was put into a fungicide solution as a holding measure before being sent to Florence for conservation. Small objects such as this would have been ideal for the quick freeze-drying method of conservation rather than the long-term soaking in a solution of polyethylene glycol. Neither of these techniques was available on Giglio. They replace the fibres which have rotted away in the sea so that, when dried out, the wood does not shrink.

Vallintine and Bound were eventually successful in locating the bronze helmet taken by a German diver from the site more than twenty years before. They were allowed to look and to take photographs, but the finder would not surrender it to them. The helmet was smooth-topped, uncrested, of Greek manufacture, and engraved with various motifs. At the front, around the chin, were engravings of wild boars, one on either side. Whether this represented the personal whim of the owner or was a unit designation, cannot now be known. Fine armour is often engraved, and this is usually regarded merely as art; but, having myself worn a steel helmet bearing on one side the emblem of a stag's head and antlers surmounting the word *Bydand* (the badge of the Gordon Highlanders) and possessing also an enemy helmet with the German eagle holding a swastika in its claws, I am less sure. Animal insignia were very popular this century at all levels, from Regiment to Army Group, and did of course serve their primary purpose of identification. Indeed, the sign of the British 30 Corps in the Normandy campaign was a wild boar charging (whereas the Greek version daintily picks its way forward round the helmet). A further point is that the ancient helmet, with two eye-slits divided by a nose-piece, would effectively disguise the wearer, unless it bore insignia.

In 1984 the Giglio project acquired a Royal Patron (as the *Mary Rose* had previously). In this case it was Crown Prince Hans Adam of Liechtenstein who, like the Prince of Wales, was an amateur diver of some experience. He had first visited us in 1983 when he had arrived with the group of mostly Swiss divers aboard the 97-ft schooner *Florette*, and I had been invited out to watch them diving Giglio by night. This year he came to dive with the Oxford expedition on the Campese wreck for a week, at a time when Richard Skelt was directing the excavation as well as handling most of the organisational tasks.

*   *   *

Clearly, another expedition would be hard (although not impossible) to organise. To find out what lies down that slope below 160 feet would require sophisticated equipment and elaborate back-up—which would not be cheap. If, in spite of that, the rewards were a few sherds from types of pottery already known from the site—then the expedition would have

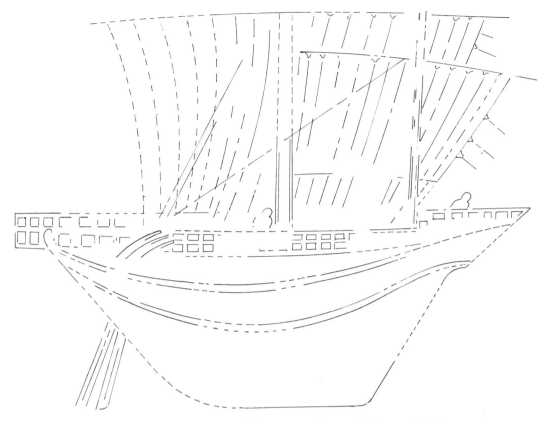

In a tomb at Tarquinia dated to the mid-fifth century BC is a partly damaged painting of a merchant ship quite unlike Greek and Roman cargo vessels, because it has two masts. There are several technically puzzling points about it, more clearly illustrated by this line drawing. *Drawn by Maurice Young*

been a waste of time. But if it produced new types of pottery and, say, another helmet? And perhaps a significant part of the hull?

On the basis of the timbers already recovered in 1983, I asked a shipwright to look again at the painting from the Tomb of the Ship at Tarquinia, dated to about 460–450 BC, which is the only evidence we have of an Etruscan merchant vessel. The shipwright was Morrie Young who had worked with me on the *Mary Rose*, since 1968. He had long had an interest in the ships of ancient times, and immediately turned to the representation in Björn Landström's classic work *Sailing Ships*. Morrie works in the mould loft of Vosper Thorneycroft at Woolston, Southampton, where modern warships are built for many navies. In one corner of the design office lurks a computer which can do many of the routine calculations—although whether the ship will be a good one or a bad one is still up to the naval architect.

From almost a lifetime of study, and especially of the *Mary Rose*, with its total lack of plans and models and only a single official picture to go on, he was convinced that almost all early ship pictures were distorted in one way or another. Usually, he felt, the detail was right, but the proportions were wrong. In the case of the *Mary Rose*, he thought that the artist had probably been rowed round the actual *Mary Rose* in a boat and been very careful of the authenticity of the details of hull, fittings, rigging, guns and decorations. But because he was looking up at a high-built hull from low down, the lines of the ship and its proportions were distorted. To this I would add that Tudor artists did not use perspective. To unscramble all that in one's mind, without an actual hull, would be complicated.

In other cases, such as the mediaeval ships depicted on town seals, in order to fit the cramped format, the hull would be shown as much shorter than it really was.

Indeed, even today, ship hulls are far too long for the ordinary photographic format used in books, magazines and newspapers. The vessel is therefore normally photographed at an angle, usually on the bow, which distorts to a greater or lesser extent according to distance and the type of lens fitted to the camera. And, of course, ships are far from being the simple box-structures most people live in. Their lines are a subtle combination of curves, altering as they go.

For this reason, and because the Etruscan painting (from which he also worked) was a flat depiction of the vessel seen from the starboard side, Morrie decided that this evidence would not warrant an attempt to work out hull sections, even with the aid of a computer.

However, using the damaged painting as a basis, he thought that both a side elevation and a plan of the hull seen from above might be attempted. His basic assumption was that the painting showed the vessel, not in the water, but in its entirety on shore. The peculiar shape of the underwater part of the hull (rather like a modern yacht with a deep keel) which had worried me in a cargo vessel, became by lengthening the keel a perfectly workable freighter's hull. The stern of the two-masted vessel was clearly indicated by the position of the steering oars. The bow was conjectural (because of damage to the painting), but Morrie believed, as I do, that many ancient cargo hulls will have been similar to the present-day caique.

Maurice Young of the original *Mary Rose* team, who is also a shipwright at Vosper Thorneycroft, Southampton, believed that the detail was right but the proportions wrong. ▶ Assuming that the painting showed the vessel, not afloat but drawn up ashore, he lengthened the keel, to produce a believable cargo-carrying hull. *Drawn by Maurice Young*

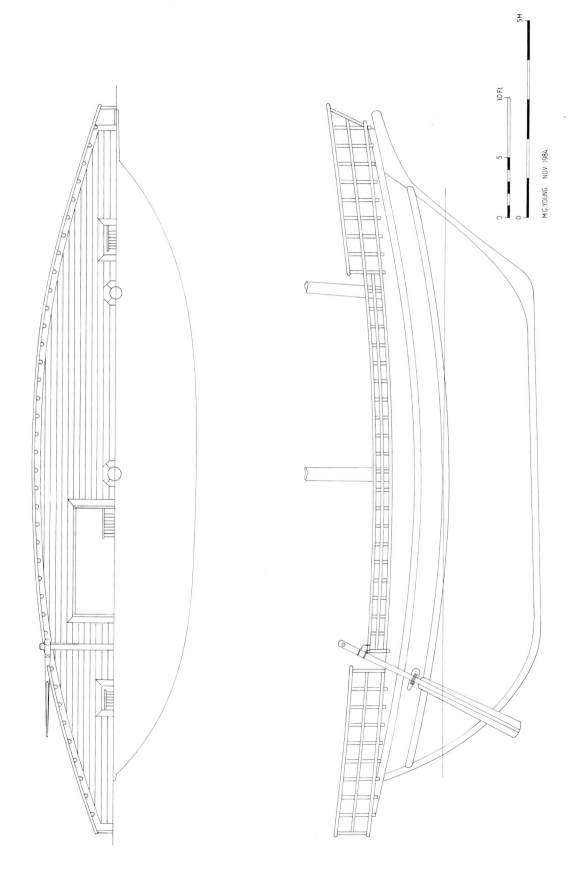

M.G. YOUNG   NOV. 1984.

5M

10 Ft

5

0

He calculated the loaded waterline accordingly, the shape of stem and stern, the boarding ladder at the stern, the low rails amidships and the higher rails required at the bow. The result was a believable ship having an overall length of slightly more than 60 feet.

*   *   *

After the example of Giglio, one might well ask, what is the future of underwater archaeology in the Mediterranean and elsewhere? One night, sitting late over drinks at Campese, Ric Wharton had made his views briefly clear. Deep wrecks (that is, 500 feet or deeper) held the real potential for the future. He personally would no longer be interested in anything easily available—that is, wrecks down to 300 feet or less.

Elefterios Yalouris, a Greek classicist who took part in Throckmorton's discovery of the neolithic wreck at Dokos, has estimated that from 1000 BC to the beginning of the Christian era, some 150,000 ships must have been built and sailed; and perhaps one in ten was lost. Many would be cast ashore or go down in shallow water, but a proportion must have been overwhelmed while far out to sea over very deep water. No one would have even seen those ships since, let alone looted them. Even if, as with most of the Giglio wrecks, the hulls were far from intact, the discovery of such uncontaminated sites would be wonderful.

But there is more to it than that. Two factors made me perservere with my search for the *Mary Rose*. Firstly, my belief that on soft seabeds ships sink deeply into the protective mud which preserves them, and secondly, that there is no such thing as 'the Sea'. Instead, there are a great variety of undersea environments, some of which are much more favourable than others to the preservation of wooden hulls and their contents. If one could link a favourable environment with a fairly rapid burial and silting up, then theoretically one might have at least some ancient ships in an almost perfect state. I sent many people to sleep in the early days of the *Mary Rose* project, while I tried to explain just why I thought we might have, very well preserved, a large part of a Tudor battleship and its contents buried under the mud and clay and basically invisible. It sounded like a tall story which, when explained in detail, produced infinite boredom. Only, it happened to be true. And it will be true also of a proportion of much, much older ships; even quite unknown vessels. A Minoan ship, for instance, or a Mycenaean, or a Phoenician. (Unless, of course, the Campese wreck turns out to be Phoenician after all!)

There are two drawbacks. First, how do you find wrecks at all in deep water, and especially totally buried and invisible wrecks? And, even if you manage to do that by means similar to those I used on the completely invisible *Mary Rose*, how do you then go about the much longer and far more daunting task of actually proving the nature of the buried wreck (which might, after all, be a modern coal barge)? In only 50 feet of water, it took me years (admittedly on a shoe-string budget). How long is it going to take in 500 feet—or 1,000 feet? Practical depths now, to be sure, but immensely expensive and not to be risked on slender evidence or mere guesswork.

The early days of the *Mary Rose* project in fact answer this objection. First-rate technical people, like Dr Harold Egerton, were so fascinated by the historic aspects of undersea work that they were prepared to gamble. To invest part of their time and some of their advanced techniques in my project, with no possibility of financial compensation. There still are such people, and it is they who will make possible even greater discoveries in the future. Without them, nothing can be done.

To my mind, there was one other approach. And this was a shallow water potential, in direct contradiction to the sorry tales to be told of France and Italy. In Greece, there are very strict laws against the looting of antiquities, and those laws, where possible, are enforced. Theoretically, the result should be a large number of unlooted sites in water shallow enough even for snorkelling, let alone aqualunging. I had been to Greece and the islands half-a-dozen times and I thought I knew an area where trade routes in the ancient world had converged and which was fanged everywhere with ship hazards. A first look at a chart revealed scores of them—or so I believed. Many were obvious. Others, because of relative changes of sea and land levels, were not.

It is one of the latter which I will describe. The weather was not too kind—the back end of a *meltemi* was still blowing the Aegean into short, steep waves; but the spray was white and warm. I had left my home in southern England at four o'clock in the morning, and at four o'clock that afternoon I was diving in Greece.

The site was a submerged hill. The first sign of a wreck was a few amphorae sherds rammed into rock crevices, which I carefully photographed with a range of exposures. This proved to be a great mistake. I had assumed that only one ship had struck this sunken reef. But no!

The few sherds became a complete field of amphorae fragments, and it went on and on as I swam round the reef. There were many different types of amphorae, some with flat bases, others pointed; fat ones, thin ones, big ones, small ones. Not one varied cargo, but many different cargoes, lost at different times.

There were plenty of amphorae necks with handles, some little pots, and complete 'cascades' of amphorae sherds spilling down the slopes and wedged into crevices and gulleys or lying piled in the open. One cache of amphorae had very thin necks—there was identification work here to keep a big team busy for a year or two.

Visibility must have been over 100 feet at times, and the site was so shallow that everything was in full colour instead of the grey of deep water at Giglio. I went down into one deep gulley—not unlike the grouper cave at Campese, whose bottom was filled with blackened amphorae and whose sides, towering high above, were vertical walls covered with red and black growths. Another such gulley ended in a cave full of broken pots, with bright bluish-purple sea urchins clinging above its sherd-filled mouth.

Various Greek governments have done history a service by protecting their undersea heritage so carefully. But inevitably, there will be increased opportunities for plunder. Not all the shallow wrecks will wait untouched another century or so to find their excavator. And not a few of them must surely be as important as the Etruscan wreck in Campese Bay was—before the plunderers got at it twenty years ago or more.

In February, 1985, I went out to Malta and Gozo to check the underwater possibilities there. The Maltese islands, athwart the narrows of the central Mediterranean, offer less of a problem to law enforcement than the long, intricate Greek coastline and its 10,000 isles. I saw one badly broken-up ship in the shallows at around 85 feet, but learned that in the nearby deeps was an intact, unlooted amphora wreck; and was assured that off Malta at least one very deep wreck—below 400 feet—had been located. And in the archaeological museum at Valletta I was shown the huge Roman anchor recovered by Comm. Salvino Scicluna from St Paul's Bay, which he believes may well be a relic from the ship shattered to pieces there in the first century after Christ. But the real historical treasures yet to be found are older—the possible remains of Greek, Phoenician and Carthaginian ships dating back to perhaps 1000–900 BC and directly or indirectly trading with the Etruscans. Malta may have been a kind of neutral ground, even when Carthaginians, Greeks and Etruscans were warring with one another.

The prospects for the next wave of historical underwater explorers—those organised to employ North Sea deep-diving techniques—seem endless; the results unguessed at.